BRITISH FOREIGN POLICY

1919–193

D1414830

MANCHESTER
1824

Manchester University Press

MANCHESTER STUDIES IN MODERN HISTORY
General editor Jeremy Black

Poverty and welfare in England 1700–1850
Steven King

Making sense of the Industrial Revolution
Steven King and Geoffrey Timmins

British fascism 1918–1939
Thomas Linehan

Origins of the Second World War
Victor Rothwell

BRITISH FOREIGN POLICY
1919–1939

'Hope for the best, prepare for the worst'

Paul W. Doerr

MANCHESTER UNIVERSITY PRESS
Manchester and New York

distributed exclusively in the USA by Palgrave

Published by Manchester University Press
Oxford Road, Manchester M13 9NR, UK
and Room 400, 175 Fifth Avenue, New York, NY 10010, USA
www.manchesteruniversitypress.co.uk

Distributed in the United States exclusively by
Palgrave Macmillan, 175 Fifth Avenue,
New York, NY 10010, USA

Distributed in Canada exclusively by
UBC Press, University of British Columbia, 2029 West Mall,
Vancouver, BC, Canada V6T 1Z2

British Library Cataloguing-in-Publication Data is available

Library of Congress Cataloging-in-Publication Data is available

ISBN 978 0 7190 4672 8 paperback

First published by Manchester University Press in hardback 1998

This paperback edition first published 2012

The publisher has no responsibility for the persistence or accuracy of URLs for any external or third-party internet websites referred to in this book, and does not guarantee that any content on such websites is, or will remain, accurate or appropriate.

Printed by Lightning Source

CONTENTS

ACKNOWLEDGEMENTS

I would like to thank my student assistants at Acadia University, Lee Barette and James Cousins, who read early typescripts of this book. Arlene Doucette helped with the final stages of the typescript. I would also like to thank my fourth-year seminar at the University of Waterloo in the autumn term of 1995, who critiqued the first chapter with an enthusiasm inspired, I suspect, by the fact that I was about to critique their essays. The class consisted of Mark Hughes, Kathy Bechtel, Monique Kaptein, Richard Farmer, Paul Gundy, Jeremy Hardie and George Spiropoulos. The map was drawn by Barry Levely, cartographer at the Mapping, Analysis and Design Department, University of Waterloo. Special thanks to those who saw this manuscript through to publication, including Vanessa Graham, Gemma Marren and Carolyn Hand at Manchester University Press, and Corinne Orde. I would also like to thank the series general editor, Jeremy Black. I owe a great debt of gratitude to Carol Cole and Aaron Cole-Doerr for their patience and support during the writing of this book. Last but not least, Tosca and Josephine provided heartening comradeship during the many long days of writing.

CHRONOLOGY

1919

18 January	Formal opening of Paris Peace Conference
22–24 March	Lloyd George's Fontainebleau meetings
28 June	Treaty of Versailles signed
24 October	Curzon becomes foreign secretary

1920

19 March	US Senate formally rejects Versailles
10 August	Treaty of Sèvres signed; Kemal seizes power in Turkey

1921

16 March	Anglo-Soviet trade agreement
27 April	Germans presented with reparations bill
12 November	Washington conference begins (ends 6 February 1922)
13 December	Four Power Treaty

1922

10 April	Genoa conference begins (ends 19 May)
16 April	Germany and Russia sign Treaty of Rapallo
1 August	Balfour Note
September	Chanak crisis
30 October	March on Rome; Mussolini appointed prime minister in Italy
19 October	Lloyd George's coalition dissolves
15 November	Conservatives win British election

1923

11 January	Ruhr occupation begins
22 May	Bonar Law succeeded by Baldwin

1924

22 January	Ramsay MacDonald becomes prime minister in Britain
1 February	Britain recognizes USSR
9 April	Dawes Report issued
16 August	Conference in London ends after approving Dawes plan
29 October	Conservatives return to power in Britain, Austen Chamberlain subsequently appointed foreign minister

1925

16 October	Locarno agreements initialled

1926

10 September	Germany enters League of Nations

1927

27 May	Britain breaks off relations with USSR after ARCOS raid
20 June	Geneva naval conference begins (ends 4 August)

1928

27 August	Signature of Kellogg–Briand pact

1929

29 May	Labour wins minority government; Henderson appointed foreign minister
6 August	Hague conference begins (ends 31 August); adopts Young Plan
29 October	Wall Street crash

1930

22 April	London naval treaty
30 June	Rhineland completely evacuated
14 September	Nazis win 107 seats in German Reichstag

1931

21 March	Austrian–German customs union proposed
11 May	Kreditanstalt bank fails
20 June	Hoover Moratorium proposed (adopted 20 July)
13 July	Danat Bank fails
18 September	Mukden incident, Japan invades Manchuria
21 September	Britain abandons gold standard
27 November	National government wins election in Britain; Simon appointed foreign minister

1932

2 February	Geneva disarmament conference begins
16 June	Lausanne conference begins (ends 9 July); reparations abolished
31 July	Nazis win 230 seats in Reichstag

1933

30 January	Hitler appointed chancellor
24 February	Lytton report on Manchuria
24 March	Hitler passes Enabling Act

1934

26 January	German–Polish treaty
25 July	Attempted Nazi coup in Austria
November	Polling begins for Peace Ballot
29 December	Japan denounces Washington naval agreement

1935

13 January	Saar plebiscite
9 March	Göring announces existence of Luftwaffe
16 March	Germany reintroduces conscription, enlarges army to thirty-five divisions
25–26 March	Simon visits Berlin
11–15 April	'Stresa front' meetings
7 June	MacDonald resigns; Baldwin returns as prime minister; Hoare becomes foreign minister
18 June	Anglo-German naval agreement

27 June	Peace Ballot ends with rally at Royal Albert Hall
3 October	Italy invades Ethiopia
11 October	League brands Italy aggressor
14 November	Baldwin's government returned
18 November	Sanctions imposed by League on Italy
9 December	Hoare–Laval plan published. Hoare resigns; Eden takes over as foreign minister

1936

7 March	German troops enter the Rhineland
9 May	Italy annexes Ethiopia
17 July	Spanish Civil War begins
1 November	Mussolini proclaims Rome–Berlin axis
25 November	Anti-Comintern pact signed by Germany and Japan
10 December	Edward VIII resigns as king of Britain

1937

2 January	Gentleman's agreement between Italy and Britain
27 April	Guernica bombed
28 May	Baldwin resigns; Chamberlain appointed new prime minister
June	Stalin purges Red Army officer corps
7 July	Japan invades China
10 September	Nyon conference begins (ends 14 September)

1938

20 February	Eden resigns as foreign secretary; Lord Halifax appointed new foreign secretary
13 March	Anschluss
16 April	Easter agreement between Italy and Britain
20 May	May crisis begins
3 August	Runciman arrives in Czechoslovakia
15 September	Berchtesgaden meeting
22 September	Godesberg meeting

29 September	Munich conference begins (ends 30 September)
9 November	*Kristallnacht*

1939

11 January	Halifax and Chamberlain arrive in Rome
15 March	German troops enter Prague
17 March	Chamberlain's Birmingham speech
20 March	Germany annexes Memel from Lithuania
28 March	Spanish Civil War ends
31 March	Britain guarantees Poland
7 April	Italy invades Albania
18 April	Soviet proposals to Britain for alliance
3 May	Molotov replaces Litvinov as Soviet foreign minister
5 August	British military delegation leaves for Moscow
12 August	British–French–Soviet military talks begin
23 August	Nazi–Soviet pact announced
1 September	Germany attacks Poland
3 September	Britain declares war on Germany

Europe 1919

CHAPTER ONE

THE BACKGROUND

In the introduction to his magisterial history of the twentieth century the historian Eric Hobsbawm writes of an otherwise intelligent American student who asked if the phrase 'Second World War' meant that there had been a first. Anyone who has taught history for any length of time can recount similar stories. We live in a fast-paced era, one of the casualties of which is historical memory. A video on the Second World War circulated to schools by the British Department of Education in 1995 only once referred to Winston Churchill. Not surprisingly, a survey of British students showed that a third of them had never heard of Churchill. Also in 1995, a postgraduate student addressing a high school in Canada on the subject of the Second World War discovered that most of the students thought the name Winston Churchill referred to another school, or perhaps a nearby street name. If Britain's most famous prime minister of the twentieth century is already fading from memory, where does that leave such of his contemporaries as Chamberlain, Baldwin and MacDonald?[1]

Such observations could easily lead to sighs of despair and foggy reminiscences of bygone days when students supposedly knew the clauses of the Treaty of Versailles like the backs of their hands. Yet I have observed that every autumn the history classes in universities are packed with students who are clearly dissatisfied with what has been imparted to them by way of history. Almost without exception, they want to know more. They are critical of media coverage of such events as the war in the former Yugoslavia: little background information is given, contradictory facts are thrown about and there are no organizational themes. One student told me that it was 'like having sand thrown in your face'. A surprising number are drawn

1

to the 1919–39 inter-war period, fascinated by the sorts of problems and issues that once were studied by diplomatic historians. Professional historians seldom use the term 'diplomatic history' any more, preferring more voguish and less embarrassing rubrics. Fortunately, students and readers of history have few such compunctions and find the inter-war period particularly interesting because it deals with many of the questions that any great novel or short story would confront: questions about the uses and limits of power, means versus ends, how to confront evil, and how to jettison lifelong beliefs and adopt a different way of thinking.

The objectives of this volume are straightforward: first, to acquaint readers with what happened during the inter-war period; second, to introduce them to some of the historical controversies of the period; and finally, to direct them to the most important historical works and documentary sources. Much of the discussion that follows focuses on debates at the highest levels of the government, but I have also attempted to draw attention to larger historical forces where it can be shown that those forces influenced the formulation of British foreign policy.

Britain and the origins of the First World War

At the dawn of the twentieth century forty-one million Britons governed a worldwide empire of twelve million square miles and a quarter of the world's population. Britain's naval supremacy was unchallenged and London served as the undisputed financial capital of the world. Queen Victoria's Diamond Jubilee of 1897 had prompted self-congratulatory celebrations of Britain's imperial attainments. The popular press was full of jingoistic slogans, such as that which described the British Empire as 'the empire on which the sun never sets'. British dominance in world affairs was taken for granted to the extent that many referred to the nineteenth century as an era of 'pax Britannica'. But some observers noted a pervasive and growing sense of unease, a fear that perhaps Britain was over-extended and past its prime. One statesman described Britain as a 'weary Titan, staggering under the too vast orb of its fate'.[2] Much of the anxiety revolved around fears that Britain now faced stiff competition as an economic power from the United States of America and from Germany. Indeed, by the turn of the century the United States and Germany were overtaking Britain in many key sectors of industrial production. Of the two, Germany posed by far the more serious threat.[3] Under the leadership of Kaiser Wilhelm II, who reigned from 1888 until 1918, Germany's economic challenge was amplified by a determination to follow a more assertive and vigorous foreign policy. In 1898 the German Reichstag passed the first in a series of naval laws designed to equip Germany with a powerful high seas fleet. The German leadership considered that a fleet, in addition to providing protection for the nation's overseas empire and worldwide trade, was a necessary proof that Germany was indeed a great power. According to the thinking of the times, a country could not claim to be a great power unless it possessed both an overseas empire and a fleet. From the British perspective, however, the emergence of German naval strength was an unwelcome development. Germany's enormous industrial strength meant that the country was in a position to realize its ambitions of attaining world power status. The concentration of the German fleet in the North Sea implied a potential threat to British security.

The Boer War (1899–1902) crystallized British anxieties about the state of the Empire and the ability of the country to face the challenges of twentieth century. Fought against the descendants of Dutch settlers living in the Transvaal and Orange Free State in South Africa, the war came as a nasty shock to the British people. British troops were routed by Boers on several occasions during the opening phases of the war. Contrary to the expectations of the British military, the Boers proved to be skilled strategists and tacticians. Many were armed with the latest German rifles. Eventually, British military might turned the tide and the Boers were thrown on the defensive. They then resorted to guerilla warfare, which prolonged the conflict by two years. In an effort to separate the Boer armed forces from their civilian supporters the British rounded up more than 120,000 Boer settlers and forced them into concentration camps. The camps were badly supplied and organized. An estimated 20,000 Boer civilians died from disease and starvation before the war ended in 1902.

The Boer War and, in particular, the concentration camp fiasco did considerable damage to Britain's international reputation. The jingoism of the Diamond Jubilee rang hollow after the savage realities of imperial conquest had come to light. Initially the war received popular approval and the government handily won the 'Khaki election' of 1900. However, the later stages of the conflict sparked bitter controversy in the press and in the House of Commons, where David Lloyd George, a young Liberal MP from Wales, emerged as one of the most forceful critics of the war. The fact that it had taken 450,000 British troops three years to defeat fewer than 60,000 Boers raised serious questions about British military competence. During the war the army had rejected large numbers of working-class recruits as physically unfit for military service, which further underlined questions about Britain's ability to defend the Empire. Not surprisingly, the post-war years saw the rise of a national obsession with efficiency. The National Service League, founded in 1902, agitated in favour of compulsory military training for all able-bodied white males in the Empire. General Baden Powell's Boy Scouts movement originated in 1908 with the general aim of preparing British youth to defend the Empire.

The Boer War also damaged relations with Germany. The Kaiser's loud and very undiplomatic support of the Boers caused much resentment in Britain and further strains in Anglo-German relations emerged in the years after 1902. Determined to maintain naval supremacy, Britain reorganized the Royal Navy in 1904, discarding dozens of obsolete vessels and concentrating the navy's remaining strength in home waters. In 1906 Britain raised the stakes with the launching of the *Dreadnought,* an entirely new type of warship designed to make all other battleships obsolete at a stroke. Built in record time, the heavily armoured, high-speed *Dreadnought* carried an armament made up exclusively of heavy twelve-inch guns. The *Dreadnought* was also much more expensive to build, almost doubling the cost of a capital ship. Unfortunately for the British, it was not difficult for the Germans to copy the basic design principles of the *Dreadnought,* and within a few years both Britain and Germany were building warships at a furious pace. The naval race between the two countries reached a crescendo between 1908 and

4

1910, both sides building warships of steadily increasing cost, sophistication and complexity. By 1914 the *Dreadnought* was obsolete and relegated to second-line duties. Britain possessed certain key advantages in the naval race: its shipbuilding industry was larger and more experienced than that of Germany and the morale, confidence and traditions of the Royal Navy conferred valuable intangible benefits. By 1914 Britain had a three-to-two advantage in terms of numbers of capital ships, although the war soon demonstrated, to the discomfort of the Admiralty, that German ships were often superior in terms of quality.

The naval race proved popular with the German and British public alike. In both countries the construction and launching of warships were followed with great interest, while suspicion of the motives of the other side intensified. The British foreign secretary Edward Grey thought that nothing after 1905 soured Anglo-German relations more than the naval race. It ranks as one of the main sources of tension in Europe during the years leading up to 1914 – though one should not conclude that war between Britain and Germany was an inevitable consequence of that race. Similarly, it would be difficult to argue that Britain's diplomatic understanding with France and Russia somehow made war with Germany unavoidable. The course of British diplomacy, conducted with considerable skill during the last decade of the peace, was in fact aimed at preserving the maximum flexibility for Britain in a crisis.

Britain's main objective in its foreign policy during the nineteenth century, or even earlier, had always been to strive for a balance of power in Europe. A rough equilibrium between the major powers in Europe meant that no power could single-handedly threaten British security. Britain would then be free to direct its energies and attention towards the Empire. The final defeat of Napoleon in 1815, followed by the peace settlement at the Congress of Vienna, ensured a long period during which a balance of power in Europe seemed to be at hand. Britain's preferred role in continental affairs was to act as a mediator or honest broker. So, for example, at the Congress of Berlin in 1878 the prime minister, Disraeli, had helped to settle a potentially dangerous dispute in the Balkans. Britain could also intervene militarily when the balance seemed threatened: in 1854 Britain had entered the Crimean War alongside France and Turkey to contain an apparent wave of Russian expansionism. The emergence of a united German empire in 1871 was, ironically, seen in Britain as a positive development. A powerful German state, it was hoped, might restrain both French and Russian ambitions in Europe.

The avoidance of formal alliances was essential to the success of British objectives in the nineteenth century. Keeping a free hand conferred a host of advantages. Britain would not be drawn into quarrels between other nations – always a significant risk in European affairs. Also, paradoxically, Britain would have more leverage over potential friends; an alliance often requires that you follow the lead of your partner, who can also restrict your freedom of action. By standing aloof, Britain stood a better chance of making other countries conform to its will.

Some of this thinking had to be revised by the turn of the century. British diplomats turned their attention increasingly to reducing the numbers of Britain's potential enemies. Accordingly, Lord Lansdowne, appointed foreign secretary in 1900, quickly set to work bolstering the country's international position and brought about an improvement in relations with the United States. In 1902 Britain signed a five-year alliance with Japan, partly to contain Russian ambitions in the Far East, but also to gain the support of an important, emerging regional power. A more significant step was taken in 1904 with the signature of the Anglo-French deal known as the Entente Cordiale.

Relations between Britain and France had been inflamed in the last quarter of the nineteenth century by a number of colonial disputes. In 1882 Britain had conquered Egypt in spite of bitter protests from the French, who owned a substantial interest in the Suez Canal. The British then attempted to extend their control southwards into the Sudan. However, an expedition under the command of General Charles Gordon was wiped out in 1885 at Khartoum by the armies of Muhammad Ahmad, better known as the Mahdi (Messiah). The British gained their revenge in 1898 when an expedition led by Lord Kitchener advanced down the Nile and won a crushing victory over the Mahdists at the Battle of Omdurman.

Kitchener continued south to the village of Fashoda, on the Nile, where he found that a small French expedition had taken up residence. The French were attempting to establish their control over the southern portions of the Sudan before the British could consolidate theirs. Thus the two towering imperial ambitions of Britain and France came face to face with each other at Fashoda in 1898 and a serious confrontation ensued, complete with the risk of war. In the end the French withdrew their expedition, but Fashoda left scars that took time to heal.

Further problems between the two countries arose in 1904 when France's major continental ally, Russia, went to war with Japan, an ally of Britain. The possibility that Britain and France might be drawn into the Russo-Japanese War served to spur talks between Paris and London, one purpose of which was to head off such an unpleasant eventuality. The resulting 1904 Anglo-French entente, or understanding, was aimed at resolving the outstanding colonial disputes between France and Britain. The main feature of the entente saw the French abandon their claims to Egypt. In exchange, Britain recognized French primacy in Morocco. The actual terms of the entente relating to Morocco were kept secret, which aroused the suspicions of the Germans. The entente resulted in an immediate improvement in Anglo-French relations and the benefits for the British were substantial: the chances of Britain becoming involved in war with France were practically nullified and British military liabilities were drastically reduced, especially in the Mediterranean.

The new entente was soon put to the test in 1905. Suspicious about Anglo-French intentions in Morocco, the Germans decided to challenge the French claim. The Germans had long felt that they had been shut out of the colonial race and that Germany had received only the crumbs of the post-1880 scramble for empire. The challenge to French domination of Morocco was designed to rectify that and perhaps drive a wedge into the new Anglo-French entente. The Kaiser visited Morocco, gave inflammatory speeches urging Moroccans to resist the French, then departed. The Germans subsequently managed to initiate a tense confrontation with France. Initially things went well for the Germans, as the French seemed easily intimidated and inclined to make concessions. The French foreign minister, Théophile Delcassé, known as a staunch anti-German, was forced to resign. The Germans demanded that an international conference be held to resolve the issue. It took place at the Spanish coastal town of Algeciras in 1906 but ended badly for the Germans, who found themselves outvoied and supported only by Austria–Hungary. The conference agreed that Morocco would fall into the French sphere of influence, with the exception of a small territory in the north previously reserved for Spain. For some in the British government the Moroccan episode served to seal Germany's image as an aggressive and reckless state. Soon after the crisis conversations took place between French and British military experts on possible military co-operation between the two states in the event of war. The talks, from the British point of view, concerned purely hypothetical circumstances and did not place obligations on either government.

Lansdowne was succeeded at the Foreign Office in December 1905 by Edward Grey. The Liberals went on to win a massive majority in the 1906 election and Grey continued the policy of attempting to reduce the number of Britain's potential enemies. In 1907 Britain signed an entente with Russia aimed at resolving outstanding colonial grievances. From that time on, Britain was counted as a member of the Triple Entente, together with France and Russia, even though the British uncomfortably insisted that the entente was not an alliance and did not involve Britain in formal commitments to go to war on behalf of any nation. According to Grey, it was simply a 'diplomatic grouping'. Within the context of European diplomacy, however, the Triple Entente now served as the counterweight to the Triple Alliance.

The origins of the Triple Alliance stretched back to the Franco-Prussian war of 1870–71, during which Prussia had inflicted a crushing military defeat on France. The conclusion of the war witnessed the proclamation of the German empire at Versailles, on conquered French territory. The Germans proceeded to annex the French province of Alsace and part of the province of Lorraine. The German Chancellor, Otto von Bismarck, realized that it was essential for Germany to keep a potentially vengeful France isolated in European diplomacy. Accordingly, he signed the Dual Alliance with Austria–Hungary in 1879. In 1882 Italy was included with Germany and Austria–Hungary in the Triple Alliance. Bismarck also tried to maintain a diplomatic arrangement with Russia in order to head off a Franco-Russian alliance that would force Germany to fight on two fronts. Initially this was done through the Three Emperor's League, which bound Germany, Austria–Hungary and Russia together. The last two, however, were bitter rivals for power and influence in southeastern Europe. As the Ottoman Empire lost its hold over the Balkans in the late nineteenth century both Russia and Austria–Hungary prepared to swoop in, hoping to expand their own spheres of influence. The Three Emperors' League went through two incarnations before falling apart in 1887. In its place Bismarck negotiated the secret Reinsurance Treaty with Russia to prevent a Russian defection to France.

In 1890, however, Bismarck was dismissed by Wilhelm II. The new Kaiser was determined to follow a more forward foreign policy, called *Weltpolitik* or 'world policy', in contrast to Bismarck, who had proclaimed that Germany was a 'satiated' power. The Kaiser allowed the Reinsurance Treaty to lapse on the grounds that it was incompatible with Germany's commitments to Austria–Hungary under the Dual Alliance. The French seized their opportunity and, after some patient diplomacy, concluded the Franco-Russian treaty of 1894, complete with military agreements. France had thus escaped the isolation that Bismarck had brought about and Germany was faced with the possibility of a two-front war. The British ententes with France in 1904 and Russia in 1907 marked the transformation of the Franco-Russian alliance into a larger, though looser, grouping of powers.

The agreement that Britain concluded with Russia in 1907 delineated spheres of influence in Tibet, Afghanistan and Persia. The Foreign Office hoped that the entente would serve as a means of restraining the ambitions of the Russians, who had been defeated in the Far East at the hands of Japan in 1905 and might – since expansion in the Far East was no longer feasible – cast covetous eyes on Central Asia, ultimately threatening the British position in India. The 1907 entente was therefore aimed at avoiding a confrontation with Russia in Central Asia.

The last few years of peace in Europe were punctuated by a bewildering series of diplomatic crises, played out against the backdrop of the continuing Anglo-German naval race. Austria–Hungary's annexation of Bosnia–Herzegovina in 1908 placed further strain on relations with Russia. The Russians protested vigorously and called for an international conference but were ultimately unable to stop the Austrians. During the crisis the Austrians received full support from Germany – and a perceptive observer at the time might have noticed how quickly a local dispute in the Balkans could draw in major powers by means of the alliance system. The annexation of Bosnia–Herzegovina also triggered a wave of unrest among Serbs in Bosnia, who resisted incorporation into the Austro-Hungarian Empire. Not surprisingly, they wanted to be united with Serbia. In 1911 the Germans returned to the fray in Morocco, sending a gunboat (the *Panther*) to the Moroccan port of Agadir to protest against the consolidation of French control in Morocco. A potentially serious crisis was averted when France granted some land to Germany in North Africa. But to many in Britain it appeared that Germany was intent on establishing a naval base on the Atlantic from which Germany's new fleet could potentially threaten British lifelines. One of those who converted to an anti-German stance as a result of the Moroccan crisis of 1911 was the Liberal government's chancellor of the exchequer, David Lloyd George.

Further crises came thick and fast. The First Balkan War, which began in 1912, saw the Ottoman Turks expelled from Europe by a coalition consisting of Serbia, Montenegro, Greece and Bulgaria. In the Second Balkan War the victorious powers quarrelled over the division of the spoils. A Russian attempt to support a Serb drive to gain an outlet to the sea was frustrated when the Austrians sponsored the creation of an independent Albania. Russia, having been humiliated twice in Europe in recent years, decided that if its status as a great power were not to be jeopardized it must not again back down against Austria–Hungary. Vienna, for its part, decided that Serbia was a menace to Austro-Hungarian security and should be reduced to the status of a satellite state at the first opportunity. Despite the potential dangers in Europe, Grey and the Foreign Office

10

seemed convinced that some sort of reconciliation with Germany was possible. Grey was nervous about the growth of German power and about Germany's long-term intentions, but he also seems to have thought, by 1912, that the entente powers had effectively balanced German power and that Britain could negotiate with Germany from a position of strength.

Meanwhile, in the wake of the Moroccan crisis of 1911, a second round of staff conversations took place between French and British military representatives. Grey insisted later that the French had nothing in writing, and the British repeatedly stated during the talks (and afterwards) that all planning was purely theoretical, but by the end of the talks the British had left the French with the impression that Britain would come to the assistance of France if it were attacked by Germany. In 1912 the British took the decision to remove their naval forces from the Mediterranean to reinforce their home-waters fleet and the French decided to remove theirs from the Channel and Atlantic in order to concentrate on the Mediterranean. The two decisions were taken independently, but together they certainly illustrate the community of interest that existed between the two countries by 1912.

As part of Grey's continuing efforts to find common ground with Germany the British colonial secretary, Viscount Haldane, travelled to Berlin in 1912 to discuss two major issues with his German counterparts. At that time Portugal stood on the brink of bankruptcy and Haldane wanted to know if Germany might be interested in a partition of Portugal's African empire. He also wanted to broach the idea of an agreement limiting further naval construction. Shortly before Haldane's arrival in Berlin the Germans announced that they had allocated further funding for the construction of additional battleships. Discussion over the Portuguese colonies led nowhere, and the Germans said they would only be interested in limiting naval construction if Britain agreed to remain neutral in the event of a European war. Significantly, the British declined to give any such assurance.

The assassination of the Austrian Archduke Franz Ferdinand in Sarajevo on 28 June 1914 gave Vienna the pretext to crush Serbia. The Austrians presented an ultimatum to Serbia on 23 July.

Although the Serbs returned a conciliatory reply, the Austrians declared war on Serbia on 28 July. The Russians mobilized in support of Serbia and Germany rallied to the support of Austria–Hungary. Grey issued a desperate, last-minute call for a conference in London to avert war, but the Germans rejected the proposal. By 3 August Germany was at war with France and Russia. The Germans had already demanded that the government of Belgium allow German troops to pass through Belgian territory as part of the campaign against France. The Belgians refused, but the Germans invaded regardless.

The German invasion of Belgium provided the legal justification for British entry into the war. In 1839 Britain had signed a treaty that guaranteed the independence and neutrality of Belgium. Belgian neutrality was considered to be absolutely essential for British security, since a hostile power in possession of the Belgian ports could easily launch an invasion of Britain. On 4 August 1914 Britain declared war on Germany. The German violation of Belgian neutrality also gave the British a strong moral cause to fight for – namely, the rights of small, independent states. Public opinion in Britain rallied quickly to the cause.

Even if Germany had not violated Belgian neutrality, it is difficult to see how Britain could possibly have stayed out of the war. In the cabinet's deliberations leading up to 4 August Grey insisted that the entente was not an alliance and that Britain had given no formal commitment to France, but he still had no trouble enumerating reasons why Britain should enter the war. Strategic considerations were certainly paramount. If Germany defeated France, Britain would have to confront a vastly strengthened Germany without allies. Despite the informal nature of the entente and the tentative nature of the Anglo-French military talks, British ministers clearly also felt a sense of obligation towards France. British honour was at stake with regard to both France and Belgium. If Britain failed to assist those countries, who would ever again take the word of Britain seriously? And how would Britain manage post-war relations with France and Russia, both of which would be irremediably hostile if Britain stood aside? Arguably, however, it was fear of the consequences of German victory that was the most persuasive reason. A German army in Belgium was not something that a British government could tolerate.

Some theories on the outbreak of war in 1914 argue that European governments resorted to war in order to deflect the attention of their subjects from severe internal problems and stresses of their own. Foreign policy, according to such interpretations, is driven largely by considerations of internal domestic politics, and rallying people around the flag always boosts the popularity of the government. Is there any evidence to suggest that the British government went to war in 1914 to escape from insoluble domestic problems?

Britain certainly faced serious internal problems during that year. A steadily escalating wave of industrial strikes had wracked the country since 1911 and showed no signs of diminishing. Britain had only recently recovered from a serious constitutional crisis in 1911, when the House of Lords tried to veto a budget passed by the House of Commons. Finally, the issue of Home Rule for Ireland had also aroused bitter controversy. In 1914 the Liberal government honoured a long-standing political promise by agreeing to grant autonomy to Ireland. Opposition from Unionists (those who favoured continued union between Britain and Ireland) was fierce, and the Conservative Party in Ireland was renamed the Unionist Party. By July 1914 thousands of Protestant Ulstermen were stockpiling arms and undergoing paramilitary training in an attempt to resist the implementation of Home Rule. When British newspapers wrote of the possibility of war in July 1914 they were referring to the crisis in Ireland, not that in the Balkans.

To prove that the British cabinet went to war in order to escape from these problems would, however, be problematic. The evidence is highly circumstantial and tenuous. The debates in the cabinet and the government were dominated by such issues as the European balance of power, the role of British honour and Britain's obligations towards France. The greatest pressure on Grey came not from any faction of 'hawks' but rather from those who wanted Britain to remain at peace. The pro-peace faction in the cabinet was led by a small but vocal minority of ministers, two of whom were to resign in protest over the British declaration of war. It could also be argued that Britain was the most prosperous of the powers in 1914 and therefore had the most to lose from resorting to war. Far from solving domestic problems, war might only intensify them.

On the other hand, students of the period should also bear in mind that war was widely regarded as an acceptable, even desirable, part of international relations in 1914. Social Darwinism, or the belief that struggle and competition between races and nations were necessary to allow the fittest to emerge, enjoyed considerable popularity in Europe in the pre-war years. The military was glorified in all European states. The years leading up to 1914 were notable for a heightened sense of nationalism and patriotism in Europe. Some intellectuals glorified war as a purifying force that would shake Europe out of its lethargy and provide the impetus needed for the creation of a new society. Finally, we should also remember that almost everyone thought the war would be short and that it would all be over by Christmas. No one foresaw four years of stalemate in the trenches. Taken together, these sorts of considerations helped to rationalize the leap into war. In the major cities of all the belligerent powers news of the outbreak of war in 1914 was greeted by spontaneous mass demonstrations of pro-war enthusiasm. The crowds numbered in the tens of thousands. Anti-war protesters were limited to a tiny, ineffective minority of pacifists.

The first task for British diplomacy during the war was to gain the support of neutral powers. The British had received an early setback when Turkey entered the war on 29 October 1914 on the side of Germany and Austria–Hungary, forming what was henceforth known as the Central Powers. Italy, by contrast, refused to enter the war on the grounds that the Triple Alliance was a strictly defensive arrangement that had been nullified by Austria's attack on Serbia. Secret negotiations between Rome, Paris and London followed. In May 1915 Italy joined the Entente (Allied) Powers and declared war on its former allies. In order to gain Italian support, Britain and France had promised Italy substantial territorial gains in the post-war settlement. These promises, written into the secret Treaty of London, caused endless complications in 1919.

The prolonged stalemate on the Western front, combined with criticisms of Asquith's leadership of the war effort, led to a political realignment in Britain in December 1916. Asquith was forced to resign as prime minister and an all-party coalition government – led by Lloyd George – emerged, determined to continue the war to a successful conclusion. Asquith, supported by a significant proportion of the Liberal Party, bitterly resented Lloyd George's coup. The events of December 1916 led to a fatal split in the British Liberal Party.

The decisive year of the war was 1917. The collapse of the Russian Empire in that year was a severe blow for the Allies. The Bolshevik seizure of power in November meant that the Eastern front could not be reconstructed in the near future. The Bolsheviks, led by Lenin, ardently opposed the war and indeed wanted to turn what they called an 'imperialist war' into a worldwide revolution of workers against capitalists. The draconian Treaty of Brest–Litovsk, which the Germans imposed on a prostrate Russia in March 1918, shocked Western opinion and seemed to confirm fears of German expansionism. Brest–Litovsk attempted to create a network of German-dominated satellite states over all eastern Europe while pushing Russia as far to the east as possible.

In April 1917, however, the United States declared war on Germany. The entry of the United States into the war more than compensated for the loss of the Eastern front, even though it took a full year to translate potential American strength into a fighting field army. A last-ditch German offensive in the spring of 1918, using troops transferred from the east, aimed to win the war for Germany before American strength could be brought to bear. The German offensive forced the Allies to give up much ground, but the latter were now building up reserves while the Germans were squandering the last of theirs. The Allies unleashed a long-awaited counter-offensive in the summer. By the autumn the Central Powers were on the verge of collapse: Turkey succumbed to a British offensive from Egypt, and Austria–Hungary surrendered after suffering a decisive defeat at Vittorio Veneto. But the German defeat was curiously indecisive: nowhere had Allied troops crossed into German territory on the Western front. German citizens had been assured by their government that they were winning the war, and as late as March 1918 German troops had been victorious, occupying large swathes of eastern Europe and forcing the Allies back in the west. Many Germans could scarcely believe in November that they had lost the war.

Historians and the inter-war period[4]

The main controversy among historians of British inter-war foreign policy has always concerned the policy of appeasement. Generally, the term appeasement refers to the policy that was pursued by the British government towards Nazi Germany, Italy and Japan during the 1930s. Appeasement is most often associated with the prime ministers Stanley Baldwin and, especially, Neville Chamberlain,[5] although there has also been spirited debate on the roots of appeasement, some historians tracing its origins back to the nineteenth century. The Munich conference of 29–30 September 1938 is generally viewed as the high point (or low point, depending on perspective) of appeasement.

Critics have always argued that appeasement entailed granting concessions to Britain's enemies in the futile hope of gaining agreements that would prevent war but in the pursuit of which long-cherished moral principles (such as the defence of small countries) were frequently sacrificed. The most extreme critics have also charged Chamberlain and his cabinet colleagues with naïveté, gullibility and carelessness.

Sympathizers of Chamberlain and defenders of appeasement have stressed the overwhelming nature of the problems that Britain faced in the 1930s and viewed appeasement as a realistic means of coming to grips with the country's substantial defensive liabilities at that time. According to this line of argument, Britain had little alternative but to pursue the sorts of policies that it did. As one historian noted, appeasement was 'massively overdetermined; any other policy in 1938 would have been an astounding, almost inexplicable divergence from the norm'.[6] Britain's weakened military and economic position in the 1930s made it imperative to avoid war. British leaders feared that war against Germany would invite attacks from Japan and Italy on the far-flung, hard to defend reaches of the British Empire. Public opinion in Britain regarded the prospect of another bloody war, only twenty years after the end of the last, with fear and horror, especially since the next war would mean the widespread aerial bombardment of civilian populations. Potential allies for Britain were in short supply in the 1930s. France was divided internally between left and right and the British leadership placed little confidence in that country's ability to conduct a war. The Dominions and the United States were in the grip of isolationism. The Soviet Union was mistrusted and, in any event, British experts held grave doubts about Soviet military capabilities in the wake of the Stalinist purges. Alternative policies put forward by the parliamentary opposition seemed hopelessly unrealistic. Given the weight of circumstances beyond his control, Chamberlain's policy of avoiding war in 1938 seems logical. The most ardent apologists for Chamberlain also argue that he was seeking time for Britain to rearm, although, as will be seen, that theory holds little water.

Critics of appeasement held sway during the period from the outbreak of war in 1939 until the mid-1960s. The tone was set by two works: *Guilty Men* by 'Cato'[7] and *The Gathering Storm* by Winston Churchill,[8] the former prime minister and the leader of the British wartime resistance. 'Cato' was the pseudonym adopted by a committee of three journalists (Michael Foot, Peter Howard and Frank Owen) who sat down during the Dunkirk disaster in May 1940 to write an account of what had led Britain to the brink of defeat. (They chose their name because they were going to clean out the British government, just as Cato had cleaned out the sewers of Rome.) They argued that the governments of the last three British prime ministers (Ramsay MacDonald, Stanley Baldwin and Neville Chamberlain) had failed to rearm Britain, had deceived public opinion about the state of British security and had remained willfully blind to the expansionist and aggressive foreign policy aims of Adolf Hitler. The book (actually not much more than a thick pamphlet) proved wildly popular and its condemnation of appeasement influenced an entire generation. Many of the criticisms in *Guilty Men* were bolstered after the war, when Winston Churchill published *The Gathering Storm*, the first volume of his six-volume *History of the Second World War*. Churchill echoed many of Cato's criticisms and somewhat misrepresented his own role in the events of the inter-war years, but his book was fundamental in setting the tone of historiography for the 1950s and 1960s. A strong stand by Britain in 1938, Churchill argued, would have stopped Hitler once and for all. The 1960s saw a continued stream of 'guilty men' publications, with titles such as *The Warped Vision*[9] or *The Appeasers*.[10]

There was a hint in the early 1960s that the accepted version of the origins of the Second World War would not remain unchallenged for ever. In 1961 the British historian A. J. P. Taylor published *The Origins of the Second World War*.[11] The book offered a new interpretation of Hitler, viewing him as a traditional German statesman who was pursuing long-standing objectives in German foreign policy. Taylor also offered a generally sympathetic portrait of appeasement. His book generated enormous controversy, but its conclusions have not withstood the test of time and the weight of evidence that has been released over the years from European archives. Taylor's most lasting legacy has been his essential way of looking at appeasement, taking it outside a moral framework. At the time, Taylor's iconoclastic views offered a taste of things to come.

In 1967 the British government reduced the closed period on access to archived government documents from fifty years to thirty. The result – beginning in the late 1960s and accelerating into the 1970s – was a wave of revisionist literature. Discounting its early critics, the new historians aimed to explain appeasement in a fuller historical context. Earlier criticisms of appeasement were dismissed as simplistic and as focusing too much on the alleged failures of individuals and their personalities. The new wave of historians emphasized Britain's economic fragility and strategic overextension in the 1930s. Highly specialized studies poured forth, illuminating every aspect of the British predicament with regard to foreign policy during that decade. Prominent members of the new generation included David Dilks, W. N. Medlicott, Donald Cameron Watt and Stephen Roskill. By no means should all the revisionists be classed as supporters of Chamberlain or apologists for appeasement, but the net effect of their work was to call into question the conclusions of the early critics of appeasement.

Unlike the fiftieth anniversary of the outbreak of the First World War, which had seen another round of debates on the issue of German war guilt, the fiftieth anniversary of the beginning of the Second

World War passed with comparatively little historical controversy. With the origins of the Second World War the issues seemed much more clear cut: guilt was squarely placed on Hitler – which lowered the temperature of the debate. For many of those who studied British foreign policy the new revisionist works seemed convincing. Even when revisionism was at its height, however, there was a certain amount of dissatisfaction with its received wisdoms. The reliance on government documentation provoked a measure of criticism. The problem with government documents is that they make it appear as though the adopted course of action was the only one possible. Yet politicians may have decided on a particular course and sought to justify their decision afterwards. On the other hand, no responsible historian can afford to ignore government documents as a source of evidence. Revisionist accounts also often seemed content to list all the possible reasons for appeasement, piling them haphazardly one on top of another without order or priority. As one prominent historian (writing of another period) noted, it is possible for historians to cast their net so widely that everything becomes relevant.[12] Individuals and their decisions disappear in such an approach to history. Not surprisingly, the new interpretations of appeasement often failed to gain credibility with the general public, who often expressed scepticism or disbelief when presented with revisionist findings.

The past few years have witnessed a modest revival of the 'counter-revisionist' view in works that attack revisionist histories of appeasement as being over-specialized to the point of irrelevance. Historians such as Sidney Aster, Anthony Adamthwaite and R. A. C. Parker have sought to restore the credibility of early critics of appeasement. Aster, for example, argues that Cato's charges against Chamberlain were essentially correct.[13] Parker's book, *Chamberlain and Appeasement: British Policy and the Coming of the Second World War*,[14] is the most sustained and comprehensive of the counter-revisionists' counterattacks. Basing himself almost entirely on primary sources, the author argues that, 'led by Chamberlain, the government rejected effective deterrence' – namely, alliances with the USSR and France. He assigns a significant role to Chamberlain's character: 'Chamberlain's powerful, obstinate personality and his skill in debate probably stifled serious chances of preventing the Second World War'.[15]

Another recent, though limited, trend in historiography has been the application of insights from political science to the events of the 1930s. Can models of bureaucratic politics, crisis management or decision-making offer new insights into the events of the 1930s? A recent study by Gaines Post, for example, argues that the chaotic nature of Britain's bureaucracy and decision-making process enormously complicated the British response to Hitler in the 1930s.[16] More studies of this nature can be expected, though there is also likely to be resistance from historians. Social science methodologies tend to result in abstract works that can be difficult to read. The statesmen and diplomats that seem so animated when historians are writing about them can in social scientific studies quickly be relegated to graphs, charts and statistics.[17]

Studies of British foreign policy in the inter-war era have been greatly assisted over the years by the wealth of official documentation that is available to historians. Students and readers should perhaps turn first to the collection entitled *Documents on British Foreign Policy*, edited by Llewellyn Woodward, Rohan Butler, W. N. Meddlicott and others.[18] Organized into three series, this collection of more than sixty volumes (each containing hundreds of documents) has a comprehensive selection of material from the Foreign Office's archives, including ambassadors' reports, instructions from London to overseas embassies and memoranda analysing various aspects of British foreign relations, as well as the occasional cabinet document. The editors have also reproduced some of the written commentaries (or minutes) attached to the documents. The material is presented chronologically according to subject. A similar series for Germany – *Documents on German Foreign Policy* – was issued in the 1950s,[19] and the Americans have issued *Foreign Relations of the United States*.[20]

In recent years *Documents on British Foreign Policy* has been supplemented by a new series entitled *British Documents on Foreign Affairs: Reports and Papers from the Foreign Office Confidential Print*.[21] This collection, which will eventually comprise 420 volumes, digs deeper into the Foreign Office's archives and contains reprints of a wider range of 'lower-level' documents – including, for instance, telegrams and reports from military attachés, embassy staff and ambassadors – that deal with domestic conditions in the host countries. Nearly all of the reprinted documents were originally intended for limited circulation within the Foreign Office. The collection is organized into eleven geographical and subject areas, such as the USSR, the Middle East, North America, Europe and the League of Nations. British Foreign Office correspondence is also available on microfilm.[22]

Cabinet material has been reproduced on microfilm, and can be accessed through university libraries. The available documentation includes minutes and memoranda from cabinet meetings, as well as records from the numerous cabinet committees that proliferated during the inter-war years. Documents from the Committee for Imperial Defence are also available on microfilm. The original cabinet and Foreign Office documents are held at the Public Record Office in London, whose website can be accessed on the Internet.[23]

Historians of the inter-war era have also been particularly fortunate in that many British government officials and diplomats kept diaries or wrote memoirs of their experiences, or both. Memoirs, of course, must be approached with caution, as the authors want to present their historical record in the best possible light, but no serious historian could choose to ignore the rich legacy left by the diplomats of the period. Some of the more detailed memoirs were produced by the most prominent figures of the time, such as the multi-volume set by Anthony Eden,[24] but a number of lesser-known individuals also wrote fascinating memoirs. Here, one could cite Fitzroy Maclean's *Eastern Approaches*,[25] F. S. G. Piggott's *Broken Thread*[26] and Ivone Kirkpatrick's *The Inner Circle*.[27] Maclean worked at the British embassy in Moscow during the worst phase of the Stalinist terror in the late 1930s. He observed the infamous Moscow show-trials of 1938, where prominent Soviet communists were put on trial and accused of fantastic crimes against the state. Maclean also made a number of surreptitious journeys into Siberia and Soviet Central Asia and through the Russian countryside. Piggott was stationed at the Tokyo embassy as a military attaché in the late 1930s and witnessed the progressive breakdown in relations between Japan and Britain, while Kirkpatrick served on the staff of the British embassy in Berlin and encountered Hitler and other leading Nazis in dramatic face-to-face meetings in 1938. Valentine Lawford's *Bound for Diplomacy* recalls the experiences of a neophyte entering the pressure-cooker atmosphere of the Foreign Office in the mid-1930's.[28] Finally, even a brief survey of the memoir and diary literature must call attention to *The Diaries of Sir Alexander Cadogan*, edited by David Dilks.[29] Cadogan, head of the British Foreign Office in the late 1930s, left a remarkable record of the seemingly endless series of crises that plagued Britain in 1938–39. Cadogan's terse writing style, combined with some unforgettable characterizations and the full historical context provided by the editor, makes *The Diaries* an invaluable source.

Those interested in the press and the unfolding of public opinion are also not lacking in material. Most of the leading newspapers of the inter-war period are available on microfilm, including *The Times*, the *Observer* and the *Manchester Guardian*. Many of the quality journals read by the political élite (such as *Round Table*) can also be found in university libraries. Another often overlooked source for newcomers to the field is *Keesing's Contemporary Archives*,[30] which provides a weekly diary of world events from 1931 on, with source references and indexes.

Historical research on British foreign policy in the inter-war period has been blessed with impressive documentary holdings. The vast extent of sources alone guarantees continuing interest. If the historical debate over appeasement continues to polarize between the 'guilty men' and the 'troubled times' schools, we will surely see an argument without end. We are more likely to witness the emergence of what historian Paul Kennedy called a 'two-tier' history: one that combines large historical forces with an appreciation of the role of individuals. The need for such an approach will best be illustrated when we turn to the British experience at the Paris Peace Conference of 1919.

The background

Notes

1 E. Hobsbawm, *Age of Extremes: The Short Twentieth Century, 1914–1991* (New York, Vintage, 1995), p. 3. Poll statistics reported in *The Globe and Mail Report on Business*, August 1995, from a report in the London *Sunday Times*.

2 Joseph Chamberlain, quoted in P. Kennedy, *The Rise and Fall of the Great Powers: Economic Change and Military Conflict from 1500 to 2000* (New York, Random House, 1987), p. 229.

3 See P. Kennedy, *The Rise of the Anglo-German Antagonism, 1860–1914* (London, Ashfield, 1980).

4 To do justice to the thousands of monographs and articles on inter-war British foreign policy would require a historiographical volume in itself. All I have attempted to do here is provide readers with some general signposts to guide them through the controversies over appeasement.

5 It was customary at one time to label Baldwin's foreign policy 'passive appeasement', whereas Chamberlain's was called 'active appeasement'. The terminology reflects the difference in style between the two leaders. Baldwin reacted to events, while Chamberlain sought to solve problems before they arose.

6 P. Schroeder, 'Munich and the British tradition', *The Historical Journal,* XIX, 1976, pp. 223–43.

7 Cato, *Guilty Men* (London, Gollancz, 1940).

8 W. S. Churchill, *The Gathering Storm* (Boston, Houghton Mifflin, 1948).

9 M. George, *The Warped Vision: British Foreign Policy and its Critics* (Pittsburgh, University of Pittsburgh Press, 1965).

10 M. Gilbert and R. Gott, *The Appeasers* (Boston, Houghton Mifflin, 1963).

11 A. J. P Taylor, *The Origins of the Second World War* (Harmondsworth, Penguin, 1964).

12 Z. Steiner, *Britain and the Origins of the First World War* (London, Macmillan, 1977).

13 S. Aster, 'Guilty men: the case of Neville Chamberlain', in R. Boyce and E. Robertson (eds), *Paths to War: New Essays on the Origins of the Second World War* (New York, Macmillan, 1989).

14 R. A. C. Parker, *Chamberlain and Appeasement: British Policy and the Coming of the Second World War* (London, Macmillan, 1993).

15 Parker, *Chamberlain and Appeasement*, p. 347.

16 G. Post Jr, *Dilemmas of Appeasement: British Deterrence and Defense, 1934–1937* (Ithaca, Cornell University Press, 1993).

17 S. Smith (ed.), *International Relations: British and American Perspectives* (New York, Basil Blackwell, 1985), especially chapter eight by C. Hill, 'History and international relations'.

18 L. Woodward, R. Butler, W. Medlicott *et al.*, *Documents on British Foreign Policy, 1919–1939* (London, HMSO, 1946–ongoing).

19 R. Sontag, J. Wheeler-Bennett *et al.* (eds), *Documents on German Foreign Policy 1918–1945*, Series C and D (London, HMSO, 1957–1964).

20 *Papers Relating to the Foreign Relations of the United States* (Washington, Government Printing Office, ongoing).

21 D. C. Watt and K. Bourne (eds), *British Documents on Foreign Affairs: Reports and Papers from the Foreign Office Confidential Print* (Frederick, Maryland,

University Publications of America, 1984–present).

22 *British Foreign Office Correspondence* (Wilmington, Delaware, Scholarly Resources, 1980 to present). Series divided into countries and time periods (e.g. Russian correspondence, 1946–1948, United States correspondence, 1930–1937).

23 The website address is *http://h-net2.msu.edu/~diplo/links/links.htm* Go to the heading 'National Archives' and click on 'UK Public Record Office'.

24 A. Eden, *Full Circle*; *Facing the Dictators*; and *The Reckoning* (London, Cassell, 1960, 1962 and 1965).

25 F. Maclean, *Eastern Approaches* (London, Jonathan Cape, 1949).

26 F. S. G. Piggott, *Broken Thread* (Aldershot, Gale and Polden, 1950).

27 I. Kirkpatrick, *The Inner Circle: Memoirs of Ivone Kirkpatrick* (London, Macmillan, 1959).

28 V. Lawford, *Bound for Diplomacy* (London, John Murray, 1963).

29 D. Dilks (ed.), *The Diaries of Sir Alexander Cadogan, 1938–1945* (London, Cassell, 1971).

30 *Keesing's Contemporary Archives* (London, Keesing's Publications, 1931 onwards; various publishers since 1970s). Currently known as *Keesing's Record of World Events*, published by Cartermill.

CHAPTER TWO

THE PARIS PEACE CONFERENCE, 1919

The British delegation to the Paris Peace Conference checked into the Hotel Majestic on the Avenue Kléber during the first few days of January 1919. On the cross-channel voyage the prime minister and other members of the British delegation had noted long lines of transport ships returning demobilized soldiers to Britain. A total of 207 delegates represented the Foreign Office, the War Office, the Admiralty, the Air Department, the Treasury, the Board of Trade and the Dominions. The Hotel Astoria, adjoining the Hotel Majestic, was taken over for use as office accommodation. The food, prepared by chefs specially imported from Britain, proved to be terrible: prices in post-war Paris were rising rapidly and vegetables, fruit and milk were virtually unobtainable. The Spanish influenza was raging and the top floor of the hotel was soon converted into a sick-bay. The British prime minister, David Lloyd George, arrived on Saturday 11 January and settled into quarters in the Rue Nitot, together with the foreign secretary, Arthur Balfour. The conference proceedings began with a meeting of the Supreme Council[1] on 12 January and the first formal session took place on the afternoon of Saturday 18 January. Nine weeks had passed since the German surrender on the Western front. The delegation from the United States was led by president Woodrow Wilson and the French by their prime minister, Georges Clemenceau. Thirty-two nations sent delegations to Paris and five hundred members of the world's press congregated on the city to report on every detail of the conference.

The members of the British contingent were confident and considered themselves well prepared for the work that they were about to undertake. This was just as well, since the tasks associated with peacemaking were formidable. The war had cost the British 723,000 dead and 1,700,000 wounded, and the horrible and futile offensives at Ypres, Loos, the Somme and Passchendaele were to scar the public mind for years to come. Between 1920 and 1923 the British government shipped thousands of headstones to France every week to mark the graves of British soldiers lost in combat – some weeks as many as four thousand.[2] During the ceremonies on 11 November 1920 marking the interment of the unknown soldier 100,000 wreaths were laid at the Whitehall cenotaph in London. Armistice days, cemeteries and cenotaphs were the legacy of the Great War, as it was then known. The financial cost was astronomical. The British Treasury estimated that the total Allied war effort had cost £24 billion. Britain had been forced to liquidate overseas investments to finance the war and was now heavily in debt to the United States. Markets and investment opportunities had also been lost – some irretrievably.

As might be expected, the mood of the people in Britain at the end of the war was not particularly generous towards the defeated Germans. The election campaign of 1918 had given rise to talk of hanging the Kaiser, putting German war criminals on trial and exacting a large indemnity from Germany. During the campaign a number of politicians, including Lloyd George, pandered to calls for retribution from Germany, but a more generous side to public opinion also emerged. Many in Britain and across Europe hoped that a new era was about to dawn in international relations; the 'old diplomacy' of alliances and secret deals had only resulted in war. The diplomats themselves – very often members of the aristocracy – now stood discredited by their spectacular failures. Idealists hoped that democracy and the rule of law would replace the anarchy and brutality that were alleged to have dominated the international arena before 1914.

Such hopes and ideals were fanned by president Wilson. In a speech to Congress in January 1918 Wilson outlined what he hoped would be the basis of a fair peace settlement. The Fourteen Points, as Wilson's principles came to be known, called for national self-determination, freedom of the seas, freedom of trade, a mutual reduction in armaments, 'open' diplomacy (open covenants openly arrived at) and a new international organization – a League of Nations – to uphold the peace. The Fourteen Points, which were later reinforced by the Four Principles and the Five Particulars, proved popular with many sectors of the British public, and few saw any contradiction between Wilson's ideals and the desires for a harsh peace. Lloyd George found it expedient to give speeches expressing views that were consistent with Wilsonism, just as he had found it expedient to play to calls for a harsh peace settlement.

Behind the scenes, however, the British government registered doubts and reservations about Wilson's programme. Lloyd George thought, for example, that Wilson's call for freedom of the seas might impede the Royal Navy's ability to impose wartime blockades. The British naval blockade of Germany, which continued until the Germans signed the peace treaty in 1919, was assumed to have been a major factor in Germany's defeat. Lloyd George persuaded Wilson to state publicly that freedom of the seas did not preclude the right to impose a blockade in time of war.

Studies of international relations should always take into account the influence of domestic politics on the formulation of foreign policy. At the Paris Peace Conference domestic politics were particularly relevant. In the United States the Congressional elections of November 1918 turned out to be something of an upset: the Republicans under the leadership of Henry Cabot Lodge gained control of Congress. They were strongly opposed to Wilson, a Democrat, attacked his ideals and opposed all future commitment in European affairs. Under the terms of the constitution, Congress was required to ratify peace treaties with foreign states. Wilson was unlikely to receive the necessary approval after Lodge's victory and he arrived in Paris with the knowledge that his authority at home was sharply restricted.

Much hard feeling existed in France, but the French had two basic, non-negotiable aims at the conference. First and foremost, they wanted security against Germany. France had endured two devastating invasions from Germany in the space of less than half a century. No significant natural geographical barriers existed in northeast France or Belgium to slow down a determined attacker.

In 1919 France's population was forty million and basically static, while Germany's numbered more than sixty million and was growing rapidly. French military planners forecast that by the mid-1930s France's manpower pool would be significantly smaller than Germany's. Something had to be done to assure France's security. Second, France needed money to rebuild the devastated northeastern regions of the country. The French government intended to make sure some of that money came from Germany.[3]

The British political landscape of 1918–19 was a particularly important factor in the determination of subsequent British actions. During the war the Liberal Party continued as the main governing party, but some Conservative and Labour Members had been invited into the cabinet in a show of national unity. In 1916 the Liberal Party split into factions led by the then prime minister, Asquith, and his arch-rival, Lloyd George. Lloyd George and his supporters deposed Asquith in December 1916 and Lloyd George became prime minister. An election was called when the war ended in November 1918, but it was an election unlike any other in British history. There had not been a vote in Britain since 1910. In 1918 the franchise was widened considerably by virtue of the Representation of the People Act. Property qualifications were eliminated, and men and women over the ages of twenty-one and thirty, respectively, now had the right to vote. Two million men and six million women voted in 1918 for the first time, making for an electorate three times the size of that of 1910.

Lloyd George wanted to continue the wartime show of unity, so his Liberal supporters fought the election in a coalition with the Conservatives. Coalition candidates had to have endorsement papers signed by Lloyd George himself. These were scorned as 'coupons' by Asquith, whose supporters ran as independent Liberals, and the election has since become known as the 'coupon election'. When the ballots were counted the coalition had won 478 seats out of 707, a great personal victory for Lloyd George. Somewhat more ominous for Lloyd George was the fact that there were now 335 Conservative MPs in the government. One observer characterized them as 'hard faced men who look[ed] as if they had done very well out of the war'.[4] Lloyd George found himself dependent on the

Conservatives for political survival. Perhaps inevitably, during the Paris Peace Conference he took stands on the basis of their popularity and in spite of his own private misgivings. His vulnerability was most evident on the issue of reparations. Government backbenchers repeatedly pushed him further in the direction of punitive reparations than he wished to go.

We must also consider the prime minister's somewhat idiosyncratic method of governing. Lloyd George hated set routines and traditional cabinet procedures. Furthermore, he had to fend off the ambitions of several discontented and strong-willed cabinet colleagues, most of them Conservative, who were quite willing to depose him as prime minister should he make the slightest misstep. Not surprisingly, Lloyd George came to rely on a small group of personal advisers known as the 'Garden Suburb' (they met in a tin hut in the back garden of the prime minister's residence), who had served him well between 1916 and 1918. The most prominent of these by 1919 included Maurice Hankey, head of the cabinet secretariat, and Philip Kerr, private secretary to the prime minister and former editor of the influential journal *Round Table*. Hankey was a particularly influential figure whose job involved much more than organizing cabinet paperwork and taking minutes. He regarded himself as an ideas man, someone who could feed Lloyd George concepts on crucial policy matters. He was also secretary to the Committee of Imperial Defence (which advised the cabinet on all matters of defence) and he remained at both posts until his retirement in 1939. His longevity can be attributed to the superb working relationships he developed with successive prime ministers. In 1937 the prime minister Neville Chamberlain described Hankey as 'that institution indispensable to the state'.[5]

Lloyd George's dislike of routine and tradition also manifested itself in his attitude towards the Foreign Office. That great institution of pre-war British government was the one branch of the government that should logically have dominated policy-making at the Paris Peace Conference. Instead, its members noticed a steep decline in its influence and prestige under Lloyd George. Foreign Office officials complained bitterly, even before the conference began, that their access to Lloyd George was being restricted by Kerr and Hankey. During the war many Foreign Office functions had been usurped by other government departments, such as the War Office, the Ministry of Information and of course the Garden Suburb. In spite of their perceived marginalization many of the younger members of the Foreign Office delegation, such as Harold Nicolson, sailed off to Paris filled with Wilsonian ideals and sure that a new, much more liberating era free from militarism and despotism was at hand.[6]

The main British objective at the conference was to end the threat posed by Germany's military power in general and its high seas fleet in particular. A major step in reducing German military prowess had already been taken when the bulk of its fleet sailed into internment at Scapa Flow shortly after the armistice. The German crews scuttled the ships, but the British still wanted to be sure that the German naval threat would never materialize again. The British government also expected reparations from the Germans, and Lloyd George was under pressure from the press to ensure that Britain was not cheated of its rightful share. The Dominions wanted to retain the German overseas colonies in Africa and the Pacific that they had conquered during the war. Finally, the British government wanted to keep military and diplomatic commitments in European affairs to a minimum, partly in reaction to the tragedy of the First World War. British leaders sincerely hoped, however, that Europe would soon return to an era of peace, prosperity and stability. Britain could then turn its attention back to the Empire.[7]

In formal terms, Britain's aims in Europe were defined as

peace and order with open facilities for trade, balance of power, territorial reconstruction based on the principle of nationality, and the maintenance of British security along the coastline opposite the British Isles.[8]

Strong hopes also existed for a continued close co-operation with the United States. Some members of the government, such as Kerr and the 'Atlanticists', hoped to build a new post-war partnership with the United States, ideally through the new League of Nations. Others, such as Hankey, were less optimistic about the chances of a successful post-war collaboration with the United States.

Europe at the end of the war

As the delegates from the victorious powers assembled in Paris they found themselves confronted by a Europe that was in a state of chaos and despair. In defeated Germany the Kaiser had been succeeded by a republican form of government that immediately came under fire from both the extreme left and the extreme right. In eastern and central Europe the disintegration of the Austro-Hungarian and Russian empires left behind a welter of successor states struggling for survival. Many in the British Foreign Office welcomed the emergence of the new East European states with open arms, seeing in them the fulfilment of the Wilsonian vision of national self-determination. They hoped that the old autocratic empires had vanished for ever. As Nicolson recalled, 'it was the thought of the new Serbia, the new Greece, the new Bohemia, the new Poland which made our hearts sing hymns at heaven's gate'.[9] Others, Lloyd George included, considered that the new states were aggressive and potentially troublesome. A few worried about the long-term viability of small states sandwiched between a resurgent Germany and Russia.

In Russia civil war continued between the Bolsheviks (later the Communists), led by Lenin and Trotsky, and the counter-revolutionary White Russians. After seizing power in November 1917 Lenin signed the Treaty of Brest–Litovsk with Germany in March 1918. Under the terms of the treaty Russia left the war and ceded vast areas of eastern Europe (including Poland, the Ukraine and the Baltic States) to German control. Given the complete collapse of the Russian armies, the Bolsheviks had no alternative but to agree to German demands. However, the loss of the vital Eastern front could not be tolerated by the Allies, who did not want the German armies stationed in Russia to be released for an offensive in the West. The British, along with the French, Canadians, Americans and Japanese, quickly despatched troops to Russia to rally the Whites and overthrow the Bolsheviks. They hoped that a new Russian government would then re-enter the war against Germany. Another reason for wanting to oust the Bolsheviks was that they had seriously embarrassed the Allies when, shortly after seizing power, they published a number of secret wartime treaties that proved that the war aims of the Allies were not as high-minded as their propaganda had made out.[10]

Despite Bolshevik propaganda proclaiming the end of the capitalist era and the imminence of a workers' revolution, Lloyd George realized that Lenin's régime was beleaguered and weak. He initially hoped to invite Lenin's government to send delegates to Paris, arguing that European peace would be difficult to attain without Russian participation, but Wilson and the ferociously anti-Bolshevik Clemenceau vetoed his proposal. France was particularly hostile to the Bolsheviks after they nationalized substantial French investments in Russia. The rationale for keeping British troops in Russia diminished after the German surrender and although Britain continued to extend assistance to the Whites in their losing struggle against the Bolsheviks, its military presence in Russia was slowly wound down during 1919. Some in Britain – especially on the right – feared that the Bolsheviks might take advantage of the disorder and devastation in eastern and central Europe to attempt a strike westwards. In 1919 short-lived communist régimes in Hungary and Bavaria seemed to confirm such fears, as did Lenin's decision to found the Communist International, or Comintern. The Comintern was to serve as a 'general staff' for what was expected to be the European workers' revolution. In subsequent years Lloyd George showed some inventiveness in dealing with the new revolutionary régime in Russia and its supra-national ideology, but for now, the Russians were strictly excluded from the proceedings in Paris.

Finally, the long-awaited disintegration of the so-called 'sick man of Europe', the Ottoman Empire, left a weakened and discredited government in Turkey. The former Ottoman Arab domains in the vast region stretching from Mesopotamia (modern Iraq) to Palestine (most of modern Israel) faced uncertainty. The future of Turkey's Arab domains had been the focus of many of the secret deals made between the Allies during the war.

Despite the nine-week gap between the German surrender and the first session of the conference, the Allies had been unable to come up with a previously agreed agenda for the conference. Nevertheless, the delegates began their work on 12 January, observed closely by the world's press. In mid-February Lloyd George and Wilson returned home to catch up on domestic business while their delegates continued without them. The leaders stayed away one month and resumed work in Paris in mid-March. April was marred by bitter disagreements on several issues. Most of the major, final decisions were taken in May. After considerable protest from the Germans the treaty was signed in the Parisian suburb of Versailles on 28 June 1919. The treaty with Germany has since become known as the Treaty of Versailles.

Negotiating the peace

In many respects analyses of the proceedings in Paris tend to focus on the slow, crushing sense of disappointment felt by adherents of Wilson's principles. First one, then another of these principles were thrown by the wayside, usually sacrificed to the ambitions of the great powers, until hardly any were left. Harold Nicolson estimated that only four of Wilson's twenty-three Points, Principles and Particulars survived the conference to be written into the final treaty. Mutual recrimination and finger-pointing abounded in the post-war years. The French were denounced for their vengefulness and determination to inflict a harsh, vindictive, 'Carthaginian' peace. The Americans received blame for abandoning Europe, retreating into isolationism and contributing little more than demands for repayment of Allied debts. The successor states were criticized for their ambitions, the Germans for their refusal to accept defeat, and the British for their unwillingness to support the French. There was plenty of blame to go around, but critics of the treaty are often hard-pressed to suggest better alternatives.

The first disappointment arose over the issue of open diplomacy, which many naïvely assumed meant public control over the diplomatic process; but open diplomacy was awfully difficult to put into practice at the Paris conference. No fewer than thirty-two nations were represented and most arrived with large delegations of experts prepared to discuss all the conceivable issues. The initial arrangement was too cumbersome to function effectively, so the conference settled on a Council of Ten. The Council comprised the leaders of the five victorious allied powers (Britain, the United

States, France, Italy and Japan) and their foreign ministers. But even the Council of Ten proved too unwieldy and it soon became apparent that Japan was only interested in issues related to the Pacific – a very small part of the proceedings. Major decisions quickly devolved to the so-called Council of Four – the leaders of the United States, Britain, France and Italy. But Orlando, the Italian prime minister, did not speak English so was quickly marginalized. The decisions of the conference were finally taken by Wilson, Lloyd George and Clemenceau, meeting privately on 145 occasions, beginning in late March. At first, no one bothered to keep a formal record of what transpired at those meetings, but so many misunderstandings resulted that Hankey assumed the role of minute-taker. To observers, the steady centralization of decision-making did not look much like open diplomacy. Critics argued that open diplomacy in fact meant little more than public discussions of decisions taken privately by the Big Three.

An equally controversial decision, made early on, was the exclusion of the Germans from the conference. Here the Allies were drawing on a lesson learned from history. In 1815 the Congress of Vienna had been called to redraw European borders after a quarter-century of nearly constant revolution and warfare, mostly at the hands of Napoleon. The French were represented in Vienna by Prince Talleyrand, a hugely talented diplomat who proved adept at manipulating the divisions between the victorious powers to the advantage of France. The Allies were determined not to let a German Talleyrand emerge at Versailles and therefore did not invite the Germans to the deliberations. Only towards the end of the conference in May did Germany receive an invitation to send a delegation. The Germans were then simply handed the completed treaty. Although they were given time to submit written reservations, no one paid much attention to their response. In subsequent years German nationalists would complain bitterly that they had been forced to sign a dictated peace, or diktat. Such arbitrary treatment was perhaps to be expected since Germany had after all lost the war. Again, the problem was that Wilsonism – with its promise of open diplomacy that was never really defined properly – had led people to expect something very different. Many Germans thought that Germany had made peace in November on the basis of the Fourteen Points and were shocked to discover otherwise. Of course, the diktat grievance was also whipped up and exaggerated by German nationalists for their own political purposes.

The League of Nations

The first major accomplishment of the Paris Peace Conference was the creation of the League of Nations. The idea of an international organization that would guarantee the peace had been much talked about in liberal circles during the war and a League of Nations Union had been founded in Britain in 1915 to promote the League. The idea of a league proved to have great popular appeal, but also generated a series of questions: What would be the characteristics of the new organization? How much national sovereignty should governments give up to the League of Nations? Would it be a strong organization with automatic collective agreements or a much looser, informal gathering of great powers? How would aggressors be punished? Should an international army be created? Would economic sanctions be an effective deterrent to aggressors? The most ardent supporters of the League of Nations favoured a powerful organization that would uphold world peace through collective security and the use of automatic economic sanctions against aggressors. A strong league could supplant traditional, pre-war means of upholding international peace, such as the balance of power. It would also impinge heavily on national sovereignty. The popularity of the League ideal reflected the extent to which the 'old diplomacy' had been discredited by 1918.

The creation of a league featured prominently in Wilson's Fourteen Points and it was well known that he wanted a league with 'teeth'. The British government set up the Phillimore Committee in March 1918 to examine proposals for a League of Nations. The committee reported back in favour of a league with limited powers and minimal departure from pre-war diplomacy, the only exception being a provision for automatic sanctions. The committee's recommendations thus fell well short of what the League's supporters in Britain envisaged. Influential members of the British cabinet and the Foreign Office were leery about the shape of the new organization. Some felt that sanctions were essentially unworkable and that collective security could never replace the Royal Navy as guarantor of British security. Government officials preferred to rely on traditional methods of ensuring British security. Lloyd George was no exception, and on the whole he did not warm to the idea of a strong league, but the enormous popularity of the League of Nations was something that recommended itself to him for political reasons, as did Wilson's unyielding insistence that it be included in the final peace treaty.

The responsibility for negotiating the charter of the new organization was given to Lord Robert Cecil, an ardent supporter of the League. In typical Lloyd George style, Cecil was given considerable latitude in his negotiating powers, and the prime minister himself showed only episodic interest in what his negotiator was doing. Cecil, by using the popularity of the League ideal as a political prod, eventually persuaded Lloyd George and the cabinet to accept a league that went well beyond what many of them wanted.

In its final form the League was composed of an Assembly, in which all member states possessed one vote, and a Council composed of five permanent members (the United States, Britain, France, Italy and Japan) and four elected, non-permanent members. Member states were required to protect one another from aggression, to respect territorial boundaries and to refer disputes to the League for arbitration. Provision was made for the punishment of aggressors by means of economic sanctions, and the Council could recommend military action. The League was also charged with undertaking international disarmament. Both Russia and Germany were initially excluded from the League, although it was expected that Germany would eventually join. The United States, as will be seen, never joined. The credibility of the League was thus significantly undermined from the start, and for many in 1919 it appeared to be no more and no less than an exclusive club of victor powers determined to uphold the peace – a perception that was heightened by the fact that the League Covenant, or charter, was written into the Treaty of Versailles.

German boundaries

The most complicated and contentious issue to be placed before the delegates concerned the future boundaries of the new Europe. On Germany's western frontiers with Belgium and France several significant alterations were made. First, Germany returned to France the annexed parts of Alsace and Lorraine, which it had taken in 1871 at the conclusion of the Franco-Prussian War. Most of the people living in these areas considered themselves French, and German rule had been a constant source of Franco-German tension and a focus for French revanchist sentiment before the First World War. Next, small areas of territory were given by Germany to Belgium (the towns of Eupen and Malmédy) and Denmark (north Schleswig). The transfers took place after local plebiscites had demonstrated the wishes of the inhabitants. Few Germans had any serious objections to the loss of those territories.

Much more difficult was the status of the Saar valley, an important coal-producing area immediately to the southeast of Luxembourg. The vast majority of the population of the Saar was German, but the area was placed under League of Nations rule in the form of a five-man commission. The coal mines were expropriated by the French. At the end of fifteen years a plebiscite would be held so that the inhabitants should determine whether they wanted to be part of Germany or France or to continue under League rule. If they voted to return to Germany, then Germany would have the right to buy back the coal mines. Initially the French wanted to annex the Saar directly, and Lloyd George may even have been sympathetic, but Wilson had no desire to create a permanent grievance in the heart of Europe. The French government wanted compensation for the damage that the Germans had inflicted on the industries in northeastern France during the war. German nationalists took offence at the apparent violation of Wilson's principle of national self-determination. The inhabitants of the Saar clearly wanted to be part of Germany and would vote overwhelmingly to do so in 1935, giving Hitler one of his earliest triumphs. The controversy over the

Saar was, however, only part of a much greater and more heated debate over the status of the Rhineland.

The Rhineland is the area of Germany that lies between the river Rhine and Germany's borders with France and Belgium. This prosperous, industrialized, urbanized region was close to the heartland of German war production in the nearby Ruhr valley. Under the final terms agreed at the conference the Rhineland was to be occupied by Allied troops. A small area near Köln in the north would be evacuated after five years and another area around Koblenz after ten, but the bulk of the region would play host to an Allied army of occupation for fifteen years. In addition, the east bank of the Rhine would be demilitarized to a distance of fifty kilometres. Fortifications in the Rhineland were prohibited in perpetuity. The occupation of Rhineland was hated passionately by all Germans, many of whom resented France's use of troops from its African colonies on racial grounds. They referred to the unoccupied areas of their country as 'free Germany'. The Rhineland settlement could have been much harsher on Germany.

Initially the French wanted to separate the Rhineland from the rest of Germany and to set up a government that would be docile and receptive to French wishes. They even went to some lengths to encourage separatist movements in the Rhineland, none of which caught on as there was absolutely no popular support for the idea. The French plan was vetoed by both Wilson and Lloyd George for some basic reasons. A separate Rhineland would violate national self-determination and serve as a source of German revanchist sentiment, in exactly the same way as Alsace–Lorraine had for the French before 1914. For his part, Lloyd George privately opposed any occupation of the Rhineland by Allied troops. He was anxious to limit British military commitments in Europe and was worried about the effect of an occupation on German nationalism. On one hand he was sympathetic to France's fears for its security, but on the other hand he did not want to strengthen France at the expense of creating a host of grievances for German nationalists to exploit.

As a compromise solution the Allies agreed on a fifteen-year occupation of the Rhineland. A French army stationed in the Rhineland could, in a crisis, easily cross the Rhine bridge-heads and march on

Berlin and the Ruhr. Occupation of the Rhineland would also serve as a means of securing German compliance with all the terms of the treaty. At the end of fifteen years, the French hoped, Germany would be purged of the influence of the Prussian military caste known as the Junkers, who were widely blamed for perceived German aggressiveness before 1914. Germany would then take its place in the comity of European nations. Others in the French government hoped that schemes for economic co-operation would promote ties between German industry and the international community and make Germany less likely to resort to war.

Another means of ensuring French security concerned a guarantee from Britain and the United States to come to the aid of France if it were attacked by Germany. Wilson and Lloyd George proposed an Anglo-American guarantee of French security at the Paris conference, but it had to be ratified by the United States Senate and that approval was never given. Clemenceau set great store by an Anglo-American guarantee, and the Anglo-American offer was one reason why Clemenceau backed down on plans for a separate Rhenish state. Despite the offer of the guarantee the French still insisted on some degree of occupation, as it would take time for their allies to mobilize and come to their assistance in the event of war.

The territorial arrangements in the east were equally controversial. The inter-mixing of ethnic populations in Eastern Europe meant that Wilson's principle of national self-determination proved notoriously difficult to apply in reality. Virtually every one of the new states that were created in 1919 contained within its borders large numbers of citizens who wanted to belong to a different state. The difficulty of drawing viable borders was most evident in the case of Poland. The re-emergence of an independent Polish state had been raised in Wilson's Fourteen Points, together with the stipulation that the new state have an outlet to the sea. A corridor to the Baltic Sea was deemed necessary for Poland's economic viability. Unfortunately, such an outlet could only be provided by granting Poland land that was heavily populated by Germans. The corridor that was finally given to Poland under the terms of the peace settlement included the former German provinces of West Prussia and Posen. Both provinces contained numerous Germans, although the Poles formed a small majority. The port city of Danzig, which was almost exclusively populated by Germans, was made a free city, governed by the League of Nations. This arrangement came about at the insistence of Lloyd George, who argued that if Danzig were included in Poland in addition to West Prussia and Posen there would be more than two million Germans in the new Polish state. The ideal of national self-determination would thus be grossly violated and the substantial, discontented German minority in Poland would undermine Polish security. Lloyd George favoured a smaller, more cohesive Polish state. In the long run, even Lloyd George's compromise proved to be no more viable. When war finally came in 1939 the immediate pretext was Hitler's insistence on the return of Danzig and the German-speaking areas of Poland. Finally, there was also the inconvenient matter of the corridor and Danzig isolating East Prussia and separating it from the rest of Germany – yet another grievance for the German nationalists.

The region known as Upper Silesia added further complications. Upper Silesia was an ethnically mixed area (German and Polish) that was rich in resources and industry. A strong case was made for assigning Upper Silesia to Poland, primarily to ensure the economic viability of the new state. Once again, however, many Germans would be left stranded outside German borders and Lloyd George in particular argued against granting the whole of the region to Poland. The dispute was not settled until 1921 when, after a plebiscite, the territory was split between Germany and Poland. Nevertheless, the new border did not in any way reflect a clear ethnic division between the two peoples.

Other aspects of Germany's eastern borders also proved worrisome. The new state of Czechoslovakia was given the horseshoe-shaped area known as Sudetenland. This region had belonged to the old Austro-Hungarian Empire and had never been considered part of Germany. There was no great call in Germany for its annexation in 1919, even though it was home to more than two million Germans and its appropriation would have been perfectly consistent with the ideal of national self-determination. Sudetenland was a hilly, semi-mountainous region with a considerable amount of industry. It was granted to Czechoslovakia to enhance the strategic and economic prospects of the new state. The large number of Germans in Czechoslovakia became an important weapon for Hitler in 1938, when he exploited the grievances of the Sudeten Germans to attempt the destruction of the Czech state.

A similar situation arose on Germany's southern borders. The largest German-speaking region of the old Austro-Hungarian Empire emerged as the new state of Austria. Again, the ideal of national self-determination argued a strong case for including Austria within a post-war Germany. Ironically, there were some in Germany who opposed the incorporation of six million Austrian Catholics within the mainly Protestant German state, but the most strenuous objections came from the French, who obviously did not want to see an even larger Germany emerge from the peace conference. The final treaty contained a strict prohibition on a German–Austrian *Anschluss*, or union. In 1938 Hitler achieved the *Anschluss* after arguing that he was only trying to right the wrongs of Versailles and carry out national self-determination.

The new borders of 1919 left a Germany that was thirteen per cent smaller in size and ten per cent smaller in population. These losses were hardly crippling and Germany still had the potential to become by far the most powerful state in Europe, a fact that was not lost on French military planners. Nevertheless, Germans felt an acute sense of grievance, and the large numbers of their country-men living outside German borders ensured that tension with Germany's neighbours would continue for years to come.

Military limitations

The treaty also imposed heavy limits on German military strength. Here, the starting-point for Wilson was the idea that all nations should reduce their national armaments to the lowest level consistent with national security. Each state should have only a pared-down frontier guard. The Treaty of Versailles limited Germany to an army of 100,000 troops, with no conscription, no air force, no submarines (a major concern to the British), no heavy artillery, no tanks and a reduced navy.[11] It also demanded the abolition of the German General Staff and War Academy. As far as Wilson was concerned, German disarmament constituted the first step on the road to universal arms reductions, Germany being the first state to make such a move. Lloyd George sympathized with Wilson's aims, but France had a completely different agenda. The French, for reasons of their own security, had every intention of restricting the German army while maintaining French strength at a comparatively high level. In the years after 1919 the German government pursued an active, secret programme of evading the arms restrictions imposed by the treaty, part of which involved the use of bases in the USSR to test tanks and aircraft. But in 1919 German nationalists were able to point to the differences in armament levels between France and Germany and to charge the victorious powers with hypocrisy.

Reparations and war guilt

Arguably the most intractable problem arose over the issue of reparations. It had long been the practice in international relations for the losing powers in wars to pay indemnities to the victors. In 1871 the Germans had forced the French to pay a large indemnity at the conclusion of the Franco-Prussian War. After surrendering in 1918 some members of the German government fully expected that Germany would have to pay at least something to the victors. The French argued that they needed reparation payments to reconstruct their devastated northeastern provinces. Some of them may well have hoped that reparations would drag down the German economy and lessen the German threat to France. Belgium had also received substantial damage and needed funds for rebuilding.

Strong demands for reparations also came from Britain, particularly during the 1918 election. Since there was relatively little direct war damage in Britain for which the Germans could be forced to pay, the idea arose instead that the Germans should contribute to pensions for widows and orphans. The author of this proposal was General Jan Christian Smuts, the South African prime minister and a member of the War Cabinet. Under his scheme the British would be assured of receiving their share of reparations and Lloyd George would score a notable political success. On the other hand, the amount of the German payments would be increased to an astronomical level. The sums being bandied around for German payments soon set alarm-bells ringing in London. A member of the British delegation to the Paris Peace Conference, John Maynard Keynes, argued that high reparations would depress the German economy, make an overall European recovery very difficult and hold back the world economy for years. Keynes was soon encouraged in his thinking by none other than General Smuts, who was having second thoughts about the wisdom of imposing reparations on Germany. The arguments put forward by Keynes and Smuts increasingly appealed not only to Lloyd George but also to the Americans, who viewed a European recovery with particular interest, since it was the best way of speeding up repayments of the wartime loans that they had extended to Britain and France. Wilson was also personally dismayed at the level and severity of the bill with which the Germans might be faced.

During the conference it became clear that the Allies would not be able to reach a consensus on the size of the bill to be presented to the Germans. Instead, they decided to demand from them an interim down-payment of 22 billion gold marks. The issue would then be referred to a special reparations commission that would report back with a final bill for reparations within two years. Lloyd George was pleased with the decision to delay the final toll. He hoped that over the next two years wartime passions would fade and that a more moderate settlement would emerge in 1921.[12]

The decision not to fix a definitive amount at the conference had several unpleasant consequences. The ensuing two years saw German nationalists spread all kinds of stories about the size of the payments that the Allies might demand, thereby gaining substantial support for their cause. But the two-year interval also contributed to financial uncertainty and an unwillingness to invest, just at the time when post-war Europe needed capital.

The legal basis for reparations was provided by Article 231 of the treaty, the notorious 'war guilt clause', which ran as follows:

The Allied and Associated Governments affirm and Germany accepts the responsibility of Germany and her allies for causing all the loss and damage to which the Allied and Associated Governments and their nationals have been subjected as a consequence of the war imposed upon them by the aggression of Germany and her allies.

The intent of Article 231 was to place moral responsibility for the war on Germany while limiting its actual liability to the damage inflicted by its army. The article may have been a well-intentioned attempt to provide a ceiling for German liability, but it backfired badly. Perhaps no single clause in the treaty was hated as much as the war guilt clause. Certainly no single clause provided German nationalists with more powerful ammunition.

The mandate system

The Paris Peace Conference also had to deal with the disposal of Germany's overseas colonies. Japan had entered the war on the Allied side in 1914 and quickly seized the German holdings on the Shantung Peninsula of China as well as the Caroline, Marshall and Mariana Islands in the North Pacific. The seizure of Shantung was especially problematic since the Chinese government made it clear to the conference that it wanted the region to be returned to China on the basis of national self-determination. In 1917 Britain and France, which badly needed Japanese help in the Mediterranean, had agreed that Japan should retain Shantung in the post-war era. At the conference Wilson was persuaded to let the deal stand, much to the fury of the Chinese government and people. The Shantung episode proved to be a costly setback for Wilson. Public opinion in the United States supported the Chinese, and Wilson stood accused of selling out his principles.

The British Dominions were especially anxious to annex the former German colonies that they had conquered during the war, much to Wilson's annoyance. The Australians wanted German New Guinea, the Bismarck Archipelago and the German Solomon Islands, while New Zealand wanted German Samoa and South Africa coveted German South-West Africa (now Namibia). According to the American president, the wishes of the inhabitants were supposed to be taken into account when the future of the former German territories was being determined. Wilson expected similar considerations to be applied to Germany's other African possessions – German East Africa (renamed Tanganyika by the British, now Tanzania), Togoland (now Togo) and the Cameroons. Armchair empire-builders in Britain wanted German East Africa so that Britain could complete the long-desired 'Cape to Cairo' empire in Africa. Lloyd George seemed generally receptive to the claims made by the Dominions.

The solution to the apparent impasse between Wilson and the Dominions was found in the mandate system, which was set up to operate under the supervision of the League of Nations. British imperialism had often been justified on the grounds that the colonial areas were benefiting from British rule: their economies were being improved and their inhabitants were being educated and 'civilized'. Hypocritical or not, the humanitarian justification for imperialism formed a bridge between Wilson and the Dominions. The occupying powers were not allowed outright annexations but were instead given mandates. They were to hold territories in trust and prepare the inhabitants for self-government. New Zealand, Australia and South Africa all received their territories as type C mandates, which meant that, owing to their remoteness of location and sparseness of population, they could be administered as integral parts of the occupying power. Critics of this arrangement alleged that there was little difference between the mandate system and the old style of pre-war imperialism. However, type B and type A mandates were quite different. German East Africa went to Britain as a type B mandate, while France received most of Togoland and the Cameroons (also as type B mandates), the remaining small slivers of both territories being granted to adjoining British possessions. A portion of German East Africa (modern Burundi and Rwanda) was similarly granted to Belgium.[13] In all cases the occupying powers were obliged to report before the League each year and outline their progress in preparing the inhabitants for independence. Arguably the worst features of imperialism were thus mitigated, and the Europeans were constantly reminded that their presence in the territories was temporary. A similar situation prevailed in the case of type A mandates, which were reserved for the Arab regions of the defeated Ottoman Empire: Palestine, Jordan, Mesopotamia (now Iraq), Syria and Lebanon.

Wilson's position here was identical to that over the disposition of the German colonies and was therefore straightforward. As might be expected, the British and French found their situation much more complicated owing to a whole series of agreements that had been made during the war. In 1916 the British and French had signed the Sykes–Picot Agreement, which recognized the long-standing French interests in Syria and Lebanon and promised French predominance there after the war. The British were to receive Mesopotamia and the Russians were given Armenia and Kurdistan. The agreement of course conflicted with Wilson's principles. If that were not enough, the British had already encouraged the Arab people of the Ottoman Empire to revolt, promising them a united Arab state with Damascus in Syria as its capital. In 1917, in an attempt to gain the sympathy of the Zionist movement, the British had issued the Balfour Declaration, which promised to look with favour on the establishment of a Jewish homeland in Palestine. The Balfour Declaration was at odds with promises the British had already extended to the Arabs. Ultimately, the mandate system was applied to the Middle East as well, whereby in 1920 Britain received mandates over Palestine, Jordan and Mesopotamia and France over Syria and Lebanon. The frustration of Arab hopes came as a tremendous disappointment to those, such as the famous T. E. Lawrence (otherwise known as Lawrence of Arabia), who had supported the cause of an independent Arab state.

Italian grievances

As an important ally during the war, Italy also had certain claims to settle at Paris. Prior to the outbreak of the First World War Italy had been a member of the Triple Alliance, alongside Germany and Austria–Hungary. When war was declared in 1914 Italy declined to join its alliance partners on the grounds that the Triple Alliance was essentially defensive in character and that German actions in 1914 could not be construed as defensive. The real reason perhaps had more to do with the vulnerability of Italy's coastline to attack by the Royal Navy. The Italians conducted secret negotiations with both sides from late 1914 to early 1915 and, in May 1915, following the signature of the Treaty of London, they entered the war on the Allied side. Under the terms of that treaty, Britain and France promised Italy extensive territorial gains in what today are Croatia, the Dalmatian coastline, Albania and Turkey. The Adriatic was to become in effect an Italian lake. Italian nationalists derived great satisfaction from these potential gains. However, the ninth of Wilson's Fourteen Points proposed an Italian frontier 'effected along clearly recognizable lines of nationality' and implied frontiers far short of those which had been promised by the Allies in 1915. Prior to the conference the prime minister, Orlando, had tried to warn Wilson that a problem might be in the offing, but when Italy's frontiers were discussed in April he failed to avert a bitter and acrimonious dispute between himself and the president. At the height of the confrontation Wilson tried to appeal over the heads of the Italian delegation, asking the Italian people to reject what he thought were the excessive demands of their leaders. Orlando was enraged and temporarily withdrew from the conference.

The Paris solution satisfied no one. Italy received territory in the north called South Tyrol, which extended Italy's borders up to the more defensible Brenner Pass but left 250,000 German-speaking Austrians in Italian territory. In the northeast it received the region of Istria and the city of Trieste, which were populated by large numbers of non-Italians. South Tyrol, Istria and Trieste were less than what the Italians had been led to expect they would receive from the peace settlement. Nationalist sentiment in the country was inflamed and tension with Italy's new neighbour, the emergent state of Yugoslavia (or the Kingdom of Serbs, Croats and Slovenes, as it was then awkwardly called), assured. In May 1919 a private army led by the Italian war hero and poet Gabrielle D'Annunzio marched into the port city of Fiume, denying it to the Yugoslavs. D'Annunzio was eventually expelled by Italian troops, but Italy did not return Fiume to Yugoslavia and the whole episode illustrates the extent to which Italian nationalist ambitions had been frustrated by the treaty. Wilson, for his part, was saddled with yet further violations of national self-determination.

Concluding the peace

By late March 1919 Lloyd George had become increasingly concerned that the treaty would be far too harsh on Germany. Kerr and Hankey shared his anxieties. Lloyd George and his advisers withdrew to Fontainebleau on the weekend of 22–24 March, where they authored the Fontainebleau Memorandum, a document that was designed to persuade Clemenceau to moderate the terms of the peace. First, Lloyd George wanted to make sure that as many Germans as possible were included within Germany's borders. Second, he thought that a harsh peace would guarantee another war when Germany recovered. Only a just peace could avert the danger of Bolshevism in Europe. Third, the League must be an unbiased arbiter of peace and disarmament must be universal. The Fontainebleau Memorandum received a cool reception from Clemenceau, who argued that Germany was a menace to European peace and must be kept under control. He also pointed to the hypocrisy of the British in their insistence that the French make concessions while Britain kept all its German colonies. The seeds of post-war Anglo-French tensions were thus planted early.

The Paris Peace Conference also attempted to establish the borders of the new Eastern European successor states. The deliberations on Eastern Europe continued after the signing of the German settlement in June. In many cases the conference could only ratify boundaries that had already been delineated by the new states. Occasionally, disputes between successor states led to calls for Allied military intervention, as, for example, during a clash between Romania and Hungary in July. But little public support existed in Britain for such adventures and, in any event, the bulk of the British army had been demobilized. British delegates travelling to Paris recalled the long lines of returning troopships in the Channel and were aware of the limits of British power in Eastern Europe.

The problem areas in Eastern Europe were daunting. Hungary was extensively carved back from the territory it had occupied under the old Austro-Hungarian Empire, which caused large numbers of Hungarians to be stranded in Romania and Czechoslovakia.[14] For its part, the new Czech state seized the industrial part of the region of Teschen, much to the dismay and alarm of the Poles. The eastern borders of Poland were not finally resolved until 1920, when the Poles turned back a Russian invasion and seized large areas of modern Belarus, but they extended far to the east of the Curzon line, the boundary originally recommended by the British.

Thus, all the new Eastern European states contained discontented minorities in large numbers. They were also divided by bitter rivalries and outstanding grievances, such as those between Poland and Czechoslovakia or Hungary and its neighbours. They were weak militarily and economically. Pre-war trade routes and economic units had all been dissolved by new borders and tariffs. Yet it was to the successor states of Eastern Europe that France turned in the post-war years to provide a second front against Germany as a replacement for Russia. The successor states were also to serve as a *cordon sanitaire* against further Bolshevik expansion to the west. The prospects for success were not good. How were the new states to maintain their viability against a resurgent Russia and Germany? Some historians have argued that the principal failure of the Paris Peace Conference was not so much the inability to stop German expansionism in Western Europe as the failure to set up a mechanism to stop German and Russian expansionism into the new power vacuum of Eastern Europe.

At the end of June the final draft of the treaty was presented to the German delegation, which had at last been invited to Paris. The Germans protested furiously, in writing, and a brief period of panic ensued when it occurred to the Allies that the Germans might refuse to sign. The Allied generals informed their political leaders that with the demobilization of their armies the Allies no longer possessed the military power to resume war with Germany. Lloyd George spent considerable time attempting to exact some last-minute modifications to the treaty, but Wilson flatly refused to reopen the issues, especially after the colossal efforts of the preceding months. Wilson was particularly stung by Lloyd George's insistence that he was only acting in the name of Wilson's own principles. Wilson did at this juncture agree to the Upper Silesian plebiscite, but that was the extent of his concessions. Despite all the last-minute manoeuvring the Germans really had no alternative but to sign the treaty. Their army was certainly in no condition to resume fighting and the Allied naval blockade had produced immense hardship in Germany. The signing ceremony took place at Versailles on 28 June 1919, the final text of the treaty having been prepared only hours beforehand. After the celebrations Harold Nicolson returned to his hotel room, full of grim foreboding and 'sick of life'. The whole conference, he wrote, had been an 'appalling dispersal of energy'.[15]

Wilson discovered on his return to the United States in early July that domestic opposition to the treaty was building rapidly. Much of the anxiety focused on the League of Nations. Lodge and the Republicans argued that the League would overrule the Constitution and drag Americans into European wars. Behind this argument was a growing swell of isolationism – the demand that the United States withdraw from European affairs. Wilson's campaign for Senate approval went poorly. The president proved to be defensive, bristly, unyielding and unwilling to compromise. In early October he suffered a serious stroke and was removed from active campaigning. During the debate over the treaty Lodge and his allies scored heavily on the 'six votes to one' issue. Lodge argued that if a dispute between Britain and the United States were referred to the League for settlement, Britain would win as a matter of course because each of the four Dominions and India would automatically side with Britain against the United States. Tensions were also building between the two nations over the repayment of British war debts to the United States and over the possibility of a post-war naval race between the two powers.

The British government saw the situation unravelling and, realizing that the Senate might reject the treaty, despatched Sir Edward Grey, the respected but ailing pre-war foreign secretary, to try to salvage a compromise. Any hint of a compromise with the Senate, however, only served to make the president even more inflexible, and Grey soon found his personal access to Wilson cut off after his assistant made slanderous remarks about members of Wilson's staff.[16] The British government tried to convince the United States that if a dispute between the two countries were referred to the League, Britain would not seek the support of the Dominions to outvote the United States – to no avail. Ironically, it could be suggested that had Lloyd George's initial concept of a loose league been allowed to prevail over Cecil's, the Republicans might have compromised. Some members of the British government, such as Kerr, argued that the United States was so crucial to the future security of Britain that it should be allowed to join the League on terms of its own choosing. But by the autumn of 1919 it was simply too late for drastic compromises. In November the United States Senate rejected the Treaty of Versailles.[17] Further attempts at compromise stalled and by early January 1920 the failure of the Treaty of Versailles to gain ratification in the United States was acknowledged. It was a failure that had far-reaching consequences. Besides refusing to ratify the Treaty of Versailles the Senate would not even consider the proposed guarantee to France. The French had therefore compromised on the Rhineland in exchange for nothing. The League of Nations was hampered from the start by the absence of the world's greatest economic power, not to mention Germany and the USSR. The British joined the League anyway, largely at the behest of the powerful League of Nations Union lobby group, but at the first session of the League in Geneva the remarks made by Curzon, the new foreign secretary, were unenthusiastic and lukewarm. Those in the British government – such as Kerr and the 'Atlanticists' – who had banked heavily on the United States to build a new post-war partnership were profoundly disillusioned. Britain's attention would instead turn to European affairs and managing a post-war relationship with France. Now that the Americans had gone, the British were left with the forlorn hope that Versailles had established an equilibrium of power between France and Germany that was acceptable to both parties.

Criticisms of the Treaty of Versailles mounted during the postwar years. In late 1919 John Maynard Keynes, who had earlier resigned from the British delegation in protest over what he thought were punitive levels of reparations, published his *Economic Consequences of the Peace*, an articulate and stinging critique of the treaty.[18] Keynes argued that reparations would drag down the German economy and inhibit European recovery. 148,000 copies of the book were sold in two years, a high number for those days. More important, Keynes' critique struck a chord, and many in

Britain who read Keynes came away persuaded that the treaty was Carthaginian – in other words, excessively harsh and vindictive. Over the next few years British statesmen were convinced that in the interests of fair play and justice the treaty had to be ameliorated and Germany appeased. Lloyd George had also come under fire from the opposite direction for allegedly being too lenient with the Germans. In the month of April 1919 in particular, the press baron Lord Northcliffe had used his papers to stir up a vituperative anti-German campaign. He also accused Lloyd George of selling out and letting the Kaiser get away with wartime atrocities. Lloyd George handled the attacks effectively in the House of Commons, but at times it must have seemed that he could do no right.

Most historians would agree that the Treaty of Versailles failed over the issues of national self-determination and reparations, both of which gave ample ammunition to German nationalists. The gap between Wilson's idealism and the requirements of French security proved unbridgeable. The Treaty might have worked if the United States, France and Britain had signed a post-war alliance and maintained an allied army of occupation in the Rhineland for fifteen years. But even this would have required a high degree of coercion and would probably have fuelled German extremist calls for revenge. Wilson had occasionally expressed the hope that the League would be able to solve some of the problems left outstanding by Versailles. Over the next few years, however, it became evident that the French thought the League existed to uphold and maintain the peace treaty, not revise it.

The British recorded many successes at Versailles. Germany's fleet had been reduced and its military threat had gone, at least for the time being. The Dominions had gained German colonies, albeit under the mandate system. Some of the more punitive aspects of the French programme had been ameliorated (such as the Rhineland and Upper Silesia). On the other hand, the British attitude over reparations was highly ambivalent and not particularly helpful. Contemporaries and some historians have criticized the British performance at Versailles for being hesitant and disorganized. The lack of organization was certainly intensified by the prime minister's style of governing. The British, according to this argument, went to Versailles with a limited number of specific objectives and, having attained those objectives, withdrew from European affairs to follow their own narrow concerns. Others have attacked Lloyd George for bowing to the winds of demagoguery, especially on the question of reparations. The critics allege that Lloyd George had no broad vision of how European peace should be arranged and was instead obsessed with maintaining his own political position at home.[19] The evidence suggests that, on balance, Lloyd George did possess a wider vision, albeit imperfectly formed. Over the next three years he made strenuous efforts to reintegrate Germany and the USSR into Europe while providing security for France; only in this way could the European economy be revived and peace maintained. Lloyd George articulated an ambitious scheme that called for an activist prime minister and an activist foreign policy. As ever, he was hampered by immutable international realities and domestic constraints.

Notes

1 In attendance were Wilson, Lloyd George, Clemenceau, Orlando and their foreign ministers.

2 See M. Eksteins, *Rites of Spring: The Great War and the Birth of the Modern Age* (Boston, Houghton Mifflin, 1989), for an assessment of the cultural impact of the First World War.

3 W. Keylor, *The Twentieth Century World: An International History* (New York, Oxford University Press, 1984), contains an excellent summary of the French position.

4 Remark attributed to Stanley Baldwin, himself a Conservative and future prime minister. R. Webb, *Modern England: From the Eighteenth Century to the Present* (New York, Harper and Row, 1980), p. 497.

5 D. Dilks, 'Appeasement revisited', *University of Leeds Review*, June 1972, pp. 28–56. S. Roskill, *Hankey: Man of Secrets*, three vols (London, Collins, 1970, 1972, 1974).

6 Lloyd George saw the Foreign Office as a bastion of aristocratic privilege. As will be seen in Chapter Six, there was a solid basis for his suspicions.

7 M. Dockrill and J. Goold, *Peace Without Promise: Britain and the Paris Peace Conferences, 1919–1923* (London, Archon, 1981).

8 Quoted in H. Nelson, *Land and Power: British and Allied Policy on Germany's Frontiers* (Toronto, University of Toronto Press, 1963), p. 370.

9 H. Nicolson, *Peacemaking 1919* (London, Constable, 1933), p. 33. Nicolson was a member of the Foreign Office contingent of the British delegation. His memoir is an invaluable source.

10 See below, p. 69.

11 The Germans were allowed six armoured ships of 10,000 tons each, six light

cruisers of 6,000 tons each, plus twelve destroyers (800 tons) and twelve tor-
pedo boats (200 tons).

12 The historian Marc Trachtenberg argues on the other hand that Lloyd George's
policy favoured a harsh reparations settlement. See M. Trachtenberg, *Reparation
in World Politics: France and European Economic Diplomacy, 1916–1923* (New
York, Columbia University Press, 1980), pp. 46–9, 61–4, 70–1 and 91–3.

13 Belgium at that time held the Congo, which was subsequently known as Zaïre
and is now the Democratic Republic of the Congo.

14 Separate treaties were signed with Austria (Treaty of St Germain, 10 September
1919), Bulgaria (Treaty of Neuilly, 27 November 1919), Hungary (Treaty of
Trianon, 4 June 1920) and Turkey (Treaty of Sèvres, 10 August 1920). As with
Versailles, these treaties received their names from the Parisian suburbs in which
they were signed. The Turkish settlement proved unexpectedly complicated and
will be dealt with in Chapter Three.

15 Nicolson, *Peacemaking*, pp. 5 and 371.

16 G. Egerton, 'Britain and the "great betrayal": Anglo-American relations and
the struggle for United States ratification of the Treaty of Versailles, 1919–1920',
The Historical Journal, XXI, 1978, pp. 885–911.

17 The United States later signed a separate treaty with Germany in 1921 that was
basically identical to Versailles, minus the League.

18 J. M. Keynes, *Economic Consequences of the Peace* (New York, Harcourt, Brace
and House, 1920).

19 Scholarly critics include Dockrill and Gold, *Peace Without Promise*; L. Jaffe,
*The Decision to Disarm Germany: British Policy Towards Postwar German
Disarmament* (Boston, Allen and Unwin, 1985); and A. Lentin, *Lloyd George,
Woodrow Wilson and the Guilt of Germany: An Essay in the Pre-history of
Appeasement* (Baton Rouge, Louisiana State University Press, 1984). Lloyd
George receives a very able defence in K. O. Morgan, *Consensus and Disunity:
The Lloyd George Coalition Government, 1918–1922* (Oxford, Clarendon
Press, 1979); Nelson, *Land and Power*; and P. Rowland, *Lloyd George* (London,
Barrie and Jenkins, 1975).

CHAPTER THREE

MAINTAINING THE PEACE, 1920–1923

With the signing of the Treaty of Versailles on 28 June 1919 many in Britain hoped that the government could at last turn its attention to long overdue social reforms. The government and Foreign Office also desired a return to prosperity, peace on the continent and a renewed focus on the Empire. These sentiments increased as Britain encountered economic problems. After a short post-war boom the economy slowed and unemployment, especially of war veterans, escalated. The international scene, however, continued to present the government with a welter of intractable problems and sudden crises. In the years following Versailles Britain had to deal with problems in Eastern Europe, the Middle East and Turkey. Relations with the new Soviet state were complicated and tense, problems arose with the United States, and insurrections broke out in Egypt and in Ireland. Particularly worrisome were Britain's relations with France, and at the centre of so many of the British government's difficulties stood the insoluble problem of reparations and French security.

Ironically, Lloyd George, who began his political career as an ardent social reformer, found himself increasingly captivated by foreign policy. The early 1920s were the heyday of the new diplomacy. Commentators on international affairs warned: 'there are grave dangers in keeping the bulk of the electorate uninstructed regarding the general character and the imperious demands of our foreign connexions'.[1] Lloyd George was determined to make the new diplomacy work and thought he could do so by attending conferences. Between January 1920 and December 1922 the victor powers held twenty-three summit meetings. Lloyd George was convinced that his personal dynamism and leadership should be employed in the creation of a new international order. His activities, unfortunately, aroused the resentment and hostility of the Foreign Office and the new foreign secretary, Lord Curzon, a senior Conservative and former Viceroy of India, who had taken over from Balfour in October 1919.[2] Lloyd George was going to make his own foreign policy, and the Foreign Office would have to play catch up.[3]

For Curzon, becoming foreign secretary was the fulfilment of a lifelong dream, and he did all he could to stay in office. Although the prime minister initially thought highly of Curzon, his admiration quickly and characteristically turned to contempt. Curzon could be pompous and snobbish, which seemed to irritate Lloyd George no end. The prime minister subjected Curzon to every conceivable insult and humiliation in cabinet meetings, knowing full well that he would not carry out his frequent threats to resign. Curzon for his part was driven to despair by Lloyd George's conduct of foreign policy. In February 1922 Curzon and the British ambassador to Paris, Lord Hardinge, discovered that Lloyd George wanted to use personal emissaries to conduct foreign policy matters without their knowledge or approval. Hardinge wrote to Curzon:

> I really felt thoroughly sickened by what I had heard and I said to myself, what is the good of diplomacy or working hard in the interests of one's country when one does not know what is going on and things are done behind the back of those who are responsible. I felt also, although this is only a minor consideration, that you and I were being made fools of.[4]

For subordinates and colleagues, Curzon could be difficult to work with. He was a learned man of immense intellectual capabilities, and his intelligence gave him a sense of confidence and easy assurance that often struck others as bordering on arrogance. He regularly lectured ministers and senior staff as though they were schoolboys. Curzon was also puzzlingly indecisive. He was always able to master the historical background to a situation or crisis, but when it came to recommending a line of action he seemed at a loss and took offence 'at the realist who dared to advance so material an enquiry'.[5] His inability to be punctual reinforced the perception of arrogance.

Curzon's most recent biographer recounts one instance:

> Impatient ministers were waiting for him before one Cabinet meeting when a servant entered with the green baize footstool that now accompanied him everywhere. 'Lord Curzon has not yet arrived', remarked Derby ... 'but we see premonitory symptoms'. And he rose and bowed at the footstool.[6]

Quirks of personality notwithstanding, Curzon took office at a particularly challenging time and his skills were soon put to the test. He took the growing field of intelligence-gathering seriously and managed to wrest supervisory control of the Secret Intelligence Service away from the Admiralty and the War Office, thereby recovering a modicum of prestige for the Foreign Office. On the international scene the challenges were more complex. Reparations came first on the agenda.

Reparations and Anglo-French relations

The debate over reparations poisoned the international economic climate in post-war Europe. Besides causing tension between Britain and France reparations also led directly to the most serious crisis between France and Germany in the early 1920s.[7] German nationalist outrage against reparations did much to undermine the stability of the post-war German government, known as the Weimar Republic. There was much controversy at the time – and there still is among historians – as to whether the German government did all that it could to pay reparations or whether it used some creative accounting to escape paying the full amount. Certainly the Allies never received anywhere near the amount of reparations that they originally hoped to obtain.

The French needed reparations to recover from the damages inflicted during the war. They wanted cash, coal and other raw materials to rebuild northeastern France. Many observers who were sympathetic to the French position contrasted the poverty and squalor in the northeast of France with the affluence of Germany's Rhineland and concluded that Germany should pay. If Germany's economic recovery were impeded, that – at least according to some in the French government – would be no bad thing. The British, however, had reservations. They had wanted money to pay for war pensions and to ensure that Britain received its share of German reparations. But they were also painfully aware that high reparations would slow German and European economic recovery. Since Germany was a major British trading partner, Britain's economic recovery would also suffer. Some members of the French government likewise worried about the long-term effects of reparations on European recovery, but the withdrawal of the United States from European political affairs, together with any possibility of the continuation of the economic co-operation that had existed during the war, meant that the French fell back on reparations, which then became central to French post-war planning.

The British dilemma was further compounded by repeated demands from the United States for the repayment of the wartime loans that it had extended to Britain. As President Coolidge said, 'They hired the money, didn't they?', as though that settled the issue. The British government concluded that some of the money might have to come from German reparation payments. During his term in office Lloyd George hoped for a moratorium on inter-allied debts, arguing that the total reparations bill would be reduced accordingly. If the British and French did not have to worry about repaying the United States, they could ask for a more realistic sum from Germany,[8] and the French would stand a better chance of collecting it. Lloyd George was to argue his case most eloquently in the Balfour Note, a letter issued by the British government to France and the United States on 1 August 1922. The prime minister's proposals would meet with little enthusiasm in either country.[9] The British embassy in Washington had long noted the rigidity of American opinion on the issue of repayment of war debts. Politicians in Congress were not above blaming the slow post-war economic recovery in America on the delay in collecting money from Britain.

The issue of reparations reached crisis point in early 1921. The bitter controversy at Versailles over compensation had been conveniently postponed for two years while the Reparations Commission tried to finalize the total bill and prepare a schedule of payment. On 27 April 1921 the commission presented the Germans with the final bill. Germany was to pay a total of 132 billion gold marks.[10] The Allies had already agreed at the Spa conference in 1920 that France would receive fifty-two per cent of the reparations, Britain twenty-two per cent, Italy ten per cent, Belgium eight per cent, and the other powers the remaining eight per cent. The details of the reparations settlement were lost in the ensuing uproar over their legitimacy. The reparations bill was to be paid in bonds divided into three classes, A, B and C. Through a complicated and poorly understood financial arrangement the C bonds, amounting to eighty-two billion marks, were largely a fiction and would probably never have to be paid. The actual reparations bill (finalized in the London Schedule of Payments presented to the Germans on 5 May 1921) totalled fifty billion marks, to be paid in annual instalments of two billion gold marks, together with a twenty-six per cent tax on German exports. The 1921 settlement was much more moderate and more conducive to economic recovery than some of the figures put forward at Versailles, but such subtleties were lost in the emotion of 1921 and nearly everyone focused on the total amount of the bill.

Implementation of the payment schedule did not go well. By the end of 1921 the Germans were already in default. After having made their first cash payment they declared that they would be unable to make any further such payments.[11] The Allies were now confronted with the question of what action to take should further defaults occur. Extending military occupation into the Ruhr was a possibility, but what would be the consequences of such drastic action?

Lloyd George knew that only by meeting French security needs could a measure of stability be restored in Europe. After the failure of the proposed Anglo-American guarantee the British government started to think seriously about offering a military alliance to France in return for concessions on reparations and a more lenient treatment of Germany. Curzon in particular seemed determined on such a course. The British offer eventually fell through in mid-1922 when it became apparent that the French wanted the British to make greater specific military commitments to European defence than they were willing to make, especially at a time when the British public was demanding reduced spending on armaments. Some cabinet ministers also feared that Britain would be expected to go to war to defend France's eastern European allies in the event of German aggression.

The underlying problem that marred Anglo-French relations was the profound distrust that existed between the two countries by 1922. For example, as Curzon noted,

> the real objection to any Alliance is this – that we cannot trust them. They are always after some success of their own. Sometimes political *éclat*, sometimes financial gains. The advantage to France is always the test ... regardless of loyalty or sincerity or candour.

On another occasion he remarked, 'the French are not the sort of people you go tiger hunting with'.[12] The British wanted to concentrate on the Empire and minimize their involvement in European affairs. The French reminded the British that they could not ignore the Continent – something that British officials deeply resented. The French dislike of the British in general and of Lloyd George in particular was equally heartfelt. Because of their diverging outlooks the two wartime allies simply could not agree on how to enforce the peace. The French remained obsessed with the German threat and sought a rigid enforcement of Versailles to assure their security, but the British increasingly felt guilty about Versailles and wanted to restore the German economy, limit military liabilities in Europe and reduce military spending. Arguably, the French might have agreed to a more lenient peace if Britain could have guaranteed to assist France, but as we have seen, a guarantee was not forthcoming. France felt obliged to enforce Versailles to the letter, playing directly into the hands of German extremists. Britain and France also entertained different conceptions on the role of Germany in Europe. The British had accepted Bismarck's unified Germany of 1871 and saw a united, disarmed and republican Germany as a useful counterweight to the ambitions of both France and Bolshevik Russia and as a valuable trading partner. The French, needless to say, held no such sympathies.

Britain's fundamental aim in its policy was to act as a mediator between France and Germany. If relations between Germany and France were cordial, disputes elsewhere in Europe could not escalate and draw in the great powers. That had been the 'lesson' of 1914; a war between small powers in the Balkans had escalated and engulfed the whole of Europe because Europe had been divided into mutually hostile blocs of alliances. So, the argument went, there was a need to resist forming alliances, to avoid surrounding Germany with hostile powers and to try to mediate disputes as they arose. Regrettably, the French, from the British point of view, were being difficult. France had created a network of alliances in Eastern Europe that was bound to be provocative to Germany. Britain had no interests in Eastern and Central Europe, areas that, sooner or later, would doubtless be dominated by Germany. British statesmen saw the forcible separation of Austria from Germany, for instance, as wholly unnatural and they felt considerable resentment at France's Eastern European connections during the inter-war period. Germany demanded only that Britain right the wrongs of Versailles, yet France could potentially drag Britain into another disastrous war because of its alliances with Eastern European states.

Disarmament and the Washington Conference

In keeping with the new diplomacy and the creation of the League of Nations the immediate post-war years saw intensive efforts at international disarmament that continued into the early 1930s and attracted considerable public interest and support. The post-war era was characterized by the deeply held belief that weapons were themselves a major cause of war. Proof could be found in the great build-up of arms that occurred in Europe during the ten years preceding the First World War – another lesson of history. Land armaments soon became very difficult to define and limit. Much time and effort were spent in trying to distinguish between offensive and defensive weapons. As one journalist noted, whether a gun was offensive or defensive depended on which end you were standing on. Naval armaments, by contrast, were much more promising. To count battleships and cruisers and place limitations on them was relatively straightforward. Battleships were to the 1920s what intercontinental ballistic missiles (ICBM) were to the 1980s. By limiting their numbers, war could be avoided. Hence, the Washington Naval

Conference was convened in November 1921 to discuss naval disarmament and issues that related particularly to security in the Pacific. There had been some grounds for concern about the possibility of a post-war naval race. Between 1917 and 1921 Japan tripled its spending on naval armaments and by 1921 the Japanese government was spending almost one-third of the imperial budget on the navy. The expansion of the Japanese fleet made the United States very nervous. It had been making plans to expand its own fleet in the post-war era, much to the alarm of the British, and aimed to have thirty-three capital ships in service by 1924, compared with thirty-two for Britain. The British government did not want to embark on a naval race with the United States and Japan at a time when the public was demanding reduced spending on armaments, and it therefore had strong grounds for supporting the Washington disarmament efforts. Moderate voices in both Japan and the United States also lent their support to the disarmament efforts.

The Washington Conference concluded in February 1922 with some major achievements. A treaty signed by the United States, Britain, Japan, France and Italy (the Five Power Treaty) imposed sharp restrictions on capital ships, which were defined as ships over 10,000 tons (mainly battleships and battle-cruisers). A ratio of strength was applied to capital ships as follows: Britain, 5; the United States, 5; Japan, 3; Italy and France, 1.67. The total tonnage of all the capital ships in the British navy was therefore to equal that of the United States (525,000 tons). Japan was allowed a tonnage two-thirds that of Britain and the United States (315,000 tons), and France and Italy trailed behind. Restrictions were placed not only on the numbers of capital ships in each navy but also on their size (not to exceed 35,000 tons) and the calibre of guns they could carry (nothing larger than sixteen-inch main guns). Similar restrictions were placed on aircraft carriers, but there were no limits on the numbers of cruisers, destroyers or submarines. A ten-year moratorium was placed on the construction of capital ships. The Five Power Treaty forced all the naval powers to scrap ships under construction as well as some older ships, much to the jubilation of pacifists. In all, the three leading naval powers were obliged to scrap more than two million tons of shipping. Militarists in Japan complained that they had been coerced by the two big English-speaking powers and argued that Japan should have been granted a navy equal to that of the two major powers. For the time being, however, a more moderate government held sway in Tokyo, and disarmament went into effect.

The Washington Conference also dealt with security issues in the Pacific. In 1902 Britain had signed an alliance with Japan. That alliance was much prized in London, especially by the Admiralty, which valued the support of a strong regional power such as Japan. To turn a potential rival into an ally is always a mark of good diplomacy. In the years leading up to the First World War British firms provided much in the way of naval technology to the Japanese, who were expanding and modernizing their fleet. During the war the Japanese assisted the Allied effort by conquering German possessions in the Pacific. In return, the British supported Japanese claims to Shantung at the Paris Peace Conference, much to the dismay of Wilson. The United States, feeling increasingly uneasy about the growth of Japanese power in the Pacific, put heavy pressure on the British government to end the alliance with Japan. By 1922 the United States had manoeuvred the British government into a position where it felt forced to choose between the friend-ship of the United States and that of Japan. It was an uncomfortable position for the British and one that caused a range of divergent opinions. The Canadian prime minister, Arthur Meighen, argued that in any future dispute between Japan and the United States Britain must be on the side of the United States. The Australians, however, favoured the alliance. Some Conservatives in Britain considered that alliance with Japan, also an island state, was natural for Britain, especially in view of the danger from the communist Soviet Union; Japan could contain Soviet ambitions in the Far East. Lloyd George and Curzon both initially favoured renewing the alliance, but Churchill expressed concerns about the effect that renewal might have on relations with the United States. Eventually, the British government, under continued pressure from Washington, concluded that a new security arrangement in the Pacific was neces-sary. Even *The Times*, a long-time supporter of the alliance with Japan, had changed its mind by 1921 and argued in favour of a new arrangement. The question then became one of how to wind up the alliance with Japan (due for renewal any time after 1921) without injuring Japanese pride.

The solution was the Four Power Treaty, signed by Britain, the United States, Japan and France on 13 December 1921.[13] The objective of the treaty was to maintain the status quo in the Pacific. The four powers were to consult with one another in times of crisis or instability, the colonial possessions of the four powers in the Pacific were recognized, and no new military bases were to be built in the Pacific, although the United States was allowed to complete the Pearl Harbor base and Britain was allowed to complete fortifications at Singapore. The prohibition on future bases in the Pacific was designed to make it easier for the Japanese government to accept the two-thirds limit on the size of the Japanese fleet. If the United States and Britain were prohibited from building additional bases closer to Japan (such as at Guam and Hong Kong), Japanese security would be assured and a larger fleet would not be needed.

The final building block in the 'Washington system', as it came to be known, was a treaty regarding China, the Nine Power Treaty. China had been in a state of internal decay and civil war for some time. It had also been under siege from European imperialists before the First World War, and during the war the Japanese government had sought far-reaching concessions there (the Twenty-One Demands of 1915), much to the alarm of the United States. The Nine Power Treaty (Japan, the United States, Britain, France, Italy, Belgium, Portugal, Holland and China) recognized the territorial integrity of China and the principle of equal trading opportunity (the Open Door). Japan was induced to give up Shantung, thus resolving a major grievance with the United States, albeit much to the fury of Japanese militarists.

Some historians have criticized Britain's decision to end the Anglo-Japanese alliance at the Washington Conference as fatally weakening its position in the Far East: Britain abandoned Japan, a proven and valuable ally, in favour of the passive neutrality of the United States – a very dubious bargain. Indeed, they argue, the concessions to which Japan agreed at Washington (the two-thirds fleet limit and the withdrawal from Shantung) strengthened the hand

64

of militarists and extreme nationalists in Tokyo. Britain's acceptance of naval parity with the United States has also been attacked.[14] On the other hand, the Five Power Treaty was a major, if rare, success in international disarmament. A post-war naval race, with all its attendant economic costs, was averted. The world economy could hardly have afforded the diversion of resources that a three-way naval race would have demanded. The British decision to opt for the Four Power Treaty did not have any immediate negative consequences, and the Washington system survived until the Great Depression of 1929, which destroyed moderate government in Japan and, for that matter, Germany. In Britain the Washington system was received enthusiastically and proved to be a welcome success for Lloyd George's government.

Britain and the Soviet Union

Lloyd George could also claim a victory in his handling of Soviet Russia. In March 1921 the British and the Soviets signed a very modest trade agreement. Numerous obstacles had arisen during the course of the negotiations that led up to it. Conservative forces in the coalition, especially Churchill and Curzon, worried about the effects of Comintern propaganda, not only in Britain but also in India. Their fears were reinforced by intercepted Soviet government telegraphs urging the Indian Communist Party to take action against British rule in India. Curzon and Churchill wanted guarantees that Comintern propaganda would cease and that Soviet foreign policy would become more amenable to Britain. From the other side of the political spectrum leftists and trade unionists demanded that the British government keep its 'hands off Russia'. In addition, the government had to consider the plight of investors who had lost money in Russia following the Bolshevik nationalization of foreign holdings. The aggrieved investors wanted compensation, which the Soviets flatly refused to consider. The Soviets turned the tables when they demanded compensation from the British government for damages done by British troops during the intervention.

The 1921 trade agreement did little to settle the issues raised during the negotiations, but it was an important step in normalizing relations with the Soviet Union. As always, Lloyd George's concern was to reintegrate Soviet Russia into the European scene to achieve long-lasting peace. He hoped that a trade agreement might help the recovery of the British economy. For their part, the Soviets remained wary of the capitalist powers. Lenin knew that the Soviet Union was isolated on the international stage. He co-operated with Western powers if the opportunity arose and an advantage was to be gained, such as in the trade agreement with Britain, but he also worked with anti-British forces in the Middle East, such as the nationalist Turks, to distract and weaken the British and head off the possibility of another intervention. Indeed, just before the signing of the trade agreement the Soviets had concluded anti-British agreements with the governments of Persia and Afghanistan.

Cannes, Genoa and Rapallo

The first few months of 1922 saw economic difficulties building in Europe. The German mark declined sharply in value and inflation ensued. Following the temper of the times, an international conference convened in Cannes in early January to discuss reparations and the European economic climate generally. A few days before the opening of the conference Hardinge discovered that Curzon had inexplicably decided to let Lloyd George attend on his own. Hardinge, fearful of what might happen if the prime minister were unaccompanied, begged Curzon to reconsider, saying: 'Heaven only knows what the decisions will be'.[15] Hardinge need not have worried; the only decision taken at the conference was to meet again at Genoa in April. At Cannes Lloyd George continued to put pressure on the French for concessions, holding out the offer of a British alliance as bait. During an adjournment in the conference proceedings the French press took photographs of Lloyd George giving a golf lesson to the French prime minister, Briand. For many in France this incident typified the patronizing, arrogant tone of the British and the subservient status of their own country; an inexperienced and naive French leader was allegedly being hoodwinked by the wily Welshman. The French cabinet refused to concede anything and Briand's government fell.

At Genoa in April the results were again disappointing. Briand had been succeeded by Raymond Poincaré, a native of Lorraine who had twice seen his village devastated by German invaders. Poincaré was a hardliner, and he soon made clear that he expected Germany to fulfil all its obligations under Versailles. He insisted that France expected both reparations and security. A reduction in reparations to aid German economic recovery would, he argued, lead to a stronger Germany that would inevitably pose a threat to France. Not surprisingly, there were a number of acrimonious exchanges between Lloyd George and Poincaré.

The Genoa conference did have one completely unexpected outcome. At its height the Soviet and German delegates scurried off to the nearby town of Rapallo where they signed the Treaty of Rapallo. The treaty had actually been negotiated beforehand and merely awaited signing. The shock to the international community, however, was considerable. On the surface the treaty did little more than proclaim German–Soviet friendship and restore diplomatic relations. But in reality Rapallo implied a joint threat to the successor states of eastern Europe and French hopes of using the *cordon sanitaire* to further French security. In fact, soon after the treaty was signed the Germans and Soviets initiated a long period of secret military collaboration, rumours of which appeared in the press. During the 1920s and early 1930s the Germans tested tanks, aircraft and poison gas at bases in the USSR. This collaboration enabled the Germans to avoid at least some of the disarmament clauses of Versailles.

The immediate aftermath of the Genoa conference witnessed a heightening of tensions in Europe. The domestic situation in Italy deteriorated during the summer of 1922, and at the end of October Benito Mussolini seized power following the so-called 'march on Rome'. As head of the world's first Fascist régime, Mussolini added elements of unpredictability and uncertainty to European affairs. A major part of Mussolini's appeal was the claim that he would recover Italy's international prestige – that same prestige which had allegedly been treated with such contempt at Versailles. If he acted in this vein of outraged nationalism, what would Mussolini contribute to European stability? Would France have to worry about Italian hostility and the possibility of fighting on a second front? In

Germany the economy continued to tumble and by the end of the year Germany was again in default on its reparation payments. Poincaré was confronted with the problem of how to handle the German defaults. Anti-Versailles agitation by German nationalists continued unabated. In late 1922 the British Consulate in Munich reported:

The eyes of most people will turn to Herr Hitler whose fame has now risen so high that five meetings, held simultaneously and addressed by him in turn, were insufficient to hold all his disciples two or three days ago. It is possible – as I have just been told by one of his admirers who has spoken to him recently – that Herr Hitler does not yet consider himself strong enough to take decisive action in the Mussolini line; but the situation does seem to present him with an excellent opportunity.[16]

The Chanak crisis

For Britain, however, much of the summer of 1922 was consumed by events in the Near East and the confrontation with Turkey. In the nineteenth century control of the Straits (the Bosporus and the Dardanelles which, respectively, connect the Black Sea to the Sea of Marmara and the Sea of Marmara to the Aegean and the eastern Mediterranean) became a major issue for British foreign policy makers. It was feared that the Russians would push south, defeat the Ottoman Turks, seize the Straits and emerge into the eastern Mediterranean, where they would threaten the British lifeline to India at Suez. The British had gone to war with Russia during the Crimean War (1853–1856) to defend Turkey and contain the Russians. From the Crimean War until the outbreak of the First World War Britain had continued to support Turkish control of the Straits. In 1914, in a move that utterly shocked the British, the Turks decided to go to war on Germany's side. The British were deeply embittered, especially as Turkey's hostility both cut off Russia from the West and threatened the British at Suez. The British tried hard to knock the so-called 'sick man of Europe' out of the war, but the sick man still packed a punch. The Turks defeated British imperial armies at Gallipoli (where they tried to seize direct control of the Straits) and at Kut (in modern Iraq). Lloyd George reckoned that Turkish hostility had caused Russia's defeat and lengthened the war by two full years.

During the war the Allies made various plans for a punitive peace against Ottoman Turkey, most of which involved stripping Turkey of its Arab possessions, establishing direct and indirect zones of control in Turkey and ending Turkish control of the Straits.[17] France would be granted a zone of indirect control north of modern Syria (then the province of Cilicia), Italy would acquire a zone on Turkey's Aegean and Mediterranean coasts as a reward for joining the war on the Allied side, and Russia would gain a substantial territory in the eastern, Armenian regions of Turkey. Early in the war the British also agreed to Russian control over the Straits. This constituted a complete reversal of British policy since the Crimean War, which had been to keep Russia bottled up in the Black Sea, but many in the British government feared a Russian defection unless the Russians were promised substantial post-war gains. The Turkish state was to be reduced to nothing more than a 'rump state' with uncontested control over only a small area of central Turkey.

When the Bolsheviks came to power in 1917 they renounced territorial claims in Turkey and published the secret wartime agreements relating to the partition of Turkey, much to the embarrassment of the Allies. The Turkish army finally collapsed in October 1918. A small Allied force was landed at the Straits. At Versailles the Allies received the Turkish Arab domains as League of Nations mandates, but a plan to grant the Straits to the United States as a mandate fell by the wayside. Incredibly, the Paris Peace Conference did not conclude a treaty with Turkey until 10 August 1920, the Treaty of Sèvres. Meanwhile, in May 1919, in a move that was particularly provocative to the Turks, a large Greek army had landed at the city of Smyrna (also known as Izmir) on Turkey's Aegean coast. Smyrna was located in the region previously assigned to Italy, but Lloyd George ruled that Italy had not contributed sufficiently to the war against Turkey.

Greece gained independence from Turkey in 1831 at the end of a long and bitter war. The nineteenth century witnessed continued tension between Greece and the Ottoman Turks. Britain had a history of sympathy for the Greek cause: Lord Byron fought for the

Greeks and the Royal Navy intervened on the Greek side against Turkey in 1827. Greece was seen as a bastion of classical and Christian values against the encroachments of Islam on Europe. Lloyd George shared those feelings and encouraged the Greek move into Smyrna (where a large Greek minority resided), but not for altruistic reasons. It was clear that he wanted to use the Greek army to enforce Allied policy on Turkey at a time when Britain did not possess adequate military means to do so. Britain's priority in dealing with Turkey was to end Turkish military control over the Straits. According to Lloyd George, the Straits were the most strategic place in the world. Never again must Turkish military power be allowed to threaten Britain's lifeline to the East.

The Treaty of Sèvres was harsh and punitive and tried to incorporate many of the elements of the wartime agreements made among the Allies. Armenia received independence and Kurdistan was given autonomy. The Greek occupation of Smyrna was to continue for five years, at the end of which a plebiscite would decide the fate of the area. The French were given Cilicia, the Italians Adalia (on the Mediterranean coast) – ostensibly to help the local inhabitants with post-war reconstruction – and the Straits were to be placed under international, mainly British, supervision. The Sultan's control was to be limited to the region around Ankara in central Turkey (Anatolia). The Turks also lost land in Europe to Greece (Thrace) and another international commission was to be set up to supervise the Turkish economy in order to ensure that Turkey paid reparations and the cost of an Allied occupation.

The Treaty of Sèvres was a dead letter almost as soon as it was signed. Together with the Greek occupation of Smyrna it provoked a nationalist uprising in Turkey that was led by General Mustapha Kemal, the hero of the successful Turkish defence of Gallipoli. Kemal overthrew the feckless Sultan in August 1920, signed a treaty of mutual assistance with the Bolsheviks, who were more than glad to help, and went on the offensive. The Armenians and Kurds were quickly crushed. Kemal then turned west and fought a longer but ultimately successful war against the Greeks. The latter were strongly supported by the British and, at one point, advanced 400 miles into the interior of Turkey before meeting defeat.

During the course of the Greco-Turkish war in 1921 first Italy then France renounced their claims on Turkey. The Italians did so because the deteriorating economic and social conditions in their country ruled out foreign adventurism. France's change of policy was for pragmatic reasons. The French government knew that the Treaty of Sèvres was dead and that it was time to make terms with Kemal. If in so doing they gained the friendship of Kemal ahead of other European powers (especially Britain), then so much the better. The French reversal revived the nineteenth-century colonial competition between Britain and France. The British saw the French action as a severe betrayal, and one more grievance was added to the list of Anglo-French antagonisms. But the hard line towards the Turks had also provoked a split in the British government. Edwin Montagu, the secretary for India, argued that a humiliation of Turkey – a Muslim state – might well provoke uprisings among Muslims in British India. Montagu voiced his criticisms publicly and, in 1922, was forced to resign from the cabinet.

In September 1922 the Greeks were literally thrown into the sea at Smyrna in scenes of great chaos and bloodshed. Kemal then turned his attention to the last area of Turkey not yet redeemed by his forces – the Straits. A tiny British contingent of three hundred troops at Chanak (on the west side of the Dardanelles, at the narrowest point in the channel) was surrounded by three Turkish armies, mustering about 65,000 troops altogether. The Turks did not fire on the British, although individual Turkish soldiers did approach the British defences to hurl insults and pull faces, but it was patently evident that a major crisis was in the making. The driving force behind British policy was the conviction of Lloyd George that the Straits were a vital strategic interest for Britain. Few questioned whether or not this judgement was as appropriate in 1922 as it had been in 1915, nor was there any effort to consult the British people on whether they wanted another war only four years after the end of the last.[18]

On 29 September the cabinet telegraphed a message to the commander of the British garrison at Chanak, General Harington, requiring him to issue an ultimatum to the Turks. They were to withdraw from the neutral zone within twenty-four hours, or British warships in the Straits would open fire. Given the odds against him, Harington did the sensible thing. He claimed that his decoding machine had broken down and that he was unable to decode messages from London. Harington's tactics averted immediate conflict and gave some room for manoeuvre to Curzon, who was trying to arrange an armistice and a new peace conference with the Turks. Significant credit for avoiding armed conflict should also go to Kemal, who declined to go to war with Britain and agreed instead to a diplomatic settlement. An armistice was arranged in October and a peace conference scheduled to open in Lausanne in November. The Treaty of Lausanne, which was concluded the following July, established the borders of the modern Turkish state. Traffic through the Straits was regulated and the Straits themselves were neutralized. The Lausanne Treaty contained nothing that could not have been accomplished four years earlier.

The Chanak crisis had two important consequences for Britain. First, it provoked changes in Britain's relations with the Dominions. At the height of the crisis the British government issued a statement that appeared to commit the Dominions to military action against Turkey. The Canadian prime minister, Mackenzie King, dismissed the statement as an exercise in pre-election posturing and refused to have anything to do with it. Similar feelings were expressed by the Australians, who had lost heavily at Gallipoli in 1915. The Gallipoli expedition had been directed by Winston Churchill, then First Lord of the Admiralty, whom many Australians held personally responsible for the defeat. Churchill was still in the cabinet in 1922 and, as a result of a maladroit and insensitive decision, was the minister responsible for issuing the controversial statement. After Chanak the British government was forced to concede complete independence to the Dominions on foreign policy issues.

Chanak further deepened Anglo-French mistrust. Harold Nicolson has provided a vivid illustration of just how poor relations were between the two countries by the autumn of 1922. He relates the scene at a meeting in Paris between Poincaré and Curzon on 20 September 1922, after British intelligence intercepts had shown, to Curzon's dismay, that the French were determined to stay one step ahead of the British in dealings with Turkey.

At the first session of the Conference Lord Curzon, in precise but cutting phrases, summarised the disloyalty of the French during the last two years, of which the betrayal of their British comrades behind the wire entanglements of Chanak was but the final culmination. In the afternoon M. Poincaré responded to this attack. His voice was dry, his words were clipped, his insults were lancets of steel. Curzon's wide white hands upon the green baize cloth trembled violently. He could stand it no further. Rising from his seat he muttered something about an adjournment and limped hurriedly into the adjoining room... He collapsed upon a scarlet settee. He grasped Lord Hardinge by the arm. 'Charley', he panted, 'I can't bear that horrid little man. I can't bear him. I can't bear him'. He wept.[19]

Chanak also had consequences for British domestic politics. Lloyd George's questionable handling of the Chanak debacle provided the coalition Conservatives with their opportunity. On 19 October, at a meeting of the Carlton Club, the Conservatives decided to withdraw from the coalition. Lloyd George was forced to resign and Canadian-born Andrew Bonar Law became the new prime minister, with Curzon continuing as foreign secretary. An election was held in November 1922, as a result of which the Conservatives formed a government, the Labour Party doubled its share of the vote and emerged as a strong opposition, and the Liberal Party entered a long period of decline and further factional infighting. Bonar Law, however, soon fell seriously ill with throat cancer. In December 1922, at a singularly inopportune moment, the Germans again defaulted on their reparations payments by failing to deliver a shipment in kind of coal and telegraph poles.

The occupation of the Ruhr

The German default meant that Poincaré's policy now came into action. On 11 January 1923 French and Belgian troops occupied the industrial Ruhr Basin. France and Belgium were determined to seize German industrial output and send it back home. The occupied area was only sixty miles deep and thirty miles wide, but it produced eighty per cent of Germany's coal and steel. The French move backfired badly. The occupation triggered economic instability and a wave of inflation in France. Since the cost of maintaining troops in the Ruhr exceeded any economic benefits to be derived from the occupation, France's international credit weakened as a result of the crisis.

The costs for the Germans were even higher. They responded to the occupation with a policy of 'passive resistance'. The workers of the Ruhr embarked on a general strike, industrial production ceased, and railways shut down. Confrontations erupted with French troops. The Germans showed almost complete unanimity in support of passive resistance, but unfortunately this policy soon led to a general economic catastrophe in Germany. Business confidence collapsed and the German currency lost all value as inflation soared to previously unheard of levels. Photographs in the newspapers showed people pushing handcarts full of money through the streets just to do the daily shopping. Government printing presses ran off bank notes at top speed and clerks with rubber stamps added extra zeroes to their values as they were rushed into circulation. By November 1923 one United States dollar was worth 630 billion German marks. Prices were adjusted hourly, always upwards. The German middle classes saw their savings wiped out, and pensioners and those with low incomes also suffered. Few ever forgave the Weimar Republic for the collapse of 1923. The ultimate political beneficiaries of the 1923 German inflation were extremists such as Hitler.

By late 1923 Hitler had decided that his time had come. He enlisted the aid of General Ludendorff, the German war hero and virtual dictator of Germany in the later stages of the war, in an attempt to overthrow the Weimar republic. His idea was to seize power in Munich so that Ludendorff could organize an army to march on Berlin. The so-called 'Beer Hall Putsch' quickly collapsed. Hitler was arrested and sentenced to five years imprisonment. He served only thirteen months of his term and used the time to write his autobiography, *Mein Kampf*, with the assistance of Rudolf Hess. Despite the ignominious failure of Hitler's plans the episode was ominous and certainly demonstrated his ability to recruit prominent members of the German élite, such as Ludendorff, to his cause. As a result of Munich Hitler decided to pursue more constitutional, legal means to power.

The Ruhr episode also ushered in the most difficult phase yet in post-war relations between Britain and France. Britain had refused to participate in the occupation. Bonar Law, Curzon and the new chancellor of the exchequer, Stanley Baldwin, thought that Britain faced two unpleasant alternatives. A breach with France would lead to chaos in Europe: Poincaré would only dig in and become more intractable, and the Germans would draw encouragement and prolong resistance, possibly to the point of war. On the other hand, British support for Poincaré's rigorous enforcement of the treaty was equally undesirable. The cabinet opted instead for 'benevolent passivity'. The Germans would be given no encouragement and every effort would be made to minimize friction with the French.

In the months leading up to the Ruhr crisis a strong body of British public opinion had been growing steadily more sympathetic towards the Germans. Many middle-class intellectuals were pro-German by 1923, as was left-wing opinion. Pro-German sympathies were predictably reinforced by guilt over the Treaty of Versailles, and the economic hardships in Germany brought on by the crisis led to the establishment of relief committees in Britain. Sympathizers and supporters included the Archbishop of Canterbury, Lord Robert Cecil and Bertrand Russell. By 1923, however, most people in Britain were war-weary and profoundly sick of international crisis. They wanted a resolution, but the deadlock continued well into 1923. In May, a seriously ill Bonar Law resigned as prime minister and was succeeded by Stanley Baldwin, the reassuring and avuncular, if somewhat dull and plodding, provincial businessman. In August 1923 Gustav Stresemann was appointed as Germany's chancellor. Stresemann controlled German foreign policy, first as chancellor then as foreign minister, until his death in 1929. He saw himself as a practitioner of realpolitik in the Bismarckian tradition. Unlike most Germans in 1923, Stresemann realized that Germany's military weakness dictated the limits of German foreign policy. Six weeks after taking power he called off passive resistance and signalled a willingness to negotiate with the French. Soon afterwards representatives from the United States were called on to act as mediators. A major breakthrough in the deadlock had been achieved, thus setting the stage for dramatic improvements in European affairs.

Britain, for the time being, continued to experience political change. Stanley Baldwin enjoyed a majority in the House of Commons and could have coasted for another four years before calling an election, but he was worried about high levels of unemployment in Britain and decided to adopt a policy of protectionism. He felt that he needed a renewed mandate from the people and accordingly called a general election late in 1923. A dramatic victory would also have solidified his hold on the Conservative leadership, but the result of that election (held in December) was an upset. The Conservatives lost heavily and the Labour Party scored a major electoral breakthrough. In January 1924 a minority Labour government took office with Ramsay MacDonald serving as both prime minister and foreign minister.[20]

Notes

1 D. P. Heatley, *Diplomacy and the Study of International Relations* (Oxford, Clarendon, 1919), p. v.
2 David Gilmour, *Curzon* (London, John Murray, 1994); H. Nicolson, *Curzon: The Last Phase, 1919–1925* (London, Constable, 1934); and G. Bennett, *British Foreign Policy during the Curzon Period, 1919–24* (London, St. Martin's, 1995).
3 P. Rowland, *Lloyd George* (London, Barrie and Jenkins, 1975), p. 516.
4 J. D. Goold, 'Lord Hardinge as ambassador to France, and the Anglo-French dilemma over Germany and the Near East, 1920–1922', *The Historical Journal*, XXI, 1978, pp. 913–37.
5 Nicolson, *Curzon*, p. 193.
6 Gilmour, *Curzon*, p. 510.
7 See W. Kleine-Ahlbrandt, *The Burden of Victory: France, Britain and the Enforcement of the Versailles Peace, 1919–1925* (Lanham, University of Press of America, 1995), for a recent survey of Anglo-French relations at this time.
8 Britain owed the United States 4.25 billion dollars, Germany owed Britain 7.2 billion dollars in reparations, and various European allies, mainly France, owed 10.5 billion dollars to Britain.
9 The document was known as the Balfour Note but was actually drafted by Lloyd George.
10 Of this total the Allies collected only about ten per cent by the time reparations were cancelled in 1932.
11 The Germans had been making interim payments 'in kind' of raw materials such as coal and building supplies.

12 Goold, 'Lord Hardinge', p. 922, and C. Andrew and J. Noakes (eds), *Intelligence and International Relations, 1900–1945* (Exeter, Exeter University Press, 1987), p. 17.

13 France at that time held Indochina (modern Vietnam, Laos and Cambodia) as a possession and was therefore considered a major Pacific power.

14 Critics include W. Medlicott, *British Foreign Policy Since Versailles* (London, Methuen, 1968), pp. 29–32, and C. Barnett, *The Collapse of British Power* (London, Methuen, 1972), pp. 267–73.

15 Goold, 'Lord Hardinge', p. 922.

16 Goold, 'Lord Hardinge', p. 930.

17 The Constantinople Agreement, 18 March 1915; the Sykes–Picot Agreement, 16 May 1916; the St Jean de Maurienne Agreement, 17 April 1917.

18 See J. Ferris, *Men, Money and Diplomacy: The Evolution of British Strategic Policy, 1919–1926* (Ithaca, Cornell University Press, 1989), pp. 119–20, for a differing view.

19 Nicolson, *Curzon*, p. 274.

20 D. Marquand, *Ramsay MacDonald* (London, Jonathan Cape, 1977).

CHAPTER FOUR

AN ERA OF STABILITY
AND PROMISE, 1924–1929

Most historians have characterized the mid- to late 1920s as an era of illusion and false hopes.[1] In view of the wreckage subsequently brought about by the Depression and Adolf Hitler, such views might appear justified. At the time, however, Europe seemed to be on the mend. The reparations impasse was breached in 1924, agreements on Western European security were signed at Locarno in 1925, and the European economy made impressive gains in the second half of the decade. The Weimar Republic in Germany seemed to have turned the corner by 1925. Even such malcontent powers as Mussolini's Italy or the Soviet Union were quiescent. To contemporaries, it appeared as though idealism, pacifism and optimism governed international relations. The new Labour government in Britain came to office embodying many of these new ideals and hoping to put them into practice.

Ramsay MacDonald remains a controversial figure, reviled by some as a traitor to his party but lionized by others as a martyr. He was a founder of the Labour Party and architect of the 1906 'deal' with the Liberals that saw Labour win its first significant block of seats in the House of Commons. A compelling orator, he recognized that Britain needed significant social reform. In terms of foreign policy he saw himself as an internationalist and during the First World War he had been a pacifist. On taking office, MacDonald's immediate objective in the field of foreign policy was to improve relations with both France and the USSR, thereby contributing to the stability of Europe. He and Poincaré exchanged a series of letters that were designed to minimize French anxieties about his own pacifist and internationalist leanings. Ultimately, MacDonald refused to enter into a firm military alliance with France: public opinion in Britain would not tolerate it, and the tradition of British foreign policy had always been to avoid alliances. Still, MacDonald wanted to leave the French in no doubt that Britain solidly supported an entente, or understanding, with France. He seems to have hoped that once the security fears of the French were assuaged they might be persuaded to depart from some of the harsher provisions of Versailles.

By the spring of 1924 moderate opinion in France was turning rapidly against Poincaré and in May his government was defeated at the polls. Poincaré had occupied the Ruhr in the hope of extracting reparations payments from Germany, but that policy had largely failed. Reparations had not been forthcoming, the occupation had proved costly and the franc was declining in value. Poincaré was replaced in early June by the more conciliatory Édouard Herriot. The new French prime minister was an Anglophile who was willing to follow the lead of the British. During his brief first term in office MacDonald was able to re-establish the ascendancy of Britain over France in the entente. Herriot realized that MacDonald would not agree to a formal alliance, but suggested that Britain and France might instead at least agree to 'a sort of moral pact of continuous collaboration.'[2] Some historians have argued that during the subsequent months France also conceded the total superiority that it had enjoyed over Germany since 1919. Never again were the French able to impose their will on the Germans as they had in early 1923.[3] From 1924 onwards, French policy became increasingly passive and defensive.

The Dawes Plan

The first step was taken with the resolution of the Ruhr crisis in 1924. Although the United States had sworn off political involvement in European affairs, its government still had substantial economic interests and markets on the continent. To seek a resolution of the Ruhr dispute was very much to the advantage of the United States. Accordingly, the American banker, General

Charles Dawes, was despatched to Europe in an unofficial capacity to mediate a settlement. Economic and reparations experts held preliminary meetings in Paris during the first weeks of January 1924. A report issued by these experts on 9 April soon became known as the Dawes Report. The recommendations of the report were then debated by an international conference that assembled in London on 16 July. The result, in August 1924, was the Dawes Plan.

The Dawes Plan was never intended to be a final resolution of the reparations issue. Its aim was simply to provide Germany with a breathing space in order to revive the economy. Accordingly, the United States granted Germany a large loan to assist its recovery. Ironically, the loan was made at a heavy cost to France. The French were obliged to give assurances that the Ruhr episode, with its attendant inflation and instability, would never happen again. French foreign policy was thus heavily circumscribed by bankers in London and Washington.[4] Without those reassurances to the banks, there would be no loan to Germany, no Dawes Plan and no European settlement. On the other hand, the French were allowed to maintain their army of occupation in the Rhineland.

The Dawes Plan also rescheduled German reparations payments. Over the next five years the payments would rise from one billion marks per year to two and a half billion marks per year as the economy improved. The size of the total reparations bill remained as set in 1921. The implementation of the Dawes Plan would proceed alongside the evacuation of French troops from the Ruhr Valley, which was to be accomplished by August 1925. When the five years had passed, a new plan would be established for a final schedule of payments.

Once put in place, the Dawes Plan was a success. Confidence in the German economy quickly returned, the currency stabilized, unemployment fell, and the French evacuated the Ruhr on schedule.

MacDonald also realized that French security needs had still not been fully addressed. During 1922 a Draft Treaty of Mutual Guarantee had been circulated by the League of Nations. Lord Cecil, operating independently of his government, was the author and a prime supporter of the treaty. Its object was to specify the duties and obligations of member states if any one state were the victim of aggression. Cecil proposed that the obligations should be binding on all the members of the League, arguing that a mutual defensive pact was necessary because certain states would not begin to reduce their armaments until they had been assured of their security.

The proposed treaty received a frosty reception in the British government – particularly from the three armed services and the Foreign Office – and also in the Dominions. Opponents of the pact argued that Britain would be forced to make worldwide commitments with limited resources. Under the terms of the proposed treaty Britain could be drawn into resolving disputes all over the globe and it was feared that the Royal Navy might have to serve as the world's policeman at a time of shrinking defence budgets. Similarly, the Dominions baulked at the prospect of involvement in disputes thousands of miles from their shores. MacDonald rejected the proposed treaty on the grounds that it was too much like an old-fashioned military alliance. It never received serious discussion and sputtered out in 1922, but hopes of assuring French security within the context of the League of Nations lingered on.

The Geneva Protocol

The idea was taken up again after the announcement of the Dawes Plan, when MacDonald and Herriot floated the 'Protocol for the Pacific Settlement of International Disputes', subsequently known as the Geneva Protocol. The Protocol, which was to be attached to the League of Nations Covenant, was designed to strengthen the League and was intended to close a perceived loophole in the Covenant, under which nations could go to war without penalty if negotiation failed. Signatories now pledged that they would not go to war except 'with the consent or at the behest' of the League and would instead submit their disputes to compulsory arbitration by the League. In addition, all members of the League were bound to offer co-operation to all victims of aggression to the best of their ability. Such assistance might include military aid, the application of sanctions, or both, depending on geographical circumstances. Under the Protocol aggression was more precisely defined: an aggressor was any state that defied the obligations of the League

Covenant, refused to abide by a League decision or resorted to war during the period of negotiation. The Protocol would come into effect after an international disarmament conference had enacted plans for general disarmament.

MacDonald thought highly of the Protocol but again encountered resistance from many sectors. The services objected on the same grounds as those on which they had objected to the Draft Treaty of Mutual Guarantee and the earlier proposed alliance with France: Britain had neither the resources nor the capability to become the world's policeman. Similar objections were raised by the opposition parties. Even some members of MacDonald's cabinet showed hesitation and reluctance to support the Protocol. Had MacDonald's government lasted, it would probably not have been able to secure the support of the House of Commons for the Protocol.

MacDonald's government also attempted to improve relations with the USSR – a policy that aroused considerable controversy. Soon after coming to office the Labour government granted formal diplomatic recognition to the Soviet state. In August 1924 the British government initialled both a commercial agreement and a General Treaty with the Soviets. Negotiations on compensation for British investors (who had lost property and investments in Russia after the Revolution) were supposed to follow. The Conservative and Liberal opposition alleged that MacDonald was being 'soft' on the Soviet Union and selling out the interests of British investors.

Baldwin returns

No sooner had the government undertaken these initiatives than Britain was again plunged into political uncertainty. MacDonald's minority government lost a vote of confidence, and yet another general election – the third in three years – was called for October 1924. The immediate cause of the fall of the government concerned the Campbell case. J. R. Campbell, the editor of the Communist newspaper the *Worker's Weekly*, published an article in which he urged British workers not to take up arms against their fellow workers during wars with other countries. He was charged with incitement to mutiny, but the charges were subsequently withdrawn by the Attorney General. Conservatives and Liberals alleged that the charges were dropped for political reasons (namely, that Labour was sympathetic to communism) and demanded a vote of confidence. Politicians are, of course, supposed to remain aloof from the judicial process. The opposition, for its part, was anxious to link the government to communism. MacDonald agreed to the vote of confidence mainly because Labour was tired of being a minority government. The government lost the vote and Parliament was dissolved. Anti-Bolshevism and Labour's policy towards the USSR played a major role in the subsequent election campaign.

On 25 October, just four days before the election, a letter allegedly written by Zinoviev, head of the Comintern, to the British Communist Party was published in the *Daily Mail*.[5] It contained directions on how to stir up the British working class and prepare it for revolution. Part of Zinoviev's purported strategy involved mustering the support of the workers for improved diplomatic links between Britain and the USSR. The Conservatives claimed that the letter proved that Labour was too soft on communism, a claim that was inadvertently reinforced when MacDonald dissociated himself from a Foreign Office note protesting against the contents of the Zinoviev letter. Labour supporters contended that the letter had been forged by anti-Labour elements in the secret service. Recent historical research inclines to the view that the letter was genuine, though this has never been proved conclusively. Anti-Labour members of the British secret service were certainly quick to use the letter as a political weapon against MacDonald's government,[6] while Zinoviev always denied sending the letter.

The election of 1924 returned the Baldwin Conservatives with a large majority. Most analyses of the election conclude that the Zinoviev letter played only a minor part in Labour's defeat. Voters focused on economic issues and thought that Baldwin's Conservatives offered the better choice, especially after Baldwin dropped the controversial protectionist plank from the party platform. The 1924 election also saw Churchill leave the Liberal Party for the Conservatives, with whom he had begun his political career.

Austen Chamberlain

Baldwin appointed Austen Chamberlain as foreign secretary.[7] Some consideration was given to reappointing Curzon, but Baldwin realized that to bring Curzon back would have a disastrous effect on relations with France. Chamberlain retained his post until 1929, making him one of the longer-serving foreign secretaries of the interwar period.

Austen Chamberlain was the son of Joseph Chamberlain, a highly successful politician from Birmingham. 'Joe' Chamberlain had dominated local Birmingham politics, defected from the Liberals in 1886 in opposition to Irish Home Rule and become a champion of tariff reform. He had held a variety of cabinet posts in the 1890s (including colonial secretary), had become enmeshed in controversy on several occasions and had often been mentioned as a potential prime minister. Joseph Chamberlain had hopes that his son Austen might become prime minister some day and strongly encouraged Austen in his political career. Austen rose to the leadership of the Conservative Party during the coalition with Lloyd George. By the time the coalition broke up in 1922 Austen was clearly in line for the prime ministership. At the last moment he was deposed as leader of the Conservatives because he did not want to break up the coalition. He never fulfilled his father's ambition and ranks as the only leader of the Conservative Party in the twentieth century to fail to become prime minister. Instead, Austen's half-brother Neville filled the post in 1937. Some attributed Austen's 'failure' to the fact that he was a mediocre, lacklustre individual who was unwilling to engage in political infighting. Even so, his years as foreign secretary were marked by a number of important accomplishments.

During his tenure at the Foreign Office Chamberlain proved to be a firm and decisive administrator. He made all the senior diplomatic appointments himself. His relationship with Baldwin had been difficult in the past (he regarded Baldwin as his junior and no doubt resented Baldwin's taking the leadership from him), but Baldwin won him back by appointing him foreign secretary and consistently supporting his policies. Baldwin was not particularly interested in foreign policy, so allowed Chamberlain considerable autonomy. On at least one occasion Chamberlain wished that Baldwin 'showed a little more interest and gave a more active support',[8] but for the most part Chamberlain seems to have been appreciative of the prime minister's hands-off approach.

Chamberlain faced difficulties with several cabinet members. Robert Cecil had been included in Baldwin's cabinet and given special responsibility for League affairs, but he complained that Chamberlain gave him little support, lacked enthusiasm for the League and the Geneva Protocol and refused to give him access to Foreign Office papers. Cecil's charges were essentially justified. Chamberlain recognized that the League was an inevitable fact of British foreign policy and that it commanded considerable public support, which he could not ignore. In his view the League did 'useful' relief work and could best serve to head off potential disputes, but a very long time would pass before it became fully effective. In the interim, the League was only one of several diplomatic tools that a foreign secretary had at his disposal.

A much more serious problem arose over Chamberlain's attitude towards French and British involvement in continental affairs. Chamberlain was strongly pro-French. In a letter from early 1925 he described himself as the 'the most pro-French member of the government'. He thought that the 'cardinal object' of British foreign policy should be the 'maintenance of the entente with France', and he clearly preferred an outright military alliance with France.[9] He admired French culture and sympathized with the French over their grievances against the Germans. Baldwin said of Chamberlain that he loved France 'like a woman'.[10] Chamberlain could go to excessive lengths, often insisting on delivering his speeches in French when he visited Paris or sessions of the League in Geneva, despite the fact that his command of the French language was rated 'a national disaster'. One of his subordinates was constantly having to devise methods of preventing the foreign secretary, who seemed blissfully convinced of the superiority of his linguistic skills, from giving speeches in French.[11]

Chamberlain's term in office overlapped with that of Aristide Briand, who served as the French prime minister from November 1925 to August 1926, then as foreign minister until 1932. The two became close personal friends. Chamberlain got along well with Stresemann too, and the press made much of the friendship between the three foreign ministers, seeing it as a reassuring symbol of the stability and relaxed tensions in Europe. For the most part, however, Chamberlain remained critical of German policy. During the lead-up to Locarno talks in 1925 (discussed below), Chamberlain saw German actions as heavy-handed and provocative.

Chamberlain's sympathetic attitude towards France placed him at odds with the cabinet and most of British public opinion. Isolation-ism was a powerful current in British foreign policy thinking at this time, and many in Britain resented France's policy towards Germany, seeing it as harsh, vindictive and liable to lead to another war – as had nearly happened over the Ruhr valley in 1923. Pro-German sympathy increased as anti-French sentiment grew in strength.

Chamberlain's overall strategy in Europe was to restore Britain's position as arbiter of the balance of power. Britain could not simply withdraw from European affairs. Advances in military technology meant that Britain's defensive frontier was now the Rhine rather than the Channel; nevertheless, the extent and limits of British involvement in Europe had to be be clearly defined. French security fears needed to be assuaged in order to promote European peace, but, as Chamberlain realized, Germany also had to be conciliated. An isolated Germany might turn to alliance with the Soviet Union, and Rapallo was a pointed reminder of such fears. The Locarno agreements of 1925 were a major step towards the attainment of Chamberlain's goals.

Locarno

Locarno originated when senior members of the German diplomatic service became dissatisfied with the results of passive resistance and tired of the constant tension with France. They proposed that Germany guarantee France's eastern borders. The concept was taken up more forcefully by Stresemann in 1925, with the encouragement of the British ambassador to Berlin, Lord D'Abernon, also a close friend of Stresemann. By the beginning of 1925 Stresemann was concerned that the French might delay the first stage of withdrawal from the Köln region of the Rhineland. The French had accused the German army of failing to comply fully with the disarmament provisions of Versailles and had evidence to back up their charges. D'Abernon also made sure that Stresemann got wind of rumours (false ones) that indicated that an Anglo-French military alliance was in the offing. Determined to calm France's fears and gain Britain's co-operation, Stresemann made proposals separately to the French and the British in early 1925, in which he suggested an international guarantee of the territorial status quo in Western Europe and continued demilitarization of the Rhineland.

Chamberlain was initially cautious and suspicious of the proposals; he worried that Stresemann was trying to drive a wedge between France and Britain. Moreover, Stresemann's proposals came at a slightly awkward moment for the British, as Chamberlain had been due to travel in March to the League Assembly at Geneva, where he would announce the British government's formal rejection of the Geneva Protocol. Nevertheless, he thought that an outright rejection of Stresemann's proposal by the British government would look bad and that Britain would be portrayed as an obstacle to the reduction of European tensions. He argued that Britain should conclude an alliance with France, but he was opposed by 'the rather stiff anti-French group',[12] which included Churchill (chancellor of the exchequer), Amery (colonial secretary), Birkenhead (secretary for India), Balfour and Curzon. The impasse between the two groups flared up at cabinet meetings in early March.

On 2 March and again on 4 March Chamberlain pressed the cabinet to accept the idea of alliance with France. Although he failed, he came away from the meetings convinced that he had gained permission to discuss with the French a Quadrilateral Pact, loosely based on Stresemann's proposals. For Chamberlain it was a fall-back position, but at least he had something to offer the French. Chamberlain then travelled to Paris and on 6 March informed Herriot that Britain was going to reject the Geneva Protocol and that there was no possibility of an Anglo-French alliance. Herriot was appalled. 'His face', Chamberlain recalled, 'turned very white and he looked suddenly a sick man'.[13] Chamberlain was so alarmed by the French prime minister's reaction that he convinced himself that Anglo-French relations were at a crucial turning-point. Before returning he telegraphed London and asked the cabinet for permission to tell the French that Britain had unequivocally accepted Stresemann's proposals. Baldwin called an informal cabinet meeting of eight ministers on 11 March. Led by Churchill and Amery, the isolationists mounted a strong attack on Chamberlain. Foreign Office advisers feared that Chamberlain's position in cabinet was becoming untenable and that he would be forced to resign. Stunned by the continuing opposition in cabinet and the depth of feeling against him personally, Chamberlain threatened to resign on 12 March. Ironically, the foreign secretary was now on the point of resigning over an idea that he had initially disparaged. Chamberlain's position was saved when Baldwin finally intervened in the debate. He threw his weight on Chamberlain's side and decided to accept Stresemann's proposals. At this juncture Curzon died suddenly, taking the wind out of the isolationists' sails. Britain's official acceptance of Stresemann's proposals was announced to the House of Commons on 24 March. Never again was Chamberlain's control of British foreign policy challenged.

Preliminary negotiations in Berlin, Paris and London made slow progress over the next few months. By September the French and Germans were working on legal texts. In October the diplomats met at the Swiss resort town of Locarno to negotiate the final pact. Initialled on 16 October 1925 by representatives from France, Belgium, Britain, Germany, Italy, Czechoslovakia and Poland, the Locarno agreements became the centrepiece of European diplomacy for the duration of the 1920s.[14]

Under the terms of the agreement the German government recognized Germany's borders with France and Belgium as established at Versailles. Germany promised never to attack France or Belgium, and France and Belgium gave reciprocal pledges to Germany. Locarno is referred to as a treaty of mutual guarantee, meaning that the obligations of guarantee were the same for all signatory powers. Italy and Britain then offered their guarantees of the French–German–Belgian borders, whereby they promised to come to the assistance of any signatory who was the victim of aggression. Arbitration agreements were signed between France,

Belgium and Germany, all of which renounced the use of force. Instead, the three states would submit disputes to peaceful arbitration. The German government also promised not to fortify or otherwise remilitarize that strategic Rhineland once the French had withdrawn their troops from the area. The continued voluntary demilitarization of the Rhineland was a guarantee of good behaviour by the German government. With Locarno Germany had renounced all territorial ambitions in the West.

Unfortunately, Germany would not give similar assurances with regard to its eastern borders. Instead, Stresemann signed arbitration agreements with Poland and Czechoslovakia. The implication was that Germany would seek territorial adjustments in the East but would at least do so peacefully. That even such a moderate statesman as Stresemann should contemplate territorial revisions in the East demonstrates the lingering German distaste for Versailles well before Hitler arrived on the scene.

The initialling of the treaty was an emotional moment for all concerned. Chamberlain and Briand embraced each other and wept with joy, while Mussolini took the opportunity to kiss Mrs Chamberlain's hand. The village of Locarno celebrated. 'Bands played; members of the assembled crowd danced in the village square; even calloused newspaper reporters applauded and cheered.'[15] The press began to speak in wildly optimistic terms about a new dawn in international relations. In London *The Times* thought that Germany and France had banned war 'forever'. The phrase 'the spirit of Locarno' became a cliché.

Post-Locarno optimism now seems hopelessly unjustified, but it is worth remembering that post-war fatigue influenced much of European public opinion. The British historian A. J. P. Taylor has argued that Locarno marked the true ending of the First World War.[16] R. H. Lamb refers to Locarno as 'the greatest achievement of British diplomacy between the two wars',[17] even though the idea originated with the Germans, while Baldwin's biographers K. Middlemas and J. Barnes note that Locarno

bound all the moves of European diplomats down to the mid 1930s, and was still so strong in 1936 that, when Hitler reoccupied the

Rhineland, it was to Locarno that the Foreign Offices of London, Paris, and Rome looked, rather than to the Covenant or the Treaty of Versailles.[18]

All four historians, as well as Chamberlain's biographer David Dutton, note that the major weakness of Locarno was the failure to stabilize the situation in Eastern Europe. As Dutton points out, Locarno's failures were not of immediate consequence in 1925. Britain did not have the military means to influence events in Eastern Europe, but France did, and France remained committed to its Eastern allies in 1925. Chamberlain simply 'could not foresee the rise of a new generation of German politicians for whom the traditional norms of diplomatic behaviour had no meaning'.[19] The foremost historian of Locarno, Jon Jacobson, notes that the three leading statesmen of Locarno all came away with different conceptions of what the treaty signified.[20] Stresemann thought that the path had been cleared for the peaceful revision of Germany's borders in the East, Briand considered that French predominance over Germany had been assured, and Chamberlain believed that since France was mollified and Germany was returned to the international community Britain would never have to assume a military role on the continent. Corelli Barnett is the most critical of Britain's actions at Locarno. He alleges that the British were guilty of duplicity and that their undertakings were 'a bogus commitment, a fraudulent IOU', given 'only because the English Government never thought for a moment that they would ever have to make it good'.[21] Barnett's evidence is the woeful state of British military preparations in 1925. Barnett takes an extreme position; as Dutton suggests, it is hard to imagine a statesman such as Chamberlain being so cunning and underhanded. But Barnett has put his finger on a crucial weakness that existed in British foreign policy by 1925.

British defence policy

By the end of 1919 it was clear that Britain had emerged from the carnage of the First World War as the world's dominant imperial power. It was certainly the only great power that could also legitimately claim to be a world power. Germany was defeated, France was weakened and preoccupied with events in Europe, the United States had withdrawn into isolationism and the Soviet Union was focused on internal affairs. Japan was a strictly regional power. Only Britain possessed a global empire and a navy in 1919 or 1920 that was still sufficiently powerful to defend it.

Britain's apparent triumph, however, failed to produce any sense of well-being. The Empire was plagued with crises and challenges to its authority in the years following Versailles. 'Hot spots', as we would say today, emerged in Ireland, India and the Middle East, not to mention in Europe where the unsettled situation obliged Britain to maintain a garrison for the occupation of the Rhineland. The British army had been reduced from a strength of 3.5 million in 1918 to only 370,000 by 1921, while British obligations and commitments had increased. Imperialists in Britain had long felt that the Empire was badly overextended – a 'weary Titan' or a 'gouty giant'.[22] Gloomy forebodings for the future grew as the Dominions of South Africa and Canada made clear their opposition to involvement in European affairs and Australia and New Zealand insisted that Great Britain maintain a commitment to their defence. The more prescient observers of the international scene also noted the enormous economic and financial power of the United States and the latent, potential strength of both Germany and the Soviet Union. Britain, by contrast, came out of the war with a national debt that had increased by more than ten times, taxation levels that had increased fourfold and an economy that was mired in recession and dogged by mass unemployment. A final source of vulnerability had also emerged during the First World War when Britain had been subjected to a number of small-scale air raids. Few observers of military developments were under any illusion that in the event of another war Britain would escape so lightly. Air power had come into its own during the war and now confronted Britain's military planners with the prospect of mass air raids on defenceless British cities, with heavy civilian casualties.

One of the more intractable problems for British defence was solved when Britain sensibly granted full autonomy (a 'Free State' within the British Commonwealth) to Catholic southern Ireland in

December 1921. The Treaty of Lausanne with Turkey in 1923 partially resolved matters in the Middle East, but Arab nationalism was growing in Palestine and, in 1920, a serious revolt erupted in Mesopotamia (Iraq). The Mesopotamian uprising was quelled, but imperial authorities then had to confront nationalist movements in both Egypt and India in the mid- to late 1920s. For military planners, the growing forces of anti-colonialism represented a long-term distraction and a significant drain on resources.

Public opinion proved to be problematic as well. As the historian Michael Howard has noted,

> after 1918 the reader becomes conscious of a new sound: the heavy and ominous breathing of a parsimonious and pacific electorate, to the variations in which the ears of British statesmen were increasingly attuned.[23]

High levels of military spending were not popular with the British public after it had made such enormous sacrifices during the war. As might be expected, the voters now wanted action on social issues and unemployment, and cuts to military spending became the order of the day. Between 1920 and 1922 British defence spending was reduced by eighty-two per cent and there were continued calls for further cuts during the rest of the decade. As Chamberlain told one of his ambassadors in 1928, 'you can have no recognition how profoundly pacific our people now are.'[24]

On the other hand, there were some avenues of escape for British military planners. The threat from Germany was long-term and could apparently be contained through the adroit use of diplomacy, as demonstrated at Locarno. That from the USSR was even more distant, although there was some anxiety about a possible Bolshevik threat to India. Relations with the United States could be recriminatory, but there was never any serious thought of war. Japan remained thoroughly friendly and co-operative in the 1920s. Air power, which was used so effectively during the Mesopotamian campaign, promised an economical and efficient means of 'imperial policing'. In order to provide for the air defence of the British Isles the cabinet decided in 1922 to create an air force of five hundred aircraft. Several months later the cabinet doubled that figure.

The keynote for post-war British defence policy had been set in 1919 when the cabinet ordered the defence services to prepare their budgets on the assumption that Britain 'would not be engaged in any great war during the next ten years'. Similar instructions were issued regularly over the next few years. In 1928 Winston Churchill, as chancellor of the exchequer, persuaded the government to adopt 'as a standing assumption that at any given date there will be no major war for ten years from that date'. At one time it was customary to blame all Britain's defence woes in the 1930s on the 'Ten Year Rule', as this clause came to be called. The rule was subject to annual review and was finally revoked in 1932, but during the 1920s the prospect of a major war still seemed sufficiently remote – especially after Locarno – to justify its assumptions. On the other hand, Locarno did commit Britain to the defence of Western Europe. The British did very little concrete planning to support their obligations under the terms of Locarno. To argue that the British were committing a fraud in signing Locarno seems to miss the point that most British statesmen were convinced that Europe's diplomatic problems had been solved.

Chamberlain and the Locarno era

Following his achievement at Locarno Chamberlain was knighted and awarded the Nobel Peace Prize. He soon cast himself into the role of elder statesman and his remaining years in office were marked by a curious lassitude or passivity. He seldom attended debates in the House of Commons, barely noticed the great British General Strike of 1926 and increasingly seemed content to rest on his laurels, to the irritation of some of his colleagues. Visits to Birmingham became less and less frequent as he began to neglect his home constituency. Even his manner of dressing gave rise to ridicule. Decked out in top hat, monocle and orchid, he seemed an anachronistic leftover from the Edwardian era. His speeches to League sessions in Geneva struck observers as condescending, patronizing and riddled with gaffes, and he developed the habit of referring to '*your* League', as though he and Britain were somehow above it all.

The remainder of Chamberlain's term in office was punctuated by a series of unpleasant controversies. Germany's entry into the League of Nations sparked a nasty debate; a breach in relations with the USSR occurred in 1927; and relations with the United States became strained over issues of naval disarmament. Chamberlain was also forced to confront anti-colonialist movements in China and Egypt. It should have been apparent to all in the second half of the 1920s that the 'spirit' of Locarno was very thin.

In February 1926, under an arrangement that had been agreed upon at Locarno, Germany applied for membership in the League of Nations. There was no question in anyone's mind that it should be allowed to join the League and, for many, Germany's entry symbolized that country's return to the international community. The ensuing controversy arose over the composition of the League Council.

Germany sought a permanent seat on the League Council in recognition of its status as one of the world's great powers. Other nations thought that they too were entitled to the same status. As soon as Germany had filed its application, the League received notice that Brazil, Spain and Poland all expected to receive permanent seats on the Council. Similar bids were made by Portugal, Persia and China. The Germans objected strongly to the Polish bid, but France supported it as Poland was a major eastern ally.

The foreign secretary's relations with Cecil and the League of Nations Union had reached a low point by 1926. Chamberlain's dismissive attitude towards the League has already been noted. The Locarno treaties had been signed outside the purview of the League. Supporters of the League had not been unduly upset by this: not only was Locarno consistent with the League's objectives but it would also strengthen the League once Germany joined. Unfortunately, Chamberlain's handling of the question of Germany's entry inflamed his relations with the British League of Nations Union.

Chamberlain decided to support Poland's application to join the League Council, partly because that was what the French wanted. He feared that a denial of the Polish bid would be seen as a triumph for Germany over France. The foreign secretary's support for France and Poland again provoked anti-French sentiments in the cabinet and the press. Some ministers charged Britain with following too closely behind France. The situation was further complicated by the fact that the cabinet had earlier decided that it would support Spain's forthcoming application. Chamberlain, an enthusiastic supporter of Madrid's bid, entertained the belief that both Spain and Poland could be admitted at the same time and publicly encouraged Spain, thinking that its application would be successful.

The imbroglio over admission procedures meant that Germany's application could not be dealt with at the March session of the League assembly and its admission was postponed until September, to the irritation of the League's supporters, who understandably wanted Germany to be admitted as soon as possible. The League of Nations Union mounted a pro-German press campaign that caught Chamberlain in a bind, and he was charged with being too subservient to France. He outlined his problems in a letter to D'Abernon.

> the Germans knew they had all the cards in their hands and were unwilling to concede anything. Public opinion here [i.e. Great Britain] accepted without question the German standpoint and the Germans were perfectly well aware, as I told them, that I was in their pocket and that my vote could be dictated by them.[25]

Chamberlain felt that the debate over the future membership of the Council could be settled by himself, Briand and Stresemann, meeting privately behind closed doors. He proposed that Germany should be admitted to the League and the League Council, whereas Poland should receive a non-permanent seat on the Council. Brazil and Spain were shut out and were deeply offended. They had been completely excluded from the discussions and the Spanish in particular felt betrayed. Both countries threatened to resign from the League.

The pattern for post-Locarno diplomacy had been set. Rather than use 'open diplomacy', the three foreign ministers were to settle European problems in a revival of the old 'concert' system. The 'Geneva tea parties' – as the meetings between the three men subsequently, and derisively, came to be known – should have had certain advantages. Private sessions to air issues outside the glare of public and media scrutiny could well have contributed to an atmosphere of trust and confidence among the 'Locarnites'. Unfortunately, the League's supporters were suspicious of the apparent revival of secret diplomacy. To the general public, the 'tea parties' contributed to the illusion that the era of pre-1914 stability in Europe had returned. Behind the closed doors, however, the meetings seem to have led to numerous misunderstandings, all rooted in the different conceptions of Locarno held by the three diplomats.

Cecil, by contrast, argued in favour of open meetings to settle the outstanding grievances of Spain and Brazil. During the summer of 1926 Cecil tried to work out a compromise deal with Poland, Brazil and Spain, under which they would take non-permanent seats on the League Council but would not be asked to step down at the end of their terms. Cecil's efforts met with partial success when Poland accepted the compromise, but by the time Germany accepted a seat on the Council in September, both Brazil and Spain were too alienated from the League. The government of Brazil carried out its threat to resign and Spain initially resigned but was later persuaded to return. The loss of Brazil dealt a heavy blow to League prestige. Chamberlain, for his part, remarked only: 'A flea can be excessively irritating [but] I suppose it remains true that it is better not to scratch'.[26]

Confronting anti-colonialism

In 1927 Chamberlain confronted anti-colonialist movements in both China and Egypt. These episodes served to remind British statesmen that worldwide defensive commitments had to be met with limited resources at a time of profound pacifism among the British electorate.

European imperialism had made substantial inroads in China during the nineteenth century. European powers, including Britain, had been granted extensive economic privileges by a weakened Chinese state, headed by the 200-year-old Manchu dynasty. European states had also been granted concessions, or blocks of territory, in all the major cities and ports of China, in which Europeans were allowed to settle and where European laws prevailed over those of the Chinese. Europeans travelling in China were said to enjoy extraterritoriality, or exemption from Chinese laws. Terrible abuses were often directed against local Chinese by Europeans, who then escaped prosecution. Extraterritoriality was further rationalized by the internal chaos and civil disorder that plagued China after the fall of the Manchus in 1912. If China had fallen into lawlessness, so the argument went, European laws should prevail. By the 1920s European gunboats regularly patrolled the rivers of China. European privileges in China soon became the focus of Chinese nationalist outrage. Signatories of the Washington Nine-Power Treaty of 1922 promised to revoke extraterritoriality once the domestic situation in China had become more stable. Chinese nationalists were not impressed, and in 1927 the British concession at Hankow was occupied by Chinese nationalists. Threats were also made against the concession at Shanghai.

Chamberlain remained passive throughout the crisis and even on one occasion denied that a crisis existed at all. He came under great pressure in the cabinet from hardliners such as Birkenhead and Amery who wanted troops sent to China in preparation for possible hostilities. Some members of the British government believed that the anti-Western protests were being stirred up by Chinese communists with the connivance of Moscow. A contingent of 20,000 troops was eventually sent to Shanghai, but the threat to the British concession failed to materialize and the danger blew over. The concession at Hankow was turned over to Chinese government control. Chamberlain's restraint was perhaps wise, since a confrontation with anti-colonialists was not necessarily in Britain's best interests, but his lack of action was rooted in passivity rather than any enlightened views on the morality of imperialism.

The British drew one important lesson from the Chinese unrest of 1927. During the crisis they tried to enlist the support of the United States, only to find themselves curtly rebuffed. Washington obviously did not want to be caught in the position of defending European colonialism in China, since the United States had always claimed to be above the grubby concerns of European imperialists. In London, however, the attitude of the United States lent credence to those who feared that giving up the alliance with Japan would throw Britain at the mercy of an unreliable United States. British leaders continued to view the United States as unpredictable and prone to sudden shifts in policy with every change in public opinion. Nationalism complicated matters in Egypt as well. Britain had established a protectorate over Egypt in 1882, mainly to safeguard the Suez Canal and the vital link to India. In 1922 Britain turned Egypt's internal affairs over to an Egyptian government while maintaining responsibility for defence. When Chamberlain came to the Foreign Office in 1924 one of his tasks was to negotiate a final treaty formalizing Britain's role in Egypt. His efforts were hampered by those in the government who did not want to turn power over to the Egyptians, as well as by the British ambassador to Cairo, Lord Lloyd, who opposed Chamberlain's attempts to reach a settlement with the Egyptians and criticized him vigorously in a private letter to Baldwin. Chamberlain refused to fire Lloyd, possibly because the two had been close personal friends.

For its part, the Egyptian government had to deal with a powerful nationalist movement, the Wafd, which viewed any agreement with Britain as a sell-out. Chamberlain was obliged to send battleships to Egypt early in 1927, at Lloyd's request, to head off a confrontation with Wafd. Chamberlain came close to achieving an agreement in late 1927 after going to Egypt in person to negotiate with the Egyptians over the head of Lloyd, but the Egyptian government was unable to muster sufficient support to sign the treaty. The British position in Egypt remained unclear through to the end of Chamberlain's tenure in office, much to the discomfort of British military planners.

Anglo-Soviet relations

The worst crisis of 1927 concerned Britain's relations with the Soviet Union. British conservatives had long been hostile towards the Soviets and believed that Soviet diplomatic representatives in London were engaged in subversive activities, stirring up British workers and attempting to incite revolution. Soviet agitation was blamed for the General Strike of 1926. Reports from the British secret service confirmed that Soviet representatives in London were going well beyond the bounds of normal diplomacy. Overseas the

Soviets were charged with subversion in India and stirring up anti-Western feelings in China. On 12 May 1927 hundreds of British police officers descended on the headquarters of the Soviet trade delegation in London, ARCOS (an acronym for All Russian Co-operative Society). Evidence of Soviet subversion was found and relations with the USSR were broken off.

Chamberlain had initially opposed the raid and the break in relations but found himself under great pressure in cabinet from anti-Communists such as Churchill and the home secretary, Joynson-Hicks. Labour denounced the government's action as provocative, while others worried about the loss of business contacts in the USSR at a time when unemployment remained high in Britain. The breach in relations with the USSR was paralleled by a worsening in relations with the United States over problems concerning additional efforts towards disarmament.

Britain, disarmament and the United States

Relations between Britain and the United States had been comparatively good between 1923 and 1926. The establishment of the Irish Free State removed a grievance for many Irish Americans who resented the British presence in Ireland. The Washington Conference and Britain's abrogation of the alliance with Japan made a good impression on the United States, as did the settlement of Britain's war debts to the United States. All that good will largely dissipated in 1927. The background to the quarrel of 1927 was rooted in the complicated history of international disarmament.

In 1926 the League established the Preparatory Commission for the Conference for the Limitation and Reduction of Armaments, which was charged with initiating preliminary discussions for a general conference on disarmament. Disagreements soon arose between the British and the French over the size of trained reserves for the armed forces. France was anxious to maintain a large standing army with conscription and a large pool of trained reservists. It could not compete with Germany's enormous industrial power and larger manpower base and wanted to maintain a quantitative advantage over Germany. Under the terms of Versailles

Germany had a much smaller army, no conscription and no significant trained reserve. France also proposed restrictions on German war-making potential by controlling budgetary spending on defence. Britain had a small army, with no immediate plans for its expansion, and favoured limitations on numbers of soldiers and trained reservists, mainly because smaller continental armies would be less likely to win sudden, lightning victories if war broke out. Britain would have time to mobilize industry and raise its own expeditionary force, as in 1914–15. The British government also argued that French proposals for limiting war-making potential were impractical. France opposed limitations on conscript armies, while Germany supported Britain. The divergences were too vast to be bridged for the time being, and it was not until 1932 that the Disarmament Conference finally met.

Meanwhile efforts at naval disarmament proceeded. Early in 1927 President Calvin Coolidge called for an international conference to discuss limitations on cruisers. The conference met in Geneva in June, the main participants being Britain, Japan and the United States. Both Italy and France declined to attend, claiming that they preferred to work for disarmament through the Preparatory Commission. Briand argued that navies, armies and air forces were components of the total defensive capabilities of a nation and should be dealt with as a whole and not through piecemeal agreements. Little advance preparation was carried out to ensure that the three participants arrived with broadly similar approaches to the subject under discussion, as is customary in international conferences. From the start the possibility of failure loomed large.

The British arrived at Geneva with strong ideas on what they considered to be adequate requirements for Britain's cruiser force. The Admiralty estimated that seventy cruisers were needed for imperial defence. The cruisers could be divided into two classes. Heavy cruisers would be limited to 10,000 tons each and carry eight-inch guns. Light cruisers would be limited to 7,500 tons each and carry six-inch guns. Britain would need fifteen heavy cruisers and fifty-five light cruisers with a total estimated tonnage of more than 560,000 tons. The British wanted to limit the numbers of ships by category rather than impose an overall limit on tonnage. They argued that the global extent of their defence commitments entitled Britain to a numerically large cruiser fleet. Some in the British government did not want any limitations on the numbers of light cruisers.

The American delegation wanted to build a smaller number of cruisers, but all large and with eight-inch guns, which would be more suitable for war in the Pacific. It also insisted on a limit of 400,000 tons on cruiser fleets, which the British opposed. The Americans argued for parity between the United States and Britain, and that the Japanese should build up to two-thirds of the 400,000-ton limit, which was consistent with the 1922 ratios for capital ships. The American proposal would have given Britain a maximum of forty cruisers, which the British Admiralty viewed as ludicrously inadequate.

Arguments continued through June and July. The Americans wanted to arm cruisers with eight-inch guns, but the British wanted a six-inch gun. There was confusion and disarray in the ranks of the British delegation. Cecil had been sent to Geneva as nominal head of the British delegation but found himself at odds with Admiralty representatives. He was given instructions to agree to the American demand for parity with Britain, which he promptly carried out, but then discovered that there had emerged in cabinet a strong faction that opposed parity with the United States. The government in London made some public statements that flatly contradicted what Cecil had told the Americans. Agreement proved impossible, and the conference broke up amidst much bad feeling.

The Americans concluded that the British were not fully wedded to the idea of parity between the two leading naval powers, and they were right. Churchill headed those in cabinet who preferred to see the conference fail rather than accept parity with the United States. For their part, the British felt that the United States had been inflexible and confrontational. As Chamberlain put it, Americans still delighted in twisting the lion's tail. Representatives of the American press covering the conference had also been filing reports that ridiculed the British proposals and accused Britain of seeking to impose inferiority on the United States. Some time later it emerged that one of the more prominent members of the American press had been accepting money from American steel interests on the understanding that he would give as much bad publicity as possible to the conference. The scandal came to light when the reporter sued the steel company for full payment.

Anglo-American relations had thus been heavily damaged by the Geneva conference of 1927. Shortly after the conference Cecil decided to call it quits and handed in his resignation, explaining that it was not that cabinet members were hostile to the League, so much as they were completely indifferent. Cecil wrote two long letters to Baldwin giving vent to his frustrations over the government's lack of enthusiasm for disarmament. 'I formed the distinct impression', he later wrote, 'that he [Baldwin] had scarcely read and had not appreciated either of the letters I had written to him. I also formed the impression that he was on the whole glad to be rid of me'.[27] Despite efforts at damage limitation, Cecil's resignation was widely interpreted as an act of disapproval of his own government's disarmament policies.

By the end of 1927 it was obvious that the blanket of peaceful dreams in which many European statesmen had cloaked themselves since Locarno was somewhat torn and frayed. Late in 1926 Briand and Stresemann had apparently come to a wide-ranging agreement at Thoiry (a small French village near Geneva) to compose the Franco-German differences. During the course of 1927 that tentative agreement fell apart, largely owing to lingering suspicions of Germany in the French government. When the opportunity came along to restore some of the Locarno spirit, supporters of the Locarno agreements leapt at it.

In 1927 Briand suggested that, on the occasion of the tenth anniversary of the entry of the United States into the First World War, France and the United States should make a joint public declaration renouncing the use of warfare. The idea had first been suggested to Briand by James Shotwell, an American professor who was head of the pacifist Carnegie Trust. The Americans feared that the French were attempting to ensnare them into a military alliance, but the popularity of Briand's proposals with American liberals and pacifists meant that outright rejection of the scheme would be politically damaging. The secretary of state, Frank Kellogg, countered with a clever stratagem designed to rid the French scheme of any practical implications. Kellogg replied to Briand by proposing that a worldwide declaration should be made by all countries, not just France and the United States. Baldwin was initially reluctant to go along with the idea, but relented when it was pointed out that rejection of the Kellogg–Briand overture would further offend the already aggrieved Americans.

The Kellogg–Briand Pact was signed with great publicity on 27 August 1928. It consisted of two articles: one whereby the signatories renounced the use of war as a means of settling disputes, and the second whereby they agreed to settle conflicts by peaceful means alone. Fifteen nations initially signed the pact, but eventually almost all independent nations did so. The Pact was little more than a statement of intent; enforcement mechanisms were non-existent. To modern ears the whole exercise sounds ridiculous and hopelessly naive, but the fact remains that the Kellogg–Briand Pact of 1928 was the perfect expression of an age.

Baldwin's government might have reaped some badly needed positive publicity, but even here it botched matters. The British government declared that its renunciation of war did not apply to undefined areas of 'vital interest'. It also refused to sign an 'Optional Clause', under which signatories were bound to submit all 'justiciable international disputes' to the Permanent Court of International Justice. The government was simply trying to be cautious and honest and not become trapped into making commitments that it would not be able to keep, but both reservations attracted much criticism and a heightened perception that Baldwin and Chamberlain were not serious about removing the causes of war.

Chamberlain's last months in office were marred by an episode concerning disarmament that called into question his basic competence. In mid-1928 the French came up with a series of proposals designed to break the deadlock at the Preparatory Commission. Chamberlain responded favourably and, by late July 1928, an understanding had been worked out. Britain would drop objections to a large conscript army for France, while France would support British positions on naval disarmament. The British made some curious concessions to the French on naval disarmament. For instance, they conceded parity to the French in heavy cruisers and large submarines, thus rejecting the Washington ratios for those categories. These concessions were bound to irritate the Americans, who had favoured an extension of the 1922 ratios to other classes of warships. Moreover, prior to discussions with the French the British had been trying to secure the abolition of submarines. The concessions may have been inspired by panic over false rumours – spread by the French themselves – of an impending French–American deal on general disarmament.

The French leaked the existence of the compromise to the press, and implied that the two countries were returning to their pre-1914 entente. Nothing of the sort had been agreed to, but the damage was done and both America and Germany were alarmed. The Germans suspected the British and the French of trying to keep them in a state of permanent military vulnerability and of violating the spirit of Locarno. The Americans thought that the French and British were ganging up on them in the naval disarmament talks. Chamberlain compounded his error when he misled the House of Commons by stating that the Anglo-French compromise was limited strictly to issues of naval disarmament. Chamberlain was again accused of being too pro-French and of resorting to the old style of secret diplomacy. Details of the Anglo-French compromise were given out slowly and ineptly. Whereas the Japanese government accepted the Anglo-French proposal in principle, Washington did not, and America's rejection killed it.

Soothing ruffled feelings in Berlin and Washington proved difficult in the autumn of 1928. Accusations that Chamberlain was pro-French were given added force by his perceived reluctance to evacuate the last British troops from the Rhineland occupation zone. Chamberlain had been seriously ill during part of 1928, and the stress of holding office was beginning to show. When he went on leave that autumn newspapers published photographs of him being carried on board ship in a wheelchair. The technical details of disarmament seemed beyond him and he was incapable of understanding that American co-operation was essential for success in the disarmament talks. Press criticism of his handling of the issues mounted, while Cecil noted acidly that the foreign secretary had accomplished the nearly impossible feat of uniting public opinion in Germany, France, Britain and the United States against him.

Matters of foreign policy are rarely of great concern in elections, but the evidence suggests that Chamberlain's record damaged Conservative prospects in the election of May 1929.[28] Numerous Labour candidates gave speeches attacking Chamberlain's performance and resentment simmered in various quarters over the deterioration of relations with the USSR and the United States. Chamberlain was perceived as being too pro-French and still wedded to the methods of secret diplomacy. Many felt that the achievement at Locarno had been squandered and that the League had been degraded. The persistent failure to make progress in the field of disarmament reflected badly on the government. In all departments, however, Baldwin's government had its work cut out for it. By 1929 the entire cabinet appeared old and exhausted, not just Chamberlain. Little progress had been achieved in the area of social reform and unemployment remained inexcusably high. The election campaign went badly for Baldwin and his chances were not helped by the execrable theme song, *Stanley Boy!* ('England for the Free; Stanley Boy! You're the man for me; Stanley Boy!'). The Conservative slogans, 'Safety First' and 'Trust Baldwin' impressed few.[29] According to J. M. Keynes, Baldwin's strategy seemed to be saying: 'We will not promise more than we can perform. We, therefore, promise nothing'.[30] The election results of 29 May 1929 exceeded even the worst fears of the experts among the Conservatives. Labour emerged to form a minority government. Chamberlain barely retained his own seat.

Ramsay MacDonald returned as prime minister, but this time he chose Arthur Henderson, a highly competent Labour stalwart, as foreign minister. MacDonald and Henderson had clashed in the past on issues of policy and a strong personal antipathy lingered between the two, but the prime minister appointed Henderson after the latter indicated that he would not accept any other cabinet position. As he was a popular figure in the Labour Party, to leave him out of the cabinet was not an option. Personal relations between the two men deteriorated further over the next two years owing to disagreements on both economic and foreign policy. Henderson, for example, was much closer than MacDonald to the pacifist wing of the Labour Party.[31]

Domestically, MacDonald's government was no more able to solve the problem of unemployment than that of his predecessor. The Labour Party followed the economic orthodoxy of the times, which demanded a balanced budget. A crisis over economic policy soon shook the party to its foundations.

In the field of foreign affairs some early successes were recorded. Henderson signed the Optional Clause, thereby reversing the policy of the previous government and reaping some positive publicity. MacDonald and Henderson also moved quickly to restore relations with the USSR, but the two sides failed to come up with any resolution of the issue of compensation for British investors. Comintern anti-British propaganda continued to be an irritation, as did the trade imbalance in favour of the USSR. Throughout the 1920s the Soviets exported far more to Britain than Britain exported to the USSR, prompting charges that the Soviets were 'dumping' goods on British markets at less than market prices. On the positive side Britain and the Soviets agreed to exchange ambassadors, something which had not been done before. MacDonald had granted diplomatic recognition to the USSR in 1924, but, as we have seen, his successors were far less enthusiastic about cultivating diplomatic links with a communist régime.

Progress was also made on the issue of German reparations. In 1929 an international commission of experts, headed by yet another prominent American banker, Owen Young, produced a scheme for reparations payments that was adopted at the Hague conference in August 1929. The Young Plan produced a final schedule for German payments. The overall amount was reduced to about one-third of the 1921 total, but the payments would continue until 1988. In exchange, the French agreed to evacuate the Rhineland in June 1930, four years ahead of schedule, although the Germans also reiterated that the Rhineland would remain demilitarized as a testament of their goodwill. The Young Plan established the Bank for International Settlements (May 1930) to collect reparations and promote co-operation between European banks.

An era of stability and promise, 1924–1929

The Hague conference of August 1929, which was called to discuss the implementation of the Young Plan, was marred by a nasty quarrel between the British and French delegations over the sharing of reparations. Philip Snowden, the British chancellor of the exchequer, accused the French of seeking to reduce the British share of reparations from 23 per cent to 17.5 per cent. The British Treasury had long feared that a new reparations agreement would result in a reduction of the British share. Snowden felt that the French wanted all the money they could get. Since the Germans wanted to pay as little as possible, the two powers, according to Snowden, hit on the idea of trying to reduce the British share for the sake of agreement. A compromise was worked out, but Anglo-French relations had again taken a battering. Henderson, who also attended the conference, inadvertently added fuel to the fire by insisting on an early evacuation of British troops from the Rhineland, regardless of French feelings. Early withdrawal from the Rhineland had been a major (and very popular) plank in the Labour Party's election campaign, and Henderson was certain that it would remove a major grievance in European affairs. The French protested, but British troops were withdrawn unilaterally by the end of 1929. French troops stayed on until 30 June 1930.

On the international scene as a whole, however, an observer could find grounds for optimism by late 1929. The Young Plan had apparently settled the reparations issue once and for all. Franco-German relations seemed stable. Had the groundwork perhaps been laid for economic prosperity? Gustav Stresemann died on 3 October 1929. Three weeks later the New York stock market went into a tailspin and finally crashed on 29 October, ushering in an era of unprecedented crisis in the West.

Notes

1   See S. Marks, *The Illusion of Peace: International Relations in Europe, 1918–1933* (London, Macmillan, 1976), and G. Ross, *The Great Powers and the Decline of the European States System, 1914–1945* (London, Longman, 1983).

2   A. Orde, *Great Britain and International Security, 1920–1926* (London, Royal Historical Society, 1978), p. 61.

3   See C. Barnett, *The Collapse of British Power* (London, Methuen, 1972), p. 327, and A. Adamthwaite, *The Making of the Second World War* (London, Unwin

Hyman, 1977), p. 30. For an alternative view of the French role, see J. Jacobson, *Locarno Diplomacy: Germany and the West, 1925–1929* (Princeton, Princeton University Press, 1972).

4 A. Cassels, 'Repairing the *Entente Cordiale* and the new diplomacy', *The Historical Journal*, XXIII, 1980, p. 146.

5 The original appeared at the Foreign Office while a copy was sent to the *Daily Mail*. Suspicions have always centred around the role of a *Daily Mail* reporter in this episode.

6 C. Andrew, 'The British secret service and Anglo-Soviet relations in the 1920's', *The Historical Journal*, XX, 1977, pp. 673–706.

7 D. Dutton, *Austen Chamberlain: Gentleman in Politics* (Bolton, Ross Anderson, 1986).

8 Dutton, *Austen Chamberlain*, p. 236

9 Jacobson, *Locarno Diplomacy*, p. 16.

10 K. Middlemas and J. Barnes, *Baldwin: A Biography* (London, Macmillan, 1969), p. 342.

11 Dutton, *Austen Chamberlain*, p. 271.

12 Jacobson, *Locarno Diplomacy*, p. 19.

13 Middlemas and Barnes, *Baldwin*, p. 352.

14 A formal signing ceremony took place in London six weeks later. The Locarno agreements technically comprised five treaties: the four arbitration agreements that Germany signed with France, Belgium, Poland and Czechoslovkia and the Treaty of Mutual Guarantee, sometimes called the Rhineland Pact.

15 Jacobson, *Locarno Diplomacy*, p. 3.

16 A. J. P. Taylor, *The Origins of the Second World War* (Harmondsworth, Penguin, 1964), p. 82.

17 R. H. Lamb, *The Drift to War* (New York, St. Martin's, 1991), p. 20.

18 Middlemas and Barnes, *Baldwin*, pp. 358–9.

19 Dutton, *Austen Chamberlain*, pp. 250–3. Dutton is also critical of Chamberlain's failure to follow up on Locarno.

20 Jacobson, *Locarno Diplomacy*, p. 44.

21 Barnett, *The Collapse of British Power*, p. 332.

22 P. Kennedy, *The Rise and Fall of the Great Powers* (London, Unwin Hyman, 1988), p. 229.

23 M. Howard, *The Continental Commitment: The Dilemma of British Defence Policy in the Era of the Two World Wars* (London, Temple Smith, 1972), p. 79.

24 Dutton, *Austen Chamberlain*, p. 272.

25 D. Carlton, 'Great Britain and the League council crisis of 1926', *The Historical Journal*, XI, 1968, pp. 354–64.

26 Dutton, *Austen Chamberlain*, p. 272.

27 D. Carlton, 'Great Britain and the Coolidge naval disarmament conference of 1927', *Political Science Quarterly*, XXXIII, December 1968, pp. 573–98.

28 The inter-war period was unique for the manner in which foreign policy concerns intruded in elections, especially 1918 and 1935.

29 Middlemas and Barnes, *Baldwin*, p. 515.

30 Middlemas and Barnes, *Baldwin*, p. 515.

31 D. Carlton, *MacDonald Versus Henderson: The Foreign Policy of the Second Labour Government* (London, Macmillan, 1970).

CHAPTER FIVE

THE IMPACT OF
THE GREAT DEPRESSION,
1929–1933

The wave of economic prosperity that swept Europe in the second half of the 1920s reinforced the good feelings that followed the signing of Locarno. Pre-war productivity levels were quickly surpassed after 1925, but, unfortunately, serious problems remained beneath the surface. The war had caused immense physical destruction in Europe. Factories, houses and other buildings had been destroyed, capital flows disrupted and labour shifted around. Conditions worsened with demobilization. Many wartime industries failed to make the transition to peacetime production and the ranks of the unemployed were swollen by demobilized veterans returning home. The prosperity of the 1920s was superficial, being based on the growth of service industries, automobile production and the manufacture of synthetic fabrics. Older industries such as the textile trade or the coal mining industry never recovered their pre-war levels of employment and profitability. The growth of large combines in Europe restricted diversification, while jobs in the service industries remained highly vulnerable to layoffs.[1]

The growth in the number of new states in central and eastern Europe also led to problems. Critics pointed out that the peace settlement had created 20,000 kilometres of new trade barriers in Europe, as a result of which pre-war trade patterns failed to revive after 1919. The new economies of Eastern Europe emerged from the war 'debt-ridden and under-developed'. The great German inflation of the early 1920s and the Russian withdrawal into economic isolation intensified Europe's problems. In 1927 the

League of Nations sponsored the World Economic Conference to negotiate reductions in European tariff barriers, but despite good intentions, the results were disappointing.

During the war Europe had lost overseas markets, trade and investments. Britain 'lost one-quarter of 18 billion dollars invested overseas, France lost half of nine billion dollars' worth of investment, primarily in Russia, and Germany lost all of its six billion dollars invested overseas'. The United States was the big winner. American investments in Europe multiplied sevenfold between 1913 and 1920. The United States raised its tariffs in 1922 and again in 1931, under the Hawley–Smoot Act, which made it profoundly difficult for Europe to sell products in the United States. The United States dominated international trade after 1919 and, as we have seen, continued to demand payment of wartime debts.[2]

Observers have noted that the international economy of the 1920s was based on a vast circular flow of paper money. The United States extended loans to Germany to help its reconstruction, especially after 1924; the Germans then gave money to France and Britain in the form of reparations; and Britain and France handed over money to the United States as loan repayments. Capital was not available for investment and the circulation of so much money may have contributed to inflation.

The world economy also faced an agricultural crisis in the 1920s. During the war the grain fields of Eastern Europe were cut off from the West. Britain had to import grain supplies from North America, whose farmers switched over to grain production and opened up vast new areas for a highly profitable method of farming. After 1919 East European farmers resumed production of grain, competing with North Americans. The result was a worldwide glut of grain, plummeting agricultural prices and mounting debt loads for millions of European and North American farmers who increasingly turned to credit for survival. Governments responded by raising tariffs and resorting to protectionism.

The war altered the demographic structure of Europe. The casualties of war left the European population 'older and more dependent on state pensions'. The post-war inflation 'shock' meant that those who had relied on savings were ruined beyond recovery.

Those who owned property or industrial concerns, by contrast, earned more wealth as properties gained in value and productivity increased in the second half of the 1920s. For the middle classes especially, the early 1920s left a sense of economic unease that lingered until the rise of Hitler.[3]

A long period of intense speculation had preceded the collapse of prices on the New York Stock Exchange on 29 October 1929. After the crash tens of millions of dollars in paper assets disappeared within days. Similar panics had certainly occurred before, but the crash of 1929 spread to Europe and hit the banks especially hard. Large numbers of them had invested heavily in stocks and real estate in the 1920s and many failed after losing all their assets. These failures triggered 'business cutbacks, consumption declined, capital dried up, factories closed and unemployment soared'. The process originated in the United States but spread overseas when the government of the United States, together with banks and businesses, started calling in loans.[4]

The near collapse of the Austrian state bank in May 1931 symbolized the arrival of the Depression in Europe. Austrian and German banks came under great pressure and the effects of the Depression spread to the whole of Europe. By 1932 'the world's industrial production was two-thirds of what it had been in 1929'. By 1932 there were an estimated thirteen million unemployed in the United States, six million in Germany and three million in Britain.[5]

The reparations system was an early casualty of the Depression. The Hoover Moratorium suspended reparations payments in 1931 and the whole system was completely abandoned, at long last, at the Lausanne conference of 1932. In Britain the government came off the gold standard (a guarantee that a unit of currency could be converted into gold at a fixed rate) in 1931 and the value of the pound promptly plummeted. Since the pound was the major trading currency in Europe at the time, the British move plunged European currency markets into complete chaos. Most countries followed Britain's lead in abandoning the gold standard and soon the entire system of international credit and exchange was in ruins.

Governments everywhere attempted to deal with the situation, with mixed results. Germany and Austria proposed a customs union in 1931, but the French, fearing an accretion of German power, immediately raised objections. International trade decreased with the establishment of tariff barriers and import quotas across Europe. Between 1929 and 1932 world trade fell by sixty per cent. Governments tried desperately to protect their economies, regardless of efficiency and productivity. With the introduction of the Import Duties Act in February 1932 the British government abandoned free trade. The act was extended at the Imperial Economic Conference, which was held in Ottawa in the summer of that year. Britain and the Dominions adopted 'imperial preference', a euphemism for imperial protectionism, to take the place of free trade.

It would be difficult to underestimate the political effects of the Depression. In the democracies of Europe conservatives, liberals and social democrats all appeared to be at a loss for answers. For many by the early 1930s democracy and capitalism appeared to have failed. Political extremism attracted more and more voters. Several European governments were embarrassed by the growth of communist parties that pointed to the Soviet Union as a model of economic growth through centralized planning. On the right, fascist parties all across Europe enjoyed great success with their attacks on liberal democracy. Authoritarianism increasingly seemed to hold the answers. Within ten years of Versailles authoritarian governments had overthrown liberal governments in eight European states (Hungary, Lithuania, Poland, Yugoslavia, Albania, Spain, Portugal and Italy). By 1936 political freedom had been suppressed in seven additional states (Austria, Bulgaria, Estonia, Germany, Greece Latvia and Romania).

The effects of the Depression were not limited to North America and Europe; the collapse of Japan's export trade with the United States – a crucial sector of the Japanese economy – caused unemployment and hardship in Japan. In the 1920s the United States had been taking forty per cent of Japan's exports. That trade virtually ceased with the Depression. The population of Japan was growing at the rate of more than one million per year in the 1920s, but the country lacked the natural resources that were needed in a modern industrial state. Emigration overseas had been encouraged by the Japanese government, but in the late 1920s the United States,

Canada and Australia all took steps to cut off the flow of Japanese immigrants to their countries. The late 1920s also witnessed the collapse of Japanese trade with China as Chinese nationalists organized anti-Japanese boycotts with the support of a sympathetic government.

Militarists in the Japanese armed forces had long argued in favour of the creation of a land-based empire by conquering portions of China. Now the Depression gave their case an added urgency. An empire would provide access to resources (especially in the northeastern province of Manchuria) and markets, enabling Japan to ride out the Depression. Support for an expansionist foreign policy in Japan grew among the unemployed and impoverished. In the early 1930s extremist elements in the Japanese armed forces gained power, prestige and influence to such an extent that they were able to transform Japan from a proto-democracy into a military dictatorship.

The Depression was a major factor in the rise of Hitler in Germany. In 1927 the Nazis were a marginal, irrelevant band of political extremists based in south Germany. During the winter of 1928 the German economy went into recession; it was in trouble even before the stock market crash. The Nazis gained their first major political success in 1930 with the circulation of a petition opposing the Young Plan that eventually gained four million signatures. In the elections of September 1930 (held just after the British and French troops in the Rhineland had evacuated the area – the French with many misgivings) the Nazis emerged with 107 seats in the German Reichstag – up from twelve before the election. They were now Germany's second largest political party, just behind the Social Democrats. The Reichstag ceased to function effectively in 1930 owing to a deadlock between President von Hindenburg and the Social Democrats over budgetary issues. From 1930 to 1933 the country was governed by presidential emergency decree. Article 48 of the Weimar constitution allowed for the suspension of parliamentary rule and had been invoked on a number of previous occasions. The president in 1930 was Field Marshal von Hindenburg, a hero of the First World War who was now eighty-five years old. Over the next three years Hindenburg appointed three successive chancellors, none of whom managed to find a solution to Germany's economic crisis and all of whom were fired by Hindenburg. Repeated German elections saw only a slow decline of middle-class liberal parties and a steady rise in Nazi strength. With unemployment at more than forty per cent, Weimar democracy was now in a terminal phase.

For France the Depression had the effect of strengthening their need to come to grips with Germany. The French undertook changes in their military planning to deal with the consequences of their withdrawal from the Rhineland – changes that had profound political implications. French military planners knew that the evacuation of the Rhineland would result in the loss of an important strategic advantage. Accordingly, in 1929, the French began the construction of the Maginot line. This was a series of massive concrete fortifications extending along the entire the French–German border. The border with Belgium was not fortified for the time being, on the assumption that Belgium would call for help in the case of an invasion and that a defensive line could then be organized along the Belgian rivers. Politically, as many commentators noted, the Maginot line implied that France's strategic posture would henceforth be defensive. France would huddle down behind the Maginot line and hope for the best in the face of growing German power.

Plans for European union

The French also resorted to diplomacy to try to contain German power, particularly in the economic field. European union was an increasingly popular idea among French and German business élites in the second half of the 1920s. The Pan-Europa Society was arguably the most influential of several groups that discussed plans for European union. These efforts were not limited to abstract discussions. In 1926 Germany and France, together with Belgium and Luxembourg, formed a steel cartel; the following year France and Germany signed a wide-ranging commercial agreement; and during late 1929 and early 1930 the French government continued to float ideas for closer economic co-operation between France and Germany. Until then, most of the plans for greater economic co-operation had revolved around tariff reform and free trade, but late in 1929 Briand began advocating a European Federal Union. In May 1930 he published a 'Memorandum on the Organization of a System for European Federal Union'. For the French the underlying motive for European union was the hope that the 'German problem' could perhaps be submerged in a larger European context. French initiatives were given urgency by the Wall Street crash and the deteriorating economic climate in late 1929 and early 1930. Both France and Germany needed some kind of economic initiative to break out of the slump. The French were also alarmed by rumours of an Anglo-American reconciliation on disarmament issues (see page 119). Some in the French government feared that such a reconciliation might lead to an 'Anglo-Saxon' hegemony over Europe. A European federation would have been one way to counter the combined power of Britain and the United States.

Briand's ideas prefigured the European Common Market, but in 1930 the time was not yet ripe. Most observers found his ideas too vague and tentative, and in any event the Depression outran the lumbering pace of diplomacy in 1930. In Britain Briand's proposals met with scepticism.[6] Although some clearly sympathized with Briand's ideas, in general the government and the Foreign Office opposed a European Union on the grounds that Britain's ties with both the United States and the Commonwealth would be negatively affected. Britain's primary ties were still with the Commonwealth, the Empire and the United States, not with Europe. The Foreign Office dismissed Briand's idea as simply a ruse to continue French hegemony in Europe and objected that a European Union might result in a weakening of the League of Nations. 'Regional initiatives,' it argued, should take place under the auspices of the League and not outside it; in any case, they were contrary to the tenets of free trade. Both Snowden and Henderson put on record their opposition to Briand's proposal.

Critics might find such objections rather disingenuous. The British government's enthusiasm for the League – as distinct from the public's – had been lukewarm in the past. Briand had announced his plans in speeches to the League Assembly in Geneva and had long acknowledged his willingness to accept League sponsorship. The Foreign Office seems to have misread the intent of French policy and suffered from the continued delusion that Britain could concern itself exclusively with the Commonwealth and the benefits of free trade.

A proposed German–Austrian customs union

By early 1931 the economic situation in Germany was so serious, and the rise of the Nazis so alarming, that the German government decided to take its own initiative. In March 1931 the German and Austrian governments, without consulting either Britain or France, announced that they had signed a protocol to create a customs union that would result in the reduction or elimination of tariffs between the two states. Briand may have been privately sympathetic: a customs union of the type proposed by Germany and Austria would fit in well with his schemes for European economic integration. The need for a dramatic step was reinforced with the near failure of the Austrian bank, the Kreditanstalt, on 11 May 1931. Since the Kreditanstalt financed more than sixty per cent of Austria's industry and Britain was Austria's main creditor (and therefore stood to lose a lot of money), the situation was closely monitored by the British government.

Viewed from France, however, the proposed customs union looked like the first step on the road to an *Anschluss*, a complete political union, which had been forbidden at Versailles. Furthermore, in 1922 Austria had accepted a substantial loan from France on the condition that it maintain strict independence from Germany. The French government opposed the customs union vehemently, as did the government of Czechoslovakia. Both states remained profoundly suspicious of German motives. The French feared that a German–Austrian union would enable Germany to completely over-awe the Little Entente.[7] Germany might use its enhanced economic power to intimidate Yugoslavia and Romania into dropping their alliances with France. An isolated Czechoslovakia would then soon follow suit. France's entire network of East European alliances would be disrupted. It should also be remembered that the proposal for customs union came on the heels of the French evacuation of the Rhineland in June 1930, which had been followed by the spectacular Nazi gains in the September 1930 elections.

116

Within the British government the proposed customs union was initially welcomed as a step towards ending the slump and boosting the political fortunes of the German chancellor, Heinrich Brüning, against the growing popularity of Hitler. Unlike Briand's proposal, the German scheme seemed to arouse some interest. The Board of Trade in particular seemed to welcome it because it would revive trade in Europe. The Foreign Office realized that British support for the customs union would damage Anglo-French relations and make further progress on disarmament impossible. On the other hand, a humiliating rebuff for Germany, and Brüning, would only rebound to the benefit of Hitler. Henderson also worried that if the customs union materialized the hand of hardliners in France would be strengthened and Franco-German relations would deteriorate.

Britain found itself in an uncomfortable position. Henderson was able to buy some time by referring the customs union proposal to the Permanent Court of International Justice in the Hague, which would determine the legality of the union. Publicly, he claimed to be acting in a mediatory capacity, trying to find a compromise that would be acceptable to both France and Germany. Henderson and the Foreign Office felt obliged to come up with a constructive alternative that would head off a defeat for Brüning, but they failed to find one that would command the support of the British public. To endorse, support or participate in a regional trade arrangement would antagonize both the supporters of free trade and those who favoured imperial preference. Britain could not simply choose Europe over the Empire. The Foreign Office was virtually powerless to advance foreign policy aims that conflicted with Britain's commercial interests. The debate over customs union provides one clear example of British commercial interests prevailing over a foreign policy goal – in this case, to avoid a German humiliation.[8]

Referring the issue of customs union to the Hague effectively took the steam out of the proposal. In September 1931 the Court ruled that it was illegal, although by that time it was virtually a dead letter as the French had succeeded in intimidating the Austrian government into withdrawing its support for the union. Unfortunately, Europe had also lost an opportunity of seeking a way out of the slump and forestalling the Nazi drive to power.

The desperation induced by the Depression also prompted the German government to appeal for help on reparations. During a visit to Britain in June 1931 Brüning told MacDonald that the collapse of the Kreditanstalt had provoked a run on German banks as panicky foreign investors withdrew their funds. An estimated £36 million was withdrawn from the Reichsbank in the first two weeks of June alone. German government credit was in difficulty and reparations could not be paid beyond November. Similar messages were conveyed by the Germans to the United States. By June 1931 the Foreign Office was thoroughly alarmed by the rise of the Nazis and declared that Brüning's government should not be allowed to fall. On 20 June 1931 President Hoover proposed a one-year suspension of all inter-governmental debts and reparations, capital and interest included.

The Hoover Moratorium was greeted with huge relief all over the world. MacDonald was certainly pleased. Like most on the British left (see Chapter Three), he had always believed that reparations were a gross injustice. He soon began advocating a 'clean slate' policy of phasing out all reparations. This put him at odds with the French, but, as he pointed out, the Germans still had a trump card in the Young Plan, under which they were entitled to declare a unilateral moratorium if circumstances warranted. Should the Germans do so, France would lose even more money. The French agreed to the moratorium with great reluctance at a conference in London on 20 July 1931.

In the short-term the Hoover Moratorium produced some momentum in the direction of improving the European economy. The failure of the prestigious German Danat bank on 13 July had underlined the need for action. As well as agreeing to the moratorium on 20 July, British and American banks extended credit to the Germans, thus stabilizing the mark for the time being. At the end of July MacDonald and Henderson visited Berlin, where there was some talk of reducing British tariffs. For the hopelessly optimistic it appeared as though fortunes were turning around by the late summer of 1931.

Besides coping with the Depression, Ramsay MacDonald's foreign policy priorities in the early part of his second period in government continued to focus on disarmament and improved relations with the United States. As with European union, the elusive goal of disarmament was given urgency in the face of the deteriorating international economic climate. The less governments spent on the military, the more money would be available for economic reconstruction.

The London naval disarmament conference

The objective of the London conference of 1930 was to continue efforts towards naval disarmament. Unlike at the Geneva conference of 1927, much preparatory work was done ahead of time. MacDonald was more amenable to agreement with the United States than his predecessors. He liked the United States, had numerous American friends and saw the United States as a country that had come closer to realizing the ideals of democracy and equality than Britain and Europe. In October 1929 he went to see President Herbert Hoover at his fishing lodge in the Virginia mountains. The visit was a great public relations success and MacDonald was praised in the American press. Later he informed Hoover that Britain was prepared to lower the number of cruisers that it considered necessary for its defence from seventy to fifty. MacDonald had secured the lower number in the teeth of tenacious opposition from the Admiralty. His determination to improve relations with the United States also led to clashes with Henderson. MacDonald was determined to conduct his own foreign policy when it came to relations with the United States, and he often rode roughshod over Henderson, neglecting to keep him informed and expressing private doubts as to his competence. In certain respects the MacDonald–Henderson relationship mirrored that of Lloyd George and Curzon.

When the conference met in London in April 1930 the Americans rewarded MacDonald by making concessions over cruiser sizes and gun calibres. The French and the Italians had also been persuaded to attend and the Americans even resolved some differences with the Japanese, who were allowed a slight increase in their ratios. In terms of results, however, the conference was only a partial success. Restrictions on cruisers were finally imposed – roughly along the lines of the Washington ratios – largely owing to MacDonald's willingness to compromise. Similar limitations were placed on destroyers and submarines. A British bid to outlaw submarines failed. The 'building holiday' for the construction of capital ships was extended to 1936 and a few capital ships were scrapped by the leading powers. France refused to sign the final agreement on the grounds that Germany had started to build a new warship outside the bounds of the treaty.[9] Italy then also refused to sign.

The Manchurian crisis

The London disarmament conference of 1930 was to have completely unanticipated, disastrous consequences in Japan. Members of the Japanese military criticized the agreement with great bitterness. Japan's navy still demanded parity with the United States and Britain, but not only did the conference fail to gain parity for the Japanese it also maintained the existing ratios and Japan was obliged to scrap a capital ship. In November 1930 the Japanese prime minister, Hamaguchi, was assassinated by a right-wing terrorist. Extremists in the Japanese military decided that the time was right to play their card.

In the 1920s the Japanese government had stationed a number of troops in the northeastern Chinese province of Manchuria, ostensibly to protect Japanese property in the face of the general breakdown of law and order in China. By 1931, however, the Chinese nationalist government had recovered a good deal of strength and was seeking to throw Japanese influence out of China. The presence of Japanese troops in Manchuria was certainly a provocation to China, and in 1931 the Chinese government began to demand that the Japanese contingent be withdrawn. The officer corps of the Japanese forces in Manchuria were strong supporters of the Imperial Way (army hardliners who favoured an expansionist foreign policy), and they were not about to give in to Chinese demands.

On the night of 18 September 1931 Japanese officers (with the connivance of the War Ministry in Tokyo) blew up a tiny portion of a Japanese-owned railway near the Manchurian capital of Mukden. The Japanese then attributed the act to Chinese terrorists and used the incident as a pretext for the full-scale invasion of Manchuria by their own troops. The civilian government in Tokyo was completely powerless and unable to restrain the army, but it soon became apparent that the invasion was a popular move in Japan and that the Japanese army enjoyed overwhelming support. In 1932 the state of Manchukuo was proclaimed in the former Manchuria. Manchukuo was a puppet state, financed and controlled by the Japanese army of occupation (known as the Kwantung Army).[10] Japan now controlled a vast province, larger than the homeland itself, that had a population of thirty million and was rich in natural resources. The Japanese takeover of Manchuria was also a blatant act of aggression. The Chinese government quickly appealed to the League of Nations for help and Manchuria was the first serious test case for the League.

Why then did the League choose to do nothing? The United States, the one power that could have taken action, was not even a member of the League. American public opinion was overwhelmingly sympathetic to the Chinese, but that sympathy did not translate into support for a war against Japan and war would have been necessary to force the Japanese to withdraw. American citizens who held investments in Japan made clear their opposition to war, and the American government itself had no vital interests in Manchuria, financial or otherwise.

As for the Soviet Union, its government was deeply concerned about the possibility of Japanese expansionism; with the conquest of Manchuria Japan now had a contiguous border with the USSR. But the Red Army was very weak in 1931 and the country was preoccupied with the Five Year Plan, a crash programme for industrialization. The Soviet Union too was not a member of the League and was not likely to act unilaterally.

France certainly had no desire to see alterations in the territorial status quo, but it was appalled at the thought of war in the Far East. Such a war would distract attention from Germany. Other powers such as Italy and Germany had absolutely no interest in Manchuria.

If the League decided to act, it would have to rely on the naval power of Great Britain. Unfortunately, Britain could hardly spare the resources by 1931, as we have seen, and the country was mired in economic crisis. The Singapore base was not completed, which ruled out a military campaign, but even if it had been ready, it was too distant from Manchuria for Britain to be able to do much. The Dominions pressed for peace. Many in the government and the press had no desire to create a powerful enemy in the form of Japan. The new British foreign secretary, John Simon (see page 124), followed a policy of complete passivity. The League was hamstrung and settled into an embarrassing pattern of evasion and inaction.

In September and October of 1931 the League Council asked the Japanese to withdraw from Manchuria. The Japanese, fully aware of League's weakness, refused. In December the League appointed the Lytton Commission to report on the Manchurian situation. The final report of the Commission was issued in September 1932, far too late to do anything. Its main conclusion was, hardly surprisingly, that Japan had been the aggressor. Retaliation by the League was confined to purely symbolic gestures. For example, it refused to recognize passports and postage stamps issued by Manchukuo. The Japanese eventually left the League in March 1933.[11]

Manchuria, not to mention the loss of another important League member, had dealt a heavy blow to the League's prestige. In Britain the Manchurian debacle caused an immediate eight per cent drop in the membership of the League of Nations Union (LNU). The LNU executive was so alarmed that it undertook door-to-door canvassing to recover lost members. Yet it was still possible for supporters of the League to put a positive spin on the Manchurian episode. The League was, after all, primarily a European institution, and might still be able to deal with crises in Europe. As the official LNU bulletin, *Headway*, argued, the League's failures in China 'would not be its deathblow'. 'If its writ does not run at the other end of Asia', it continued, 'that is no proof that its writ does not run in Europe'.[12] The optimistic forecasts of the LNU were soon to be tested.

The crisis in Manchuria coincided with an economic and political crisis in Britain that did much to restrict Britain's ability to act in 1931. By the beginning of the year there were more than 2.6 million unemployed workers in Britain – about twenty per cent of the workforce. In order to cope with the Depression, MacDonald's government was under intense pressure to maintain a balanced budget, which, according to the economic orthodoxy of the time, would be one way out of the Depression. In August 1931 MacDonald was forced to propose a ten per cent cut in Unemployment Assurance to save £12,250,000 and balance the budget. Cuts in government spending were urged on MacDonald by the Bank of England. The gold reserves of the Bank by then were dangerously low because of a run on sterling prompted by the continuing wave of bank failures in central Europe (whose ripples originated in the failure of the Kreditanstalt in May). The Bank of England lost £45 million during July. Historians still debate the seriousness of the crisis and MacDonald's handling of it. Allegations were certainly made at the time that financial circles exaggerated the situation to discredit Labour. MacDonald's cutbacks resulted in a fatal split in the Labour Party, which depended heavily on working-class support. The bulk of the Labour MPs, led by George Lansbury, refused to follow MacDonald's leadership and went into opposition. MacDonald then formed a 'National' coalition government with Conservative and Liberal support.

In the election of 27 October 1931 the National government won an overwhelming victory. No fewer than 554 National MPs were elected, of whom 473 were Conservative, thirteen National Labour, and sixty-eight Liberals. The Labour Party was shattered, returning only fifty-two MPs, although the Labour share of the popular vote had declined less precipitously, from thirty-six per cent to thirty-one per cent. Labour was to spend the next few years wandering in the political wilderness with minimal representation in the House of Commons, trying to repair the damage inflicted by the events of 1931. MacDonald stayed on as prime minister, dependent on Conservative support, just as Lloyd George had earlier. Baldwin, who had retained the leadership of the Conservative Party in spite of serious challenges, was given the cabinet post of Lord President of the Council, a position with no specific duties and no salary. (As the years passed he increasingly came to fill in for MacDonald as the prime minister's health declined.) Neville Chamberlain was appointed chancellor of the exchequer. The new foreign secretary was John Simon, a member of the Liberal Party.[13] Simon held the post until June 1935.

John Simon

Simon was one of the most mistrusted and disliked cabinet ministers of his time. His biographer compiled a list of some of the remarks that his contemporaries made about him. It is worth quoting.

Duff Cooper confessed that he hated Simon, while Harold Nicolson called him a 'foul man' and likened him to a 'toad and a worm'. For Brendan Bracken the appropriate comparison was with Uriah Heep. Sir Ronald Lindsay compared Simon to an adder; for Anthony Eden he was merely 'snaky'. As far as Beatrice Webb was concerned, he was among the most unpleasant personalities she had met.[14]

Obviously not everyone felt the same way, but Simon possessed a sycophantic quality and almost pathetic desire to please that seem to have prompted the reptilian metaphors. The most famous story of Simon has him trying to overcome his social awkwardness by approaching a prominent political ally in a London club, slapping him on the shoulder and calling him by the wrong name in front of an embarrassed crowd of onlookers.

Born in Manchester in 1873, Simon came from a Nonconformist background and did extremely well at school, achieving high academic grades and winning all sorts of prizes. He became a lawyer and his formidable intellectual talents won him a strong reputation. He won election to Parliament for the constituency of Walthamstow in the great Liberal sweep of 1906. Over the succeeding years he held a couple of minor cabinet posts. From 1927 to 1930 Simon led a commission on the future direction of British rule in India. He emerged in 1931 as leader of the National Liberals, commanding the support of thirty-six MPs. His appointment as foreign secretary in 1931 was his greatest triumph to that time. In 1931 the Liberal Party and Simon still had the reputation of being strong upholders of League principles, a perception reinforced by the many pro-League speeches Simon had given. A Foreign Office memorandum that crossed Simon's desk shortly after he took office outlined Britain's position as follows:

> World recovery (the aim of our policy) depends on European recovery; European recovery on German recovery; German recovery on France's consent; France's consent on security (for all time) against attack.[15]

Simon thought the initial step would be to promote 'appeasement' to achieve a reconciliation between Germany and France. The French had to be persuaded that a German recovery would not jeopardize their security. France could not count on a guarantee from Britain, but Britain would continue to support disarmament. Simon's foreign policy goals accorded well with those of his colleagues, although MacDonald had appointed Simon with a distinct lack of enthusiasm, explaining cryptically that in appointing the new cabinet he had to take political realities into account.

It has often been said that Simon approached foreign affairs in the same manner as that in which he approached a legal case. He could argue a case one way or the other with consummate skill, but he did not appear to show any passion or emotional engagement with the issues at hand. He was one of those rare politicians whose intellectual abilities left others questioning his sincerity. In many respects his personality and style most resembled those of Curzon. In both we see the combination of brilliant intellectual abilities and dubious social skills. His talents were to be sorely tested during his first weeks in office when he was confronted simultaneously with the Manchurian crisis and the 1932 disarmament conference. Manchuria in particular was a difficult episode for Simon. His completely passive performance during the crisis earned him the sobriquet 'Man of Manchukuo'. Disarmament produced another set of challenges.

The 1932 disarmament conference

The Preparatory Commission had produced a draft report on disarmament in 1930, but it was not until 2 February 1932 that the disarmament conference finally met in Geneva. The first session of the conference lasted until July. Almost from the start it was apparent that the difficulties in attaining agreement would be overwhelming. Again the basic dispute concerned the levels of armaments that Germany and France would be allowed. Germany wanted either that all nations reduce their armaments down to Germany's own level or, more alarmingly, that it should be granted the right to rearm to a more substantial level. The French were naturally opposed to both options. The British felt that Germany should be given some latitude to rearm but that France should undertake some degree of disarmament. Paris might have agreed, but Britain still refused to commit itself to the defence of France. The specific proposals put forward by Brüning in April, which featured a German army of 200,000 troops, were actually rather modest, but the French government was in the middle of an election campaign and could give no ground. In late May Brüning's cabinet was dissolved and Brüning was replaced as chancellor by the even more feckless von Papen. The new German cabinet proclaimed the right for Germany to rearm without being bound by the restrictions of Versailles.

A variety of highly technical proposals were circulated at the disarmament conference to try to reconcile France and Germany. None were successful, but the plan that attracted the most attention was put forward by Tardieu, the French premier. He argued in favour of an international army under League control that would guarantee the security of all states. Furthermore, all civil aviation would also be internationalized to prevent the use of aircraft for aggressive designs. Tardieu's plan was not rejected outright but rather put on the back burner. As the Soviet delegate Maxim Litvinov pointed out, a way would have to be found of preventing the new international army from being used by the dominant League powers for their own ends.

When the conference adjourned in July it was apparent that breakdown was close. The Germans hinted that they would not return to a future session unless they were granted the right to equality of armament with other powers. That was the last thing the British government wanted to hear.

Indeed the British performance at the conference left much to be desired. Simon had taken office less than two months earlier and it was apparent that he was still learning the ropes. MacDonald, who desperately wanted a foreign policy success to crown his career (and distract the memory away from his split with Labour), was sidelined by glaucoma and generally deteriorating health. The British delegation failed to circulate any concrete proposals in Geneva. Simon had invited Cecil to serve as an adviser to the British delegation, but Cecil, after meeting Simon, concluded that the British government was incapable of formulating a coherent policy and declined the invitation. Simon's opening address to the conference focused on the need for 'qualitative disarmament', by which he meant the total abolition of certain types of offensive weapons. His delivery was poor and one observer commented that Simon had the most irritating set of gestures that he had ever seen in a public speaker. Simon quickly cultivated a distaste for the city of Geneva itself, calling it 'a dreadful place, well worthy of Calvin'.[16]

The basic problem at Geneva went beyond Simon's mannerisms and lack of preparation. Britain had no significant army and therefore no bargaining chips. Six weeks before the opening of the conference the cabinet had again decided that Britain could not give the French a guarantee that would involve its troops in a war in Europe. Britain's unwillingness to give a continental commitment (Simon did not want British troops 'called upon to maintain the status quo of the Polish Corridor')[17] implied a basic lack of interest in the affairs of Central Europe beyond ensuring that disputes did not get out of hand and lead to war. The British had much to say on naval disarmament but nothing on land disarmament. The perceived French intransigence over disarmament and other issues, especially reparations and the customs union proposal, did nothing to diminish the resentment that British statesmen felt towards France. MacDonald said of the French delegates at Geneva: '[they] never seemed straight; and certainly pursued crooked diplomacy and worked behind our backs'.[18] Vansittart, the new permanent under-secretary at the Foreign Office, thought: '[France has] of late attained the very thing that we have traditionally sought to avoid in Europe, hegemony, if not dictatorship, political and financial'.[19] Vansittart, it should be noted, was a pro-French member of the Foreign Office.

In the meantime it was apparent that something had to be done about reparations. The Hoover Moratorium would end in June, but no one seriously expected that Germany would be in a position to resume payments after the expiry date. A conference was held at Lausanne on 16 June at which it was eventually agreed to abolish reparations after a final payment of £150 by Germany. (The final payment was never made.) On the face of it von Papen had scored a considerable victory, but voters in Germany did not see it that way. Von Papen came to Lausanne pleading that only the total and immediate abolition of reparations would give him the political leverage needed to head off the Nazis. In the spring of 1932 Hitler challenged von Hindenburg at the presidential elections. Hitler lost, but more than thirteen million Germans had cast their votes for him. The Reichstag elections of 31 July gave the Nazis 230 seats with thirty-seven per cent of the vote. The Nazis had emerged as the largest single party in Germany, and it was only a matter of time before Hitler was appointed chancellor. When the votes of the Communist Party (fourteen per cent) and the right-wing Nationalist Party (six per cent) were added to the Nazi total, it was clear by that the autumn of 1932 an absolute majority of the German people had rejected the Weimar democracy. The Western powers were at last motivated to do something. In December Britain, France, the United States and Italy agreed that Germany should be given the right to equal armaments. A new session of the conference was scheduled for March 1933. It was a truly last-minute gesture. On 30 January 1933 Adolf Hitler was appointed chancellor of Germany, which changed the rules of the game completely.

Adolf Hitler

Hitler was born in Austria on 20 April 1889 at Braunau am Inn, near the German border. His father was a foul-tempered, hard-drinking minor customs official. As a child Hitler was a lazy, bossy brat and a playground bully at school. He imagined himself to be a great artist and twice sought admission to the Vienna Academy of Arts. Twice he was refused, much to his fury. As a young man, following the death of his mother (his father had died much earlier), he drifted into the Hapsburg capital city of Vienna. He was immediately repelled by the cosmopolitan, multi-ethnic character of the Austro-Hungarian Empire but absorbed instead the anti-Semitic politics of the Viennese mayor, Karl Lueger. He spent the pre-war years in Vienna as a drifter, living in dosshouses, occasionally selling watercolours and playing the role of a bohemian artist. Uncertain of what to do with his life, Hitler chose to remain unemployed. His life in Vienna was never as impoverished as he led everyone to believe in *Mein Kampf*. He had money left over from his mother's estate, and regularly attended the opera.

By 1913 Hitler had moved to Munich, where he could feel more at home in a 'pure' German state. He was later to remember – in common with many others – the outbreak of war in August 1914 as being an emotional highlight in his life. His war service was well above average. He served as a *Meldegänger*, a runner whose job it was to convey messages between company and regimental head-quarters. It was a hazardous occupation, and to his credit he served with considerable bravery. He was promoted to lance corporal and received the Iron Cross, Second Class, in 1914. In 1918 he received the Iron Cross, First Class, for 'personal bravery and general merit'. The latter was very rarely awarded to corporals. Hitler seemed to relish his time in the trenches, finding there (as did many veterans) a solidarity and purpose that he had never experienced in civilian life.

When the war ended in 1918 Hitler was in a hospital on the Baltic coast, recovering from the after-effects of a British gas attack. The German surrender came as a complete shock to him, as it had to many Germans who had been told until only a few months previously that Germany was winning the war. After recovering from his wounds and a mental breakdown characterized by hysteria, Hitler returned to Munich. The surrender left Hitler and many other Germans convinced that Germany had been stabbed in the back by liberals, pacifists, socialists and members of an imagined inter-national anti-German Jewish conspiracy. In Munich he volunteered to act as an army informant and report on the activities of a number of extreme nationalist political groups that were cropping up all over Germany in 1919. He quickly joined one such group, the German Workers' Party (DAP), founded by Anton Drexler, a

Munich locksmith. Hitler dominated the party and turned it into his own political vehicle. In 1920 he renamed it the National Socialist German Workers' Party (NSDAP), or Nazi for short.

From 1919 to 1923 Hitler spoke in Munich beer-halls, perfecting his style of speaking, which consisted of delivering brutal accusations and falsehoods in an increasingly hysterical manner. He attracted a considerable following (see Chapter Three, page 68) and chose to make his move during the chaos of 1923. The failure of the 1923 putsch only convinced Hitler of his need to gain power by legitimate means.

Hitler's 'world-view', so-called, was elaborated in *Mein Kampf*, in his speeches and in his assorted writings and rantings. First, and most basic, was his anti-Semitism. His consuming hatred of Jews ran like a red thread through his entire career, from the dosshouses of Vienna to the writing of his last will and testament in the Berlin bunker shortly before he committed suicide. He also hated Marxism, viewing it as a manifestation of a Jewish conspiracy. Throughout his life his coarse vulgarity, loutishness and anti-Semitism – all given vent in his oratory – impressed his most violent supporters while generating revulsion in his opponents. Hitler also subscribed to a barely coherent dogma known as Social Darwinism, which achieved a considerable measure of popularity in Europe towards the end of the nineteenth century. He considered that the concepts of evolution and the survival of the fittest could be applied to international relations. Nations and races, he suggested, were engaged in a titanic struggle for survival. The fittest races and nations were those which deserved to survive; the rest should be condemned to extinction. In Hitler's mind the greatest struggle was between the Aryan race and the Jewish conspiracy to destroy it. In order to survive Germany must expand and obtain *Lebensraum* (living space) in Eastern Europe. If it failed to expand it would lose the struggle. As far as Hitler was concerned Eastern Europe was populated by inferior races and Jews, and they must all be enslaved, exterminated and annihilated. Hitler's ambitions, needless to say, culminated in the Holocaust.

None of this was new, and Hitler was not an original thinker. What he brought to the fore was a violent obsession with destroying the Jewish people and a focus on Eastern Europe as the target for *Lebensraum*. Keeping in mind that Hitler was a skilled opportunist, (as shown by the Nazi–Soviet pact of 1939) and had a cunning sense of the weakness of his opponents (as is characteristic of bullies), most of what Hitler did in foreign policy in the 1930s can be understood in the light of his obsessions and warped beliefs. He identified France and its eastern European ally, Czechoslovakia, as the key upholders of the status quo and of the Versailles settlement. Czechoslovakia and France must be destroyed first. He had no quarrel with Britain and indeed thought (in a serious misreading of British history) that Britain would be content to remain isolated from Europe. After he had destroyed France and Czechoslovakia, he would march east to conquer *Lebensraum* in Poland and the USSR. He hoped that a new German empire might initially be able to maintain friendly relations with the British Empire. He admired Mussolini and hoped to enlist Italian ambitions. Japan would be another powerful ally. Following the conquest of Eastern Europe a much longer war would ensue between the new German empire and the Anglo-Saxon nations for world supremacy.

Hitler's ambitions were fantastic and delusional, but he was now in control of potentially the most powerful single state in Europe. How were the British going to deal with him?

Notes

1 This account is based on the analysis in M. Chambers, R. Grew, D. Herlihy, T. Rabb and I. Woloch, *The Western Experience*, second edition (New York, Knopf, 1979), pp. 967–9, still the best short overview of the effects of the Depression.

2 Chambers *et al.*, *The Western Experience*.

3 Chambers *et al.*, *The Western Experience*.

4 Chambers *et al.*, *The Western Experience*.

5 Chambers *et al.*, *The Western Experience*.

6 R. Boyce, 'Britain's first "no" to Europe: Britain and the Briand plan, 1929–30', *European Studies Review*, X, 1980, pp. 17–45. Boyce places the blame for the failure of the Briand initiative squarely on Britain.

7 The Little Entente was a French-sponsored alliance between Czechoslovakia, Yugoslavia and Romania that was formed in 1921. It was designed to contain a bitter and vengeful Hungary and was part of the French policy of building a *cordon sanitaire* in Eastern Europe.

8 M. Newman, 'Britain and the German–Austrian customs union proposal of 1931', *European Studies Review*, VI, 1976 pp. 449–72.

9 This was the *Deutschland*, the first of the so-called 'pocket battleship' class that later included the *Graf Spee*. These ships were referred to as 'pocket' battleships simply because they were smaller and lighter than other battleships of the era – small enough, metaphorically speaking, to fit in your pocket.

10 For the sake of appearances, the Japanese placed Pu Yi, the last of the old Chinese Manchu dynasty, on the throne of Manchukuo. A film by Bernardo Bertolucci about the life of Pu Yi, *The Last Emperor*, was released in 1988. See also Edward Behr's biography, *The Last Emperor* (London, Futura, 1987).

11 The crisis has been most definitively studied in C. Thorne, *The Limits of Foreign Policy: The West, the League and the Far Eastern Crisis of 1931–1933* (New York, Putnam's, 1972).

12 Quoted in M. Pugh, 'Pacifism and politics in Britain, 1931–1935', *The Historical Journal*, XXIII, 1980, pp. 641–56.

13 The position of foreign secretary was held very briefly by Lord Reading for the period from Henderson's resignation in August 1931 to Simon's appointment in November 1931.

14 D. Dutton, *Simon: A Political Biography of Sir John Simon* (London, Aurum, 1992), p. 2.

15 Dutton, *Simon*, p. 154.

16 Dutton, *Simon*, pp. 154–5.

17 C. Barnett, *The Collapse of British Power* (London, Methuen, 1972), p. 127.

18 D. Marquand, *Ramsay MacDonald* (London, Jonathan Cape, 1977), p. 718.

19 D. Reynolds, *Britannia Overruled: British Policy and World Power in the Twentieth Century* (New York, Longman, 1991), p. 118.

CHAPTER SIX

THE FOREIGN OFFICE

An early practitioner of the history of international relations once argued that in order to understand international relations the historian must first understand the nature of the diplomatic process itself.[1] How was diplomacy practised, and by whom? What was their 'habit of mind?'. What were the limitations of and constraints on diplomacy? Within the British government the Foreign Office was the institution responsible for the formulation and execution of Britain's external relations. It operated in conjunction with the Diplomatic Service, the designation for the staff of Britain's overseas embassies. At the risk of stretching a rather obvious metaphor, the Foreign Office establishment in London can be seen as the 'brain' of Britain's foreign policy apparatus, with the embassies acting as 'nerve endings'. Ambassadors sent back reports, or despatches, which made their way up the ladder of the Foreign Office hierarchy in the same way that a nerve impulse travels through the nervous system. At some point the 'impulse' or despatch was dealt with. It could be filed away, it could be ignored, or it could prompt a response. The most serious despatches were dealt with by the cabinet itself, surely the metaphorical equivalent of a cerebrum. Following the path of these despatches offers the easiest introduction to Britain's foreign policy hierarchy.

The most prestigious postings for British diplomats in the inter-war era included the embassies in Rome, Paris and Berlin, the so-called 'inner circle'. Washington and Tokyo were less desirable, while Moscow was positively loathed. The ambassadors themselves were usually men of upper-class background who had served for many years in a wide variety of overseas postings, working their way up from embassy counsellors. Sir Nevile Henderson, appointed British ambassador to Berlin in 1937, began his career in 1905 and served in ten different embassies before his appointment to Berlin. He spent very little time in Britain during his thirty-two years of climbing up the ladder. Lord Chilston, the British ambassador to the USSR in the 1930s, entered the Diplomatic Service in 1899 and served in seven embassies before arriving in Moscow in 1933. Ambassadors administered their embassies, conducted interviews with the foreign ministers and heads of state of their host country and assisted British citizens. Normally they worked in harmony with the cabinet and the Foreign Office, but occasionally problems arose. According to some historians, Henderson's disagreements with Robert Vansittart, head of the Foreign Office and Chief Diplomatic Advisor in 1937–38, did much to disrupt British policy towards Hitler.

The Foreign Office ladder

Despatches from ambassadors were first opened and read in the Third Room of the Foreign Office by the most junior member of the department.[2] Departmental heads and their assistants were given their own offices (the First and Second Rooms), but junior clerks worked together in the Third Room, and one veteran remembers it as 'usually fairly noisy, with several telephones ringing and people coming in and out all the time'.[3] Valentine Lawford, who worked as a Central Department clerk in the 1930s, had the rotten luck to draw a desk

> exactly opposite the door communicating with the room of the head of the department: in the best position, that is, to be seen by [Ralph] Wigram whenever he came through in search of someone to run an errand.[4]

Over the next two years, Lawford remembers, 'I was rarely to sit at my desk for more than five minutes on end'. In less stressful times the Third Room had something of a 'frat-house' atmosphere to it. Ivone Kirkpatrick recalls being censured by his departmental head, Gerald Villiers, for 'joining Neville Butler in practising mashie shots against the door whilst he was receiving the Spanish Ambassador'.[5]

There was little in the way of formal behaviour and superiors were seldom addressed as 'Sir'. Junior clerks could offer their comments (called minutes) on despatches or, better still, simply initial the document and pass it on to the next clerk for further sorting and minuting. Departmental heads supervised the day-to-day functioning of the department and decided which despatches warranted further attention at higher levels or different branches of the Foreign Office. Normally, only twenty per cent of despatches were passed from the departmental level to the upper bureaucracy.

The next rung on the ladder consisted of deputy under-secretaries, and assistant under-secretaries (the distinction between the two being fairly thin), whose main responsibilities lay in the supervision of two or more departments. These were key positions, as one historian of the Foreign Office has noted:

> It is they, in consultation with their heads of departments, who evolve and formulate and recommend courses of action and lines of major policy on the basis of general directions from the Secretary of State, or in the light of what is known to be his general outlook, or on the strength of what, in their judgment, would best meet the public interest.[6]

The numbers of deputy (and assistant) under-secretaries varied from one year to the next, as did their responsibilities. Under-secretaries were, however, free to fish outside their own waters should they so choose. The assistant under-secretary for the Southern Department could, for example, comment on relevant despatches handled by the Northern Department.

One of the most influential and important under-secretaries was Orme Sargent. Sargent entered the Foreign Office in 1906 at the age of twenty-one. He had a very high reputation among his contemporaries, all of whom praised his formidable intellect. One thought him 'a philosopher strayed into Whitehall. He knew all the answers; when the politicians did not want them he went out to lunch'.[7] Another remembered Sargent as a 'brilliant and rather passionate character', something of a loner 'who never left the Foreign Office except for a brief excursion to the Ambassadors' Conference in Paris'.[8] Lawford also referred to Sargent as a 'philosopher' and remembered his coolness under pressure. Sargent was so cool, in fact, that Lawford initially thought him without emotion; someone

> coolly prepared for the world to come crashing about his ears and give him his cue for the 'What else did you expect?' that would have been his only comment; and in the meantime disinclined, if the policy which he advocated was not adopted by the government of the day, to do more than shrug his shoulders as though to say: if they wished to go the shortest way to perdition, who was he to prevent them?[9]

Sargent worked up a 'secluded flight of stairs', from which he periodically scurried forth.[10] He thus earned the nickname 'Moley'. He ended his career as permanent under-secretary of the Foreign Office from 1946 to 1949.

The permanent under-secretary oversaw the whole structure. His official duties were to

> ensure the efficient administration of the Office, to be responsible to Parliament for the spending of the sums voted, to recommend promotions and dismissals, to receive Ambassadors and, most important of all, to advise the Foreign Secretary on issues of policy.[11]

He could request that a despatch from an embassy be circulated to the other deputy (or assistant) under-secretaries aside from the department heads. He could then send it on to the foreign secretary or request that a department head draw up a memorandum incorporating the views of the commentators. In 1934 the permanent head of the Foreign Office bureaucracy was Robert Vansittart. Together, Vansittart and the Treasury's permanent under-secretary, Warren Fisher, were the two most influential civil servants in Britain in the mid-1930s. Tempestuous, energetic, egotistical and volatile, Vansittart was an important formulator of British foreign policy during the 1930s. He was born in 1881 and entered the Foreign Office in 1903. He rose through the ranks very quickly to become permanent under-secretary in 1930, before he had reached the age of fifty. His brother-in-law was Eric Phipps, who served as British ambassador to France and Germany in the 1930s. Vansittart lived 'in a large and luxurious house in Mayfair where he and his wife entertained on an almost regal scale', and his well-known 'unquenchable gusto for life' evidently included a penchant for gambling.[12] He still represented the Foreign Office in tennis tournaments in his late forties, earned a reputation as an ardent Francophile (and Germanophobe) and in his youth wrote a play in French that was produced at the Odéon in Paris. Vansittart's baptism by fire as head of the Foreign Office came in early 1933 when he steered the British government through the difficult and acrimonious Metro-Vickers crisis with the USSR.[13] In January 1938 Vansittart was 'kicked upstairs' and given the meaningless position of chief diplomatic adviser, from which he churned out lengthy memoranda that were seldom read. He was replaced as permanent under-secretary by Alexander Cadogan.

An exclusive institution

The various steps on the Foreign Office ladder were linked by a vast flow of paper, a small portion of which sieved its way from the Third Room to the foreign secretary's desk. But Foreign Office personnel were united by much more than their paperwork. The Foreign Office in the inter-war period was an institution of remarkable homogeneity and no small measure of social exclusivity. The senior figures of the 1930s were born to wealthy, aristocratic families of the late-Victorian and Edwardian periods. Vansittart writes that he 'was born on the border between the second and third Victorian eras, the heyday of the squires, when a man could still be passing rich on a few thousands a year'.[14] In fact, Vansittart's view of diplomacy was relentlessly Edwardian. He viewed the international arena as a vast extension of London's clubland, where all the members obeyed certain accepted rules. Cadogan's family lived in a home of baronial proportions in London and owned a rural estate of some eleven thousand acres. Throughout the nineteenth century the aristocracy provided the largest single social pool of recruits for the Foreign Office, and between 1898 and 1907 (the period during which Vansittart and Sargent began their careers) more than half of the recruits came from the aristocracy and the gentry. In terms of education it was Eton and 'Oxbridge' that dominated. Cadogan, a product of Eton and Balliol College, Oxford, was typical. Vansittart also attended Eton. As late as 1919 twenty-two of the forty-four Foreign Office clerks were Etonians. Apologists for the Foreign Office explained that it was 'not because any special favour was shown to Eton, but because the sort of people who wanted nomination mostly came from Eton'.[15]

Membership in the aristocracy was not in itself enough to guarantee entry into the Foreign Office. In the pre-war era the Foreign Office and the Diplomatic Service were still separate institutions. Qualifying examinations for both services had been introduced as early as 1856, but nomination by the secretary of state for foreign affairs was required before the exams could be taken. This usually meant that the parents of the candidate had to be known to the secretary or to his advisers. If the candidate wanted to enter the Diplomatic Service he had to prove that he had a private income of at least four hundred pounds per year (known as the 'property qualification'). During his first two years in the service the new recruit held the post of attaché, a probationary rank that carried no salary. New recruits also had to pay out of their own pockets for the endless round of social engagements they were expected to attend. (Recruits to the Foreign Office, however, were granted a salary of two hundred pounds on entry). Moreover, by 1905 the entrance exams called for a good command of French and German, and it was generally felt that one or two years of study abroad was necessary to attain sufficient competence in these languages. Together, all these prerequisites ensured that only a very small and wealthy élite entered the Foreign Office and Diplomatic Service.

Mr Diptitch Scoones

Preparation for the qualifying exams meant 'cramming'. This was best done at the school of Mr Diptitch Scoones in Garrick Street. Some who came through Mr Scoones's tutelage, such as John Tilley, chief clerk at the Foreign Office during the First World War, spoke very highly of him. Tilley took the exam of 1892.

> When I went up for the examination, I believe that in twenty years there had not been more than one successful candidate for the Foreign Office who had not been to that famous crammer. Of the dozen or so candidates who went up with me, there was one from

another crammer, and he got no marks at all. The teaching was certainly very good, and I believe the Private Secretaries had considerable confidence in Scoones's personal opinion about the candidates. He, of course, knew the tricks of the trade, but he had teachers both for foreign languages and history who were highly qualified.[16]

Others were much more critical, both of Mr Scoones and of the whole pre-war examination system. 'The products of this system', Harold Nicolson drily noted, 'were not at all the products that the State required. It was found that these young men might be extremely proficient in languages, but that they knew little else'.[17] Owen O'Malley, another prominent Foreign Office veteran, recalled in his memoirs that he attended Scoones's school very briefly in 1910 but abandoned it in favour of a private tutor. O'Malley paid the price when he failed the exam, although he did rebound to first place in the 1911 exams. After 1908 the Foreign Office made a point of seeking university graduates, and the importance of Scoones's school slowly diminished.

Assuming that the candidate passed the examination, what awaited him in the Foreign Office? In general, recruits seemed to have experienced a crushing sense of disappointment after taking up their jobs. Vansittart describes his first days in the following terms:

> I had started without ambition but with dreams of at least sharing in the interests and intrigues of some modern Talleyrand ... Instead I was told to fag off and decipher, to fill the Cabinet's pouches with papers, to copy out telegrams in violet ink and rub them into scores on stacks of decomposing 'jellyfish', whose fragments were pervading. Once I sought escape, for under a tarpaulin like the gun at Dover Harbour was a typewriter; but as I sat down to explore it, the Head of the Department burst in exclaiming: 'Leave that thing alone! Don't you know we're in a hurry'. Disheartened by these sweats, I could bring no zeal to my new work.[18]

Another clerk from the pre-war era claimed that 'the only original work' that he could remember having done was 'a small contribution to the annual departmental memorandum'.[19] One prominent historian of the Foreign Office found an instance of a grown man whose work after nine full years at the Foreign Office was still 'to copy out despatches, to put numbers on papers, to sort confidential prints, and, more especially to do up despatch bags with sealing wax and red tape'.[20] Cadogan's first job in the Foreign Office – after Eton, Oxford and two years of private preparation – was to copy out manuscripts. Not surprisingly, the brighter and more active recruits, such as Vansittart, escaped to a foreign posting as soon as they could. The lack of challenging work for newcomers became a serious problem by 1910, when university graduates started to arrive in large numbers. On his return to the Foreign Office in 1911 Vansittart discovered that junior clerks were now allowed to 'have a little say in high matters however wide of the mark at first. This was an enormous advance, for a man is resentful of being thought young at thirty, and still more resentful if he is not'.[21]

Reforms in the Foreign Office

The last few years of peace saw a period of modest, though not insignificant, reform in the Foreign Office. The examination system was overhauled in 1904, as a result of which candidates were required to take the same exams as the Home Civil Service, but with added emphasis on modern languages; they also had to have attained the age of twenty-two before they could apply. After 1906 efforts were made to give senior clerks more responsibility by relieving them of routine administrative chores.

In 1907 a selection board was set up to process applications. The intention was to broaden the base of applicants, but, as it turned out, the board chose pretty much the same type of applicants as before. Nevertheless, increasing numbers of university graduates were accepted, and it is possible to detect in the last two or three years of peace a very slight widening of the social base of candidates. This trend should not, however, be exaggerated. When Owen O'Malley turned up for his first day on the job in the Western Department in 1911, he discovered that four of his six colleagues were 'the offspring of noble families'. In fact, O'Malley created something of a sensation for being 'the first member of the Foreign Office to live in the suburbs and go up and down to London every day'.[22]

The historian D. C. Watt has argued that the general decline of the landed aristocracy in British politics in the immediate post-war years was mirrored by changes in the foreign and Diplomatic Service. For example, in 1909 Reader Bullard, whose father had been a London dock worker at one stage in his life, entered the Foreign Office after serving in the Levantine consular service.[23] Members of the professional and middle classes also gained entry. A very long time would pass before any of these individuals attained sufficient seniority within the Foreign Office to effect policy decisively. Vansittart, Cadogan and Sargent monopolized the position of permanent under-secretary until 1949. The sponge-like ability of the Foreign Office to soak up change was noted by the historian John Connell. The pre-war reforms, Connell thought,

> were all within the framework of long-established, useful and proper conventions and traditions. The Office was never resistant to changes; it bowed to them courteously and manfully and then proceeded, in its own subtle fashion, to absorb and modulate them.[24]

One typical recruit of the pre-war era was Laurence Collier. Collier headed the Northern Department (which included the Soviet Union) during the 1930s and ended his career as British ambassador to Norway in the late 1940s. His father, John Collier, had been a relatively well-known Edwardian portrait painter. Between 1908 and 1913 the Foreign Office and Diplomatic Service admitted thirty-seven recruits to their ranks. Collier was the only candidate whose father's occupation was listed as 'artist'. He was also the only candidate from those years who attended Bedales School. He fitted the mould in that he attended Balliol College at Oxford (where he earned a first-class honours degree in modern history and a Brackenbury Scholarship) and his family must have had sufficient credentials to impress the selection board, but his appointment was also part of a slow trend on the part of the Foreign Office towards a broader social base. In a brief article that Collier wrote for *Blackwood's Magazine* in 1972 one can detect a lingering resentment towards the aristocrats who dominated the foreign and Diplomatic Service.[25] Collier pointed out that he entered The Foreign Office because he 'had neither the money nor the social graces then thought necessary' for the Diplomatic Service. In the pre-war years he noted:

> [the] Foreign Office was commonly regarded as the place for 'brains and no money' and the Diplomatic Service for 'money and no brains'. This may have been unfair to the diplomats; but I certainly encountered some remarkably unintellectual specimens ...

Collier then goes on to recall one unintellectual specimen, this one serving in the Foreign Office.

> Hope Vere, a melancholy dyspeptic little man, had distinguished himself on his first day in the cyphering room by sitting alone for about half an hour before suddenly announcing in his high squeaky voice: 'This telegram is marked Very Urgent and is totally indecipherable'. He also, on a later occasion, had a celebrated conversation with the kitchen, from which in those days one could order teas. We heard only his side of it, which ran like this: 'No, I said nothing. No, I didn't say muffin, I said nothing. No I said *nothing*, not a muffin. Oh well, if you must send up a muffin, I'll have it'.

In spite of the Foreign Office's efforts to give increased work to clerks, Collier remained singularly unimpressed. The office, he found, 'was still the place where no junior clerk was supposed to concern himself with foreign policy or do much more than file papers and index the Confidential Print'. From Collier's perspective, the reforms of the preceding years had had little practical effect. 'A few years previously', he noted, 'what were known as "the Hardinge reforms" had introduced such things as typewriters and even an occasional typist'. Working hours were not demanding. For some time it had been the practice in the Foreign Office to begin work around mid-morning or even later, and end at six o'clock (five in the summer) with, as Collier relates, a

> generous break for lunch – long enough to allow for a walk across St. James's Park and Green Park and back, so as to get a good lunch at the St. James's Club in Piccadilly, the regular resort of the foreign diplomats in London, who saw to it that the cooking was of a Continental standard.

Collier also repeated a long-standing joke that likened Foreign

Office officials to the fountains in Trafalgar Square because they played from ten to four.

Despite these shortcomings, Collier concludes his article on a rather nostalgic note and seems to have held genuinely fond memories of 'the Old Foreign Office'. Many of his colleagues expressed similar sentiments. O'Malley, for example, recalled that in 1911 'the Foreign Office and the Diplomatic Service were surrounded by a nimbus of prestige and romance'.[26] Office morale was very high in the last years of peace and The Foreign Office stood at the peak of its power and prestige. It had evolved from a nineteenth-century clerical body to 'an emergent department of state'.[27]

The MacDonnell Commission

There were some voices of discontent. Labour had emerged as a force in the House of Commons in the years following the 1906 election, after Vansittart and Sargent had begun their careers.[28] By 1914 Foreign Office elitism had become a major target of Labour criticism in the Commons. Discontent with the Foreign Office was not confined to the left: increasingly, business representatives complained that British diplomats displayed aristocratic prejudice towards commercial activity and were not interested in promoting British business interests overseas. Consequently, in 1914 the MacDonnell Commission on the civil service made some important recommendations: the property qualification should be eliminated, the selection board broadened, and the Foreign Office amalgamated with the Diplomatic Service. Considerable time passed before the recommendations were carried out.

The war years witnessed internal reorganization (the addition of a War Department and a Contraband Department) and the influx of dozens of clerical assistants and new staff members. Collier remembered the war years as a time of opportunity:

> for the first time in my life, I was allowed to 'minute' papers – that is, to write on the 'jacket' enclosing a despatch or telegram my suggestions for dealing with the questions raised in it. But for the war it might have been years before I could have done this. As it was, however, we juniors had the chance of our lives, and some of us had

some really bright ideas, particularly Nicolson, whose fertile brain turned out a prodigious mass of minutes and memoranda. He had learned how to dictate and virtually monopolised the services of our one typist.[29]

If the pre-war years marked the high point of the Foreign Office in terms of its prestige and influence, then (as we have seen earlier) the immediate post-war years marked its nadir. It found itself under attack from all directions, which must have been a bewildering experience. Lloyd George marginalized the Foreign Office in favour of other agencies. For a brief period in 1919–20 intense public interest was focused on foreign policy issues and Foreign Office experts felt sidelined. Rival agencies within the government, such as the War Office, the Treasury, the Cabinet Office and the prime minister's staff all became involved in foreign policy issues. Predictably, the Foreign Office soon developed the 'atmosphere of a garrison under siege'[30] and insiders felt that they were no longer masters in their own house.

Intense pressure was placed on the Foreign Office to implement the recommendations of the MacDonnell Commission of 1914. Accordingly, in 1919 the selection board was expanded, the property qualification was finally dropped and, most controversial of all, the Foreign Office was amalgamated with the Diplomatic Service. Amalgamation was intended to encourage greater interchangeability between the Foreign Office in London and the embassies and missions overseas. For the purposes of promotions and transfers the two services now worked from a common seniority list. Laurence Collier was one of those transferred in 1919 – in his case to Tokyo. Pressure for further changes came from the Treasury, 'which was anxious to sweep away the existing quasi-independent status of the Foreign Office and bring it into line with the rest of the domestic departments'.[31] Outside the government, reformers hoped that the post-war changes might result in a more democratic Foreign Office, or at least one that was more representative of British society as a whole.

The hopes of the reformers were cruelly disappointed. Public interest in foreign policy waned sharply after the Paris Peace Conference. In 1920 the principle of amalgamation was quietly dropped by Curzon without any public discussion. A strong core of opposition within the Foreign Office stymied attempts at reform, arguing that the Foreign Office and the Diplomatic Service were two distinct enterprises that required different personalities, and so amalgamation must go. Nevertheless, the reforms of 1919 were not completely abandoned. In subsequent years there was a greater tendency to send Foreign Office personnel overseas for short spells and for Diplomatic Service staff to spend time in London. The proportion of Etonians among new entrants slowly diminished and the social net of recruits continued to widen. In 1919, for example, William Strang, the son of an Essex farmer, passed a special qualifying exam for servicemen. He gained admission on the basis of a strong academic record (University College, London) and a strong war record. Ivone Kirkpatrick was also admitted in 1919. His father had served in the British Army in India and Kirkpatrick himself had been severely wounded at Gallipoli.[32] Neither had come through the Eton–Oxford circuit. By contrast, Gladwyn Jebb, also a post-war recruit, came from an aristocratic background and had attended both Eton and Oxford.[33]

The partial success of the 1919 reforms also allowed publicists for the Foreign Office to make some notable claims. John Tilley's account of 1933 maintained that amalgamation had been a complete success and that social exclusivity was a thing of the past. Arthur Willert's article in *The Strand Magazine* (doubtless designed to give the Foreign Office some badly needed positive publicity in the wake of the Hoare–Laval disaster[34]) made similar claims, asserting that the newly democratized Foreign Office had changed 'from a small and select club whose pastime was work of a specialised nature in which outsiders were not encouraged to take an interest, into a great public office run on up-to-date lines'.[35]

Critics on the left were not impressed. Robert Nightingale of the Fabian Society charged that 'the British Foreign Office and Diplomatic Service [were] a preserve for the sons of the aristocratic, rentier and professional classes' and 'one of the last strongholds in which the aristocratic principle [had] withstood the advance of democracy.[36]

Arguably the most serious challenge that the Foreign Office faced in the inter-war era came from the Treasury. Many in the Foreign Office clearly felt threatened by the Treasury and its head, Warren

Fisher, and accorded them considerable hostility. Throughout the 1920s and 1930s the two departments fought bitterly on a number of issues. The economy-minded Treasury was reluctant to sanction any additional expenditures by the Foreign Office and attempted to limit salaries in the Foreign Office and Diplomatic Service. It also guarded jealously its authority over economic issues such as reparations. The stage was set for a major battle in the 1930s when the Foreign Office attempted to establish an Economic Relations Section. This arose out of an initiative by Victor Wellesley, a deputy under-secretary who felt, not unreasonably, that economic issues were of growing importance and should be taken into account in the formulation of British foreign policy. The Treasury resisted Wellesley's proposals, and although a Foreign Office Economic Relations Section was established under Frank Ashton-Gwatkin in 1931, it fell far short of Wellesley's original aims. As Ashton-Gwatkin later wrote, his section had only one or two members of staff and barely survived as a 'one man liaison bureau'.[37] So bitter was the experience that, well into the 1950s, Foreign Office personnel involved in the struggles with the Treasury continued to publish memoirs in which they charged Fisher (unfairly) with wrecking the whole course of British foreign policy in the 1930s.[38] The ascendancy of the Treasury over the Foreign Office in the inter-war era can be attributed to the overriding priority of economic issues in domestic British politics, especially after the onset of the Depression.

The Foreign Office in the inter-war years

Aside from these larger issues, how had life in the Foreign Office changed from the pre-war era? The establishment itself employed many more people. The staff of 185 in 1913 had expanded to 880 in 1926. The volume of work had also risen dramatically. In 1901 the Office processed just under 50,000 incoming papers, despatches and telegrams. By 1934 that number had more than tripled. Although the dates are not quite comparable, it is interesting to note that staff increases were approaching forty per cent each year while paper-work was expanding at the rate of nearly ten per cent. A number of new departments emerged. Vansittart strengthened the position of the Central Department, which was under the command of Ralph Wigram by the time Lawford joined. As Lawford was informed, the Central Department dealt with 'France and Germany – and Poland and Belgium and much else beside – and if any department could claim to be in a perpetual state of crisis it was this'.[39] By comparison, those who worked in the Northern Department in the early 1920s recalled it as an agreeable and congenial place in which to work.[40] The workload on departmental heads and their superiors had increased substantially by the mid-1930s. To judge from Lawford's account, Ralph Wigram, the head of the Central Department, spent most of his last years in a state of constant overwork and nervous exhaustion. Vansittart could still enjoy long weekends, but by 1939 his successor, Alexander Cadogan, had no such luck. A typical day for Cadogan began at nine in the morning and went on past midnight. Gladwyn Jebb, Cadogan's private secretary in 1939, recalled in his memoirs that 'Alec Cadogan was a tremendous worker and most methodical; but the red-labelled boxes piled up on his desk like mountains and often seemed to get him down'.[41]

In certain respects, not much had changed for the entry-level junior clerks in the Third Room. Passing the qualifying exams was still an ordeal. Valentine Lawford (a Cambridge graduate and non-Etonian) failed his first attempt:

> A day or two later there came an official letter, enclosing the complete Table of Results, from which I learned that I had been placed ninth, with three marks less than Fitzroy Maclean, who had been only one mark below the last successful candidate. Fitzroy at once very sensibly called at the Foreign Office to represent that it would be absurd to expect him to take the examination all over again for the sake of one mark out of a total of two thousand; and just as sensibly he was admitted.[42]

Lawford's father was outraged and clearly believed that personal influence still counted for something in the Office: '"Say the word," said my father, "and I'll write to Vansittart".' Lawford declined. His next attempt was successful, and his sense of relief and joy at having passed was as overwhelming as it had been for O'Malley twenty-three years earlier. 'I cannot think of any bit of news I was ever so glad to get in all my life', O'Malley recalled later.[43] Jebb likewise referred to the exams as an ordeal and also had to make two attempts.

Lawford had no way of knowing it, but privately the Foreign Office still preferred to find the right sort of candidates, irrespective of their ability to do well in the exams. In 1936 Lord Cranborne, a parliamentary under-secretary, argued against a civil service proposal to alter Foreign Office examinations so that they placed less emphasis on the interview part. Cranborne observed:

> personality counts for far more in diplomacy than in any other public service. It is no question of enabling socially favoured candidates to obtain jobs. It is a question of securing candidates for the very special work they have to do'.[44]

On his arrival in the high-pressure atmosphere of the Central Department Lawford found the work frenzied and hectic but also disappointingly mundane. Much of his time was spent running up three flights of stairs to fetch papers for Wigram ('the departmental volcano') from the impassive clerks of the Central Registry: 'Ground between their boredom and Wigram's impatience, I didn't much fancy my new role as a bellhop in Whitehall.' He experienced moments of near despair: 'even at my most bitter I couldn't believe that it was Wigram's intention to humiliate the youthful, would-be diplomatist'. Less menial duties were not always much compensation. Minute writing 'could paralyse [his] faculties for hours'. If he thought there was 'nothing much' in a particular despatch he was invariably wrong. 'Alternatively,' he commented, 'if I was foolhardy enough to suggest some such action myself, my recommendations would as like as not be countermanded'. Then, suddenly, 'one red letter day in November 1935', an astonishing development took place. Vansittart praised one of his minutes! Soon afterwards Sargent acknowledged Lawford's earthly existence while strolling through the Third Room. Finally, the arrival of a newcomer in the Third Room meant Lawford 'was no longer the neophyte; and oh, the subtle change'.[45]

Lawford's experiences were fairly typical. Ivone Kirkpatrick's departmental head was also a stern task-master.

Unsatisfactory efforts were returned to the third room with cryptic little slips which compelled the delinquent to find out what was wrong. 'Accuracy is precious and inaccuracy misleading' or 'too tired to read the previous papers?' or even 'rejected with contumely' or 'this is too much'. On one occasion Villiers wrote: 'I really do not know. So I speak with the utmost reserve. But this seems to me the bloody limit of blatant imbecility'. These written complaints were sometimes reinforced by oral reproofs of great vehemence.[46]

On another occasion, much earlier in his career, Kirkpatrick was reprimanded by none other than Eyre Crowe, then permanent under-secretary.

> I was paralysed one day to pick up the telephone to hear his voice: 'I have just r-r-read your minute. Either you do not mean what you say, in which case you are wasting my time. Or you do mean it, in which case you are wr-r-riting r-r-rot'. And with that he put down the receiver.[47]

As Lawford noted, approval from higher-ups for a good minute or memorandum was always regarded as a major breakthrough. A memorandum by O'Malley in 1924 attracted the attention and praise of the foreign secretary, Austen Chamberlain. 'I was excited and pleased, and thought to myself that I was now getting on in the world. So I was'.[48]

One of the most universally disliked jobs for junior clerks involved drafting answers to Parliamentary Questions. This was a delicate task that required great precision. Any slip could get the offender into a great deal of trouble. Kirkpatrick regarded 'PQs' as his 'principal affliction' during those years, but Gladwyn Jebb discovered the 'right technique'.

> Clearly it was impossible, in the general interest, always to tell the plain truth in answer to a question on foreign affairs. To do so might result in a perfectly unnecessary deterioration of our relations with a friendly power. On the other hand it was not only against the rules but clearly counter-productive ever to give expression to anything resembling a lie. The right solution as often as not therefore was to compose in crisp and convincing English some answer which was not untrue.[49]

Lawford, Maclean and Kirkpatrick all spent substantial portions of their careers in overseas postings, reflecting the general inter-war trend towards 'interchangeability'. Even so, there was a sense that some postings were preferable to others. Kirkpatrick recalls a joke which likened the foreign service to 'the London Underground Railway and it was said that once a man was launched on the Inner Circle (London, Paris, Berlin, Rome) it was impossible to leave the track'.[50] Kirkpatrick also relates his relief at not having been transferred from Berlin to Tokyo (outside the inner circle) in 1936.

At its senior levels in the 1930s the Foreign Office remained dominated by individuals from a restricted and exclusive social background whose intellectual development had taken place during the late-Victorian and Edwardian periods. In the lower ranks (some departmental heads and clerks) it was possible to notice a somewhat greater degree of diversity, but overall the Foreign Office as an institution had retained the core of its pre-war traditions and ethos. It never recovered its pre-war position of prestige within the structure of government, however. The Hoare–Laval debacle did much damage, and by 1937 the prime minister (Neville Chamberlain) seemed once again to be assuming a primary role in foreign policy-making to an extent not seen since the days of Lloyd George.

Influences on the Foreign Office

The bureaucrats in the Foreign Office and their political masters comprised only two of the elements that had a bearing on the formulation of foreign policy. The historian D. C. Watt has identified two additional groupings in Britain's political élite that impinged on the making of foreign policy. First, there were the bureaucrats of the domestic civil service whose 'co-operation [was] necessary in the taking and implementing of decisions in the field of foreign policy'.[51] Reference has already been made to the not inconsiderable tension that existed between the Foreign Office and the Treasury. Historians have generally recognized that by the later 1930s the influence of the Treasury waned as the urgency of rearmament grew. A second important category of influence was found in the various groups of military advisers, which included military attachés stationed in

Britain's overseas embassies, the War Office located in London and, most important of all, the Chiefs of Staff.

Watt also identifies groupings outside the ranks of the foreign policy élite whose interest in foreign policy issues allowed for a measure of influence. First, and most obvious, was the British press. The newspaper with the largest circulation in Britain in the 1930s was the *Daily Express*, owned by Lord Beaverbrook, which enjoyed a circulation of more than 2.3 million. The second largest paper was the *Daily Mail*, owned by Lord Rothermere, with a readership hovering around 1.6 million. Rothermere also owned the *Daily Mirror*, which was read by more than one million people. In contrast to the mass-circulation papers were *The Times* and the *Observer* with print runs of 187,000 and 201,000 respectively. Both papers were owned by Viscount Astor and were read mainly by the political élite of Britain. The Beaverbrook and Rothermere papers, by contrast, catered to the middle- and working-class markets. The Rothermere papers in particular were targeted at the lower middle-class and skilled workers. Both Beaverbrook and Rothermere personally directed the editorial content of their papers on a regular basis, whereas Astor largely left his editors alone. Editorially, the press was overwhelmingly sympathetic to the Conservative Party, although this did not stop it from disagreeing with the government on specific issues. In 1938 Geoffrey Dawson, the editor of *The Times*, was a particularly strong supporter of Chamberlain's policies. In 1939, on the other hand, many papers disagreed with the government's line towards the USSR and mounted a vociferous campaign to have Winston Churchill appointed to the cabinet. Two papers, the *News Chronicle* and the *Manchester Guardian* (which had circulations of 1.4 million and 45,000 respectively) supported the Liberal party. The sole supporter of the Labour party was the *Daily Herald* (with more than one million readers), which was partially owned by the Trades Union Congress.[52]

One final source of pressure on the Foreign Office was the House of Commons. One thinks immediately of the junior clerks struggling with the dreaded 'PQs'. Many questions served as a constant reminder that dissident Conservatives, Liberals and Labour members had no intention of being shut out of the foreign policy process.

It seems clear that the Foreign Office of the inter-war period was much more restricted in its freedom of action than it had been before 1914. Public opinion, the press and the rise of the Treasury and other governmental bodies all served to limit what the diplomats and statesmen were able to do. Edward Grey, according to some historians, conducted his foreign policy virtually on his own. Those rarefied days had vanished forever by 1919. Much of this, of course, reflected the suspicion that it was the secretive style of the old diplomacy that bore the brunt of responsibility for the First World War. In this, as in many other respects, the lessons of what had happened in 1914 cast a shadow over the inter-war period.

Notes

1 D. P. Heatley, *Diplomacy and the Study of International Relations* (Oxford, Clarendon Press, 1919). See also G. Craig, 'On the nature of diplomatic history: the relevance of some old books', in P. Lauren (ed.), *Diplomacy: New Approaches in History, Theory and Policy* (New York, The Free Press, 1979).

2 The Foreign Office divided Europe into regions, each of which was dealt with by a separate department. The Central Department, for example, was responsible for the central European states.

3 Letter from Sir Fitzroy Maclean to the author, 6 May 1993.

4 V. Lawford, *Bound for Diplomacy* (London, John Murray, 1963), pp. 236 and 239.

5 I. Kirkpatrick, *The Inner Circle: The Memoirs of Ivone Kirkpatrick* (London, Macmillan, 1959), p. 34. Kirkpatrick was in the Western Department from 1919 to 1929 and occupied the same desk for the duration – possibly a Foreign Office record.

6 W. Strang, *The Foreign Office* (London, George Allen and Unwin, 1955), p. 154.

7 R. Vansittart, *The Mist Procession* (London, Hutchinson, 1958), p. 399.

8 G. Jebb, *The Memoirs of Lord Gladwyn* (London, Weidenfeld and Nicolson, 1972), p. 73.

9 Lawford, *Bound for Diplomacy*, pp. 268–9.

10 Lawford, *Bound for Diplomacy*, p. 269.

11 D. Dilks (ed.), *The Diaries of Sir Alexander Cadogan, 1938–1945* (London, Cassell, 1971), p. 20.

12 Jebb, *The Memoirs of Lord Gladwyn*, p. 59, and Lawford, *Bound for Diplomacy*, pp. 269–72.

13 See Chapter Seven, p.156.

14 Vansittart, *The Mist Procession*, p. 15.

15 J. Tilley and S. Gaselee, *The Foreign Office* (London, Putnam's, 1933), p. 88.

For figures on Foreign Office recruits see R. Jones, *The Nineteenth Century Foreign Office: An Administrative History* (London, Weidenfeld and Nicolson, 1971), pp. 60–4.

16 Tilley and Gaselee, *The Foreign Office*, p. 88.
17 H. Nicolson, *Diplomacy* (London, Thornton-Butterworth, 1939), pp. 207–8.
18 Vansittart, *The Mist Procession*, p. 43.
19 Tilley and Gaselee, *The Foreign Office*, p. 128.
20 Z. Steiner, *The Foreign Office and Foreign Policy 1898–1914* (Cambridge, Cambridge University Press, 1969), p. 14. Steiner notes that the work done by clerks had not changed much since the days of Palmerston.
21 Vansittart, *The Mist Procession*, p. 98.
22 O. O'Malley, *The Phantom Caravan* (London, John Murray, 1954), pp. 34 and 51.
23 D. C. Watt, *Personalities and Policies: Studies in the Formulation of British Foreign Policy in the Twentieth Century* (London, Longman, 1965), p. 41.
24 J. Connell, *The Office: The Story of the British Foreign Office, 1919–1951* (New York, St Martin's Press, 1958), p. 18.
25 L. Collier, 'The Old Foreign Office', *Blackwood's Magazine*, no. 312, 1972, pp. 256–61.
26 O'Malley, *The Phantom Caravan*, p. 37.
27 Steiner, *The Foreign Office and Foreign Policy*, p. 209.
28 Most British senior civil servants of the 1930s, including Maurice Hankey, Warren Fisher, Horace Wilson and others, similarly began their careers prior to the emergence of Labour.
29 Collier, 'The Old Foreign Office', p. 261
30 A. Sharp, 'The Foreign Office in eclipse, 1919–22', *History*, LXI, 1976, pp. 198–218.
31 Z. Steiner and M. Dockrill, 'The Foreign Office reforms, 1919–21', *The Historical Journal*, XVII, 1974, pp. 131–56, and C. Larner, 'The amalgamation of the Diplomatic Service with the Foreign Office', *Journal of Contemporary History*, VII, 1972, pp. 107–26.
32 Kirkpatrick, *The Inner Circle*, pp. 1–2, and W. Strang, *Home and Abroad* (London, André Deutsch, 1956), pp. 19–22 and 46.
33 Jebb, *The Memoirs of Lord Gladwyn*, pp. 5–14.
34 See Chapter Seven for a discussion of this topic.
35 A. Willert, 'The Foreign Office from within', *The Strand Magazine*, XLV, 1936, pp. 398–405.
36 R. Nightingale, 'The personnel of the British Foreign Office', *Fabian Tract* no. 232, 1930.
37 F. Ashton-Gwatkin, 'Thoughts on the Foreign Office, 1918–1939', *Contemporary Review*, CLXXXVIII, 1955, pp. 374–8.
38 See especially W. Selby, *Diplomatic Twilight, 1930–1940* (London, John Murray, 1953).
39 Lawford, *Bound for Diplomacy*, pp. 235 and 260–2.
40 O'Malley, *The Phantom Caravan*, p. 60.
41 Jebb, *The Memoirs of Lord Gladwyn*, p. 72.
42 Lawford, *Bound for Diplomacy*, p. 191
43 O'Malley, *The Phantom Caravan*, p. 34.

44 V. Cromwell and Z. Steiner, 'Reform and retrenchment: the Foreign Office between the wars' in R. Bullen (ed.), *The Foreign Office, 1782–1982* (Maryland, University Publications of America, 1984), p. 98.
45 Lawford, *Bound for Diplomacy*, pp. 242–3 and 263–4.
46 Kirkpatrick, *The Inner Circle*, p. 32.
47 Kirkpatrick, *The Inner Circle*, p. 32.
48 O'Malley, *The Phantom Caravan*, p. 67.
49 Jebb, *The Memoirs of Lord Gladwyn*, p. 39.
50 The London Underground Railway's Circle Line route was known at that time as the Inner Circle. See Kirkpatrick, *The Inner Circle*, p. x.
51 Watt, *Personalities and Policies, passim*, but see especially pp. 1–15.
52 P. Kyba, *Covenants Without the Sword: Public Opinion and British Defence Policy, 1931–35* (Waterloo, Wilfrid Laurier University Press, 1983), pp. 36–7; B. Morris, *The Roots of Appeasement: The British Weekly Press and Nazi Germany during the 1930's* (London, Frank Cass, 1992); F. Gannon, *The British Press and Germany, 1936–9* (Oxford, Clarendon, 1971).

CHAPTER SEVEN

FROM THE RISE OF HITLER TO THE CRISIS IN ETHIOPIA, 1933-1936

Following his installation as chancellor, Hitler wasted little time in seizing the initiative, either on the domestic front or in the field of foreign policy. By July 1933 domestic opposition to Hitler had been crushed remorselessly and within a few months he had gained more power in Germany than Mussolini had ever held in Italy during his eleven years in office.[1]

In the light of the foreign policy programme that Hitler had in mind, the resumption of the disarmament conference at Geneva in February 1933 resembled a quaint exercise in futility. In October of that year Germany withdrew from both the disarmament conference[2] and the League of Nations. Hitler called a referendum that produced a ninety per cent vote of confidence in his foreign policy. Although that figure is of course suspect, few doubt that the vast majority of Germans supported Hitler's foreign policy in 1933. The withdrawal of Germany from the League was seen by that organization as a heavy blow – the second serious loss that it had suffered in 1933 (in March Japan had resigned in protest over the League's adoption of the Lytton report).

The apparent failure of the disarmament conference caused a wave of anxiety amongst many British voters; the League of Nations seemed to be slipping into irrelevance. Again the possibility arose that a financially ruinous arms race would follow and that Europe would inevitably be plunged into Armageddon. Isolationism, or the demand that Britain withdraw completely from the affairs of Europe, briefly gained ground both on the left and in the columns of conservative newspapers. The *Daily Express* in particular emerged as an advocate of isolationism.

Simon reacted to Germany's withdrawal from the League and the disarmament conference with apparent apathy. According to many critics, already by early 1933 he was simply going through the motions as far as disarmament was concerned. The first months of that year had in fact been a stressful period for him. On 12 March six British engineers working on a construction project in the USSR for the Metro-Vickers company were arrested by Soviet authorities and charged with espionage.[3] The Foreign Office denied the charges, recalled the British ambassador from Moscow and imposed a trade embargo on the Soviet Union. The Soviets retaliated with a trade embargo on British products. Vansittart insisted that a tough line be taken and that no concessions should be made to the Soviets. Simon agreed. Although five of the British engineers were convicted (and two sentenced to terms of imprisonment), they were soon released, largely through the intercession of the Soviet foreign minister, Maxim Litvinov. The incident was smoothed over by June (and the embargoes lifted), but it was neither forgiven nor forgotten and only intensified the mistrust between the two countries.

Simon was feeling the strain of work at the Foreign Office by the summer of 1933 and decided to offload some of his duties on to his parliamentary under-secretary, Anthony Eden. He had decided that the long stays in Geneva to attend League sessions were not to his liking, so Eden was given responsibility for League affairs, an appointment that provided a substantial boost to his career. Eden was associated with League principles and enjoyed a solid reputation within League circles in Britain. He was young, handsome, charismatic and a complete contrast to Simon, who grated on everyone's nerves. He received rapturous reviews in the press and was increasingly mentioned as an ideal replacement for Simon. Not surprisingly, Simon resented Eden's easy success and popularity, and the talk of Eden as the new foreign secretary drove him to distraction. The two men agreed on the fundamentals of foreign policy, but many observers saw important differences in style. Eden seemed frustrated by Simon's indecisiveness and inability to 'take a lead'. Perhaps more serious was Simon's failure to define the exact areas of responsibility dividing Eden's job from his own. Eden developed the habit of reporting to Baldwin directly, over the head of Simon, which further irritated the foreign secretary. It was perhaps unfortunate that things did not go more smoothly at the Foreign Office, since 1933 was a crucial year for Europe.

Perceptions of Hitler

What did Simon and others in the British Foreign Office think of Hitler's accession to power? Hitler's appointment as chancellor does not seem to have prompted any immediate reordering of British priorities. In April 1933 the British ambassador in Berlin, Horace Rumbold, sent Simon a five-thousand word despatch analysing the role of ideology in Nazi foreign policy. For Rumbold, the views that Hitler expressed in *Mein Kampf* were ominous with regard to the future peace of Europe. Simon himself was deeply disturbed by the anti-Semitism displayed by the Nazis and made speeches in the House of Commons that condemned the new régime and attacked its dictatorial direction. It is worth remembering that Simon, in company with many others in 1933, failed to recognize that Nazism represented something fundamentally new in European history and that Hitler's government was not just another authoritarian régime. Baldwin brusquely dismissed the ideological content of the Nazi régime and thought of Hitler as another Philip II or, at worst, another Napoleon. Simon, Baldwin and indeed most people in Britain simply could not comprehend the implications of such concepts as *Lebensraum* or Hitler's warped Social Darwinist vision of history, at least not in 1933 or 1934.

At one time it was commonly said that the Foreign Office and the government ignored *Mein Kampf* and that a copy of the book sat, unread, on a shelf in the Foreign Office library after it was placed there in 1933. If cabinet ministers had only read the book they would have been aware of Hitler's objectives. Unfortunately, cabinet ministers seldom have the time to read works as vast and obtuse as *Mein Kampf*, and in any case they have advisers to do that for them. Even if Simon had read the book, that is not to say Hitler's intentions would necessarily have become clear. Hitler had after all called for British–German friendship in *Mein Kampf*, so it is conceivable that Simon would have seen grounds for reassurance. Nevile Henderson, the British ambassador to Berlin from 1937 to 1939, did read *Mein Kampf* and he concluded that once the grievances arising from the Treaty of Versailles had been resolved, Hitler and the Nazi régime would have no further function and would disappear.

Hitler as a person seemed as difficult to decode as his book. Eric Phipps, Rumbold's successor in Berlin, had only three or four meetings with Hitler over the course of his first two years in Berlin.[4] In conference Hitler was taciturn, remote and unhelpful. When he did speak, it was in the form of long, rambling and boring monologues. Other senior Nazis, such as Göring and Ribbentrop (initially German ambassador to London, later foreign minister), who might have been expected to illuminate Hitler's thinking, were often difficult to take seriously. Phipps regularly described Göring as buffoonish and childlike, while Ribbentrop was dismissed as a complete 'windbag'. According to the historian W. N. Medlicott, Baldwin 'later reflected that Phipps' despatches from Berlin had too much wit and not enough warning: they did not alarm the Cabinet enough'.[5]

Some saw Hitler as a passing phenomenon – one who could not possibly last. Others thought him a puppet of industrialists or the generals. 'Moderate influences' in the German government (such as the army, or the leading industrialists, or Göring) would try to restrain him. At times Hitler seemed to denounce the goals of *Mein Kampf*, attributing the book to a youthful radicalism that he had long since left behind. On 21 February 1936 he told the French journalist Bertrand de Jouvenel that *Mein Kampf* was outdated and that 'the correction of certain pages in his book would be made upon the page of history'.[6] A few days later, on 28 February, he told the British historian Professor Toynbee that Britain and Germany would soon be firm friends. On 7 March Hitler remilitarized the Rhineland, overturning Versailles and Locarno at a single stroke.

Foreign diplomats were constantly encouraged to think that the excesses of the Nazi régime would moderate with the passing of the years. Hitler was careful to cultivate such hopes: Rumbold concluded in his last despatch on 30 June 1933 that Hitler would evolve into a moderate whose main concern would be to reduce German unemployment. Hitler's diplomatic methods caused further confusion. After initiating crises he would proclaim that peace was on the horizon – provided that a few more problems be solved. For example, ten days after Germany left the disarmament conference, Phipps reported that a disarmament agreement with Hitler was still possible. The reintroduction of conscription in 1935, the expansion of the German army in the same year and the remilitarization of the Rhineland in 1936 were all followed by promises that a European settlement was imminent.

For those who did realize the full extent of Hitler's ambitions clues were no easier to find. Even casual observers of the international scene soon understood that it was impossible to call Hitler's bluff and that he would go to war if pushed. The construction of alliances to maintain the balance of power was simply not an option.[7] The old diplomacy had been tried before and had failed disastrously in 1914. Instead, British statesmen chose to employ a different tradition in their country's foreign policy. Britain would act in a mediatory capacity to find solutions to European problems – as had been customary in nineteenth-century British diplomacy, or so it was believed. The more recent examples of Lloyd George's conference diplomacy and the Locarno treaties also came to mind. British leaders argued moreover that, were it not for the harsh Treaty of Versailles, the Nazis would never have come to power. Hitler found a responsive chord in Britain when he claimed that he was only trying to right the wrongs of Versailles. The Versailles settlement was frequently denounced in Foreign Office minutes as 'untenable' and 'indefensible'. Although Hitler's régime was distasteful, it was still important to deal with him, to resolve Germany's outstanding grievances and to reconcile Germany to the existing order. (Pro-German sympathy – as distinct from pro-Nazi sympathy – was widespread in Britain in 1933.) In any event, there did not appear to be any alternative. The British economy was weak and could not support a major rearmament drive. The armed forces were badly depleted and needed strengthening. If nothing else, Britain needed time.

Simon certainly subscribed to these views, but so did the vast majority of those in Britain who had any opinion on foreign policy.

A deal with Germany would have had the additional benefit of boosting the government's popularity. Anti-war sentiments still seemed very strong among the general population. The government could also point to the economic benefits of a relaxation of tension in Europe. So the search for an agreement with Germany began.

Anti-war sentiment in Britain

How deeply rooted was pacifism in Britain in 1933? Since reliable opinion polls did not yet exist, it is difficult to assess public opinion at the time. The only real evidence is in the newspapers, the results of by-elections and anecdotal material. In the late 1920s and early 1930s the British reading market had been flooded with a number of memoirs from First World War veterans, many of which made clear the absolute horror of war in the trenches. Edmund Blunden's *Undertones of War* appeared in 1928, followed by Robert Graves' *Goodbye to All That* in 1929 and Siegfried Sassoon's *Memoirs of an Infantry Officer* in 1930. Most successful by far was *All Quiet on the Western Front*, written by a German veteran, Erich Maria Remarque. Initially published in German, it was immediately translated into English and sold 3.5 million copies within the first fifteen months of publication. But did such anti-war feeling translate into opposition to rearmament? And what did the government think was the temper of the times?

In later years, especially in his 'appalling frankness' speech to the House of Commons on 12 November 1936, Baldwin argued that the people's opposition to rearmament in 1933 was so strong that he could not even raise the issue in public. According to critics, Baldwin delayed rearmament efforts because, by implication, it would have meant taking an unpopular political stand. He thus left himself open to accusations that he had put party interest ahead of national interest, a charge that seemed to dovetail with his image as a procrastinator. Baldwin and his defenders have cited as evidence of the state of public opinion the October 1933 by-election at East Fulham, the Oxford Union 'King and Country' resolution of 9 February 1933 and the Peace Ballot of 1935.

In addition, one could cite the Peace Pledge Union (PPU), which was founded in 1934 by Canon Richard Sheppard, a popular radio personality who had also served as vicar of St. Martin-in-the-Fields in London and as dean of Canterbury. During the war Sheppard had been an army chaplain. In October 1934 he sent a letter to the editors of British newspapers in which he asked readers to send him a postcard if they agreed with his resolve never to support war again. Only three papers published the letter, but the results were astonishing. Within days the local post office was having to use a special van to deliver the replies to Sheppard's house. One year later replies were still pouring in at the rate of 400 per day and by October 1935 he had collected no fewer than 80,000 pledges. In May 1936 he established the PPU to promote anti-war activity. The PPU set up a newspaper named *Peace News* and gained the support of such prominent intellectuals as Bertrand Russell and Aldous Huxley. By 1939 it enjoyed a membership of 130,000.[8]

The PPU was a spectacular success, but it is not the only evidence of anti-war sentiment. One of the best-selling books in Britain in the mid-1930s was *We Did Not Fight*, an anthology of recollections by conscientious objectors in the First World War, and by the mid-1930s an estimated fifty anti-war organizations were active in Britain. But what exactly did this blizzard of anti-war activity signify? The Peace Ballot and the confused state of British public opinion in 1935 will be covered later, but for the present, the Oxford 'King and Country' debate and the Fulham by-election deserve closer study.

The Oxford debate and the Fulham by-election

Ten days after Hitler became chancellor of Germany, the Oxford Union debated the resolution 'That this House will in no circumstances fight for its King and Country'. The motion was passed by a vote of 275 for, 153 against. News of the vote was received with incredulity by the sensationalist right-wing press, and some Oxford graduates, led by Randolph Churchill, son of Winston, mounted a campaign to have the resolution expunged from the Union's records.

The campaign failed and a few weeks later the Union again re-affirmed its support for the original motion. Since Oxford was seen as the training ground for the ruling élite of the British Empire, events at that university tended to assume national significance. The 'King and Country' resolution is cited as an example of the deep-seated pacifism that existed in Britain just after Hitler gained power, a pacifism that limited the government's range of options. In 1948 Winston Churchill alleged that the Oxford debate had conveyed to Hitler and Mussolini the message that the youth of Britain would not fight.

A closer look at the Oxford debate reveals a different story.[9] The motion of 9 February was passed on the strength of a strong and highly entertaining speech by the widely known speaker and author C. E. M. Joad. The students appear to have reacted mainly against the mindless jingoism and militarism of 1914 and wanted to ensure that a similar mistake would never be made again. 'Pacifism' in 1933 was not precisely defined, and virtually everyone who was opposed to 'militarism' described themselves as a pacifist. The Oxford Union reaffirmed the original motion a second time in response to outside criticism led by a pushy and deeply disliked Randolph Churchill, who had attended Oxford from 1929 to 1932 but left without a degree to enter journalism. The students also felt that they were victims of a malicious and deceitful press campaign and thus rallied round their leaders. Right-wing papers campaigned against the Union primarily because they were dismayed at the growth of Labour Party and left-wing thinking at Oxford. The 9 February resolution was a convenient excuse for right-wing journalists to lash out at those students who did not appear to be following in the respectful footsteps of their elders. Winston Churchill attacked the Oxford Union after the war for two reasons: first, his son Randolph had lost the 'expunging' debate, and second, Winston himself was laughed at during a speech advocating rearmament at the Oxford Conservative Association in 1934, an episode he apparently never forgot. No evidence has ever been produced to show that Hitler even learned of the Oxford debate. Although Mussolini may have heard an account, he certainly did not base any policy decisions on what happened at Oxford in 1933. Furthermore, none of the students who voted in favour of the motion in 1934 registered as conscientious objectors in 1939. In the interim they were convinced that Hitler was a greater menace to world peace that British jingoism. At bottom, the students who voted in favour of the 'King and Country' resolution did so because they recognized the first-rate debating skills of C. E. M. Joad, topped off with a protest against 1914-style jingoistic 'militarism', and little more.

The orthodox version of the East Fulham by-election result holds that a pro-rearmament government candidate was soundly defeated by a Labour candidate who campaigned mainly on the 'pacifist' issue.[10] The swing against the government was one of the biggest in British electoral history and East Fulham ushered in a string of by-election disappointments for the National government. Although the National government candidates won subsequent by-elections, their share of the vote dropped dramatically.

Analyses of the East Fulham result suggest that the voters were concerned with local and domestic issues, such as housing conditions, and that pacifism played a comparatively minor role.[11] The East Fulham by-election was also skewed by the fact that the Liberals did not put forward a candidate. The East Fulham Liberal organization endorsed the Labour candidate John Wilmot because he had responded favourably to a questionnaire on disarmament. For East Fulham Liberal voters disarmament was probably the main issue (and they were numerous enough to put Wilmot over the top), but most Labour supporters had more immediate concerns. Labour was also assisted in its campaign by having a candidate who was effective and articulate. The Conservative candidate, William Waldron, was inept and hampered by poor organization.

Some members of the cabinet suspected as much and few ministers expressed any concern about the East Fulham result. Baldwin, by contrast, chose to regard the by-election as hugely significant and continued for the rest of his life to cite it as an example of the public mood in 1933. However, he may have been seeking to justify a passive foreign policy during his third term as prime minister (1935–37). The work of some historians suggests that although substantial anti-war sentiment obviously existed in Britain, it was not what we understand today as pacifism (opposition to all war).

Support for 'pacifism' in 1933 was confused, comparatively soft and flexible enough to allow for a change of direction on the part of the government.

Military policy

Even if British politicians had wanted to rearm fully in 1933, could they have done so? Was British industry in any condition to embark on a full-scale rearmament drive? Historians have identified a number of economic limitations that faced Britain, not only in 1933 but during the whole period leading up to 1939. Skilled labour was in short supply. A rearmament drive might 'distort' the economy and take resources away from the export trade. Export earnings would decline and leave less revenue for further rearmament. The economy might also become overheated and prices would rise, which would lead to crippling strikes and possibly another slump. Treasury objections produced much frustration in military circles, some soldiers complaining that the main concern of the Treasury was to ensure that payment of reparations could be met after Britain lost the war. Not all historians have been convinced by such arguments, but in the mid-1930s concerns over the viability of the British economy acted as a real restraint on rearmament.[12]

Hitler's accession to power, combined with the Japanese threat in the Far East, prompted a modest rethinking of British defence policy. Although the government had scrapped the Ten Year Rule in 1932, the future direction of British defence planning remained unclear. In the autumn of 1933 the Chiefs of Staff warned the cabinet that substantial German rearmament was under way and that British defences were seriously depleted. The cabinet decided to set up a committee, subsequently known as the Defence Requirements Committee (DRC), to take stock of the world situation and recommend measures to promote British security. The committee included Vansittart from the Foreign Office, Fisher from the Treasury, the three Chiefs of Staff and Maurice Hankey in the chair. Deliberations began in November and the report was issued on 28 February 1934.

The DRC report of 1934 identified Germany as the 'ultimate potential enemy against whom our "long range" defence policy must be directed'.[13] German rearmament was the most serious threat to British security in Europe and considerable attention was drawn to the air threat to British cities, industry and shipping. Japan was identified as a second major threat. The report argued that Britain could do little to counter the rise of Japanese power in the Far East. The base at Singapore was incapable of supporting a fleet as it lacked infrastructure, supplies and personnel. The deterioration in Anglo-Japanese relations was blamed by Fisher on Britain's decision to end the Anglo-Japanese alliance in 1922 and draw closer to the United States. Vansittart was much more preoccupied with the menace from Germany. He was increasingly inclined to see Hitler as a 'mad dog', capable of unleashing a 'knock-out blow' from the air that might cripple Britain within hours.

The DRC argued that Britain should create a 'Regular Expeditionary Force' to be sent to the continent within one month of a declaration of war. This force should consist of four infantry divisions, one cavalry division, two air defence brigades and one tank brigade. Its function was to defend Belgium and France and prevent the Germans from setting up air bases that would be within striking distance of London. The DRC recommended an expansion of the Royal Air Force to fifty-two squadrons, with another twenty-five in reserve if Germany should continue to rearm. The cost of expanding both army and air force was estimated at £82 million over eight or nine years. Upgrading of the Royal Navy was also needed, which would also be a costly exercise. The bulk of the funding for remedying Britain's defence deficiencies would go to the army, the navy coming next in line and the air force trailing well behind. The DRC report triggered a long debate within the British government on the direction of defence policy. A series of cabinet debates followed the tabling of the DRC report, during which Neville Chamberlain emerged as a powerful force.

Neville Chamberlain

Neville Chamberlain was the younger half-brother of Austen Chamberlain. Born in 1869, Neville initially set out on a career in business. In his youth he managed a family sisal plantation in the

Bahamas and spent seven years working doggedly at a venture in which his father had invested £50,000 before conceding that sisal could not grow in the Bahamian climate. He returned to Birmingham and embarked on a career in municipal politics. By 1915 he was mayor of Birmingham – an astonishing rise that testified to the future prime minister's considerable political skill. In 1916 he was appointed Director of National Service, a position of great responsibility, but quickly incurred the wrath of Lloyd George, who fired him seven months later. Chamberlain never forgave Lloyd George, and the latter referred to Chamberlain contemptuously as 'that pinhead'.[14] The war years were difficult for Chamberlain in another respect: in 1917 his cousin Norman, with whom he had forged a close friendship, was killed on the Western front.

Chamberlain bounced back quickly, winning election to the House of Commons as a Conservative in 1918. He served briefly (in 1923–24) as minister of health and chancellor of the exchequer before returning as minister of health in Baldwin's second government (1924–29) and made an impression as a capable, efficient and progressive minister. His ascent continued under the National government when he was again appointed chancellor of the exchequer in 1931. Following MacDonald's decline Chamberlain emerged as a major force in the cabinet, second only to Baldwin. Like many politicians, he was convinced of his own indispensability and sometimes wondered how the rest of the cabinet could function without him.[15]

Chamberlain was supremely self-confident and had his own ideas on defence. His starting-point was that finance, or the economic health of the country, was the fourth arm of defence. The lesson of World War One had been that a sound economy would enable Britain to fight a long war. For Chamberlain a sound economy meant a balanced budget and a strong export trade. As a fiscal conservative he staunchly opposed the idea of taking out a loan to finance rearmament.

In a series of cabinet and committee meetings following the tabling of the DRC report Chamberlain managed to gain acceptance of his views on defence priorities. His main focus was on the German air threat. He certainly recognized that Japan posed a danger but always felt that Japan could best be dealt with by patient diplomacy. As for Germany, Chamberlain thought that Britain should build up a deterrent bomber force so powerful that Germany could only deliver a knockout blow to Britain at the cost of receiving a retaliatory knockout blow from Britain. By the autumn of 1934 Chamberlain had effectively reversed the spending priorities outlined in the DRC report. Scheme A, the first in a long series of schemes for the expansion of the Royal Air Force, called for an air force of seventy-five squadrons. The army would receive half the funds requested in the DRC report. The Royal Navy upgrades would have to await the results of discussions with Japan and the United States on the future of the Washington Treaty. Strengthening the RAF had the added benefit of being the cheapest form of rearmament and an effective method of countering public fears of a knock-out blow in the next war.

The road to Stresa

In the meantime, Germany had not remained idle. Hitler's foreign policy received a significant boost with the conclusion of the German–Polish non-aggression treaty in January 1934. Although the treaty contained some economic clauses allowing Polish access to German markets, Germany emerged as the main beneficiary. At a single stroke Hitler had significantly reduced tension on his eastern border. Poland had signed an earlier alliance with France in 1925, and the German–Polish treaty of 1934 contained a clause acknowledging Poland's obligations to France, but few observers doubted that Hitler had taken a major step in undermining France's eastern European alliance system.

The German–Polish treaty jolted France and inspired a renewed search for allies to contain Germany. Two candidates immediately presented themselves: Italy and the Soviet Union. The Soviets, long outcast by the European community, felt profoundly threatened by the rise of Hitler and, by 1934, seemed anxious to end their isolation. Mussolini, while being deeply sympathetic towards the Nazi régime for ideological reasons, remained apprehensive of any revival of German power. Such a revival might lessen the influence of Italy on Europe as a whole. More specifically, a resurgent German nationalism might once again threaten Austria, which served as a buffer state between Italy and Germany, and Italy had an interest in ensuring that Austria maintain its independence. The Treaty of Versailles had given Italy an area known as South Tyrol (Alte Adigio) in which about half a million German-speaking citizens resided. Germany might demand the incorporation of these people once Austria had been absorbed.

The threat to Austria surfaced in 1934. In July of that year Austrian Nazis (encouraged and supported by the German embassy in Vienna) attempted a coup d'état. The coup was crushed, although not before the Austrian chancellor, Dollfuss, was murdered by Nazi supporters. During the coup the Italian army had mobilized troops along the Italian–Austrian border in a show of force that was meant to give a warning to Hitler. He, however, immediately denied any German involvement in the coup. The incident served to accelerate co-operation between France and Italy. In the first week of January 1935 the French and Italians signed a pledge of co-operation in the event of a German threat to Austria. In return for Italian assistance France agreed to give Mussolini a 'free hand' in 'economic matters' in the independent African kingdom of Abyssinia.[16]

The French enjoyed similar success in cultivating ties with the Soviet Union. Having foolishly ignored Hitler during his rise to power, Stalin was now deeply alarmed by the potential growth of German military power. The League of Nations, which had been formerly denounced in Soviet propaganda as an imperialist conspiracy, suddenly became a force for containing fascism. In September 1934 the Soviets joined the League at France's prompting but with only the most grudging support of the British. The Soviets had now apparently joined the ranks of those advocating 'collective security'. The Soviet foreign minister, Maxim Litvinov, was very strongly identified with the new Soviet line.

By the end of 1934 French policy had made considerable head-way. It seemed that France was about to recreate the coalition that had defeated Germany in the First World War. Unfortunately, in the early months of 1935 Hitler regained the initiative. In January the Saar Valley plebiscite produced an overwhelming vote in favour of unification with Germany. The plebiscite was a notable victory for Hitler, who exploited it for all it was worth.[17]

Meanwhile, Simon had spent the last few months of 1934 trying to work out a policy on German rearmament. In December 1934 the cabinet had set up a Committee on German Rearmament, chaired by an ailing MacDonald and dominated by Simon. In general, Simon believed that little could be done to stop German rearmament. The military clauses of Versailles were dead and Britain should accept German rearmament as an inevitable fact. Simon proposed making an agreement with Germany, under which Britain would accept a limited degree of German rearmament. In exchange Germany would have to return to the League and to the disarmament conference. Simon pointed out to his colleagues that if his policy were successful, the government would score points with the electorate: the government could argue that it was promoting disarmament and international security by achieving agreement with Germany. France, however, might be a stumbling block: Simon suspected that Paris would not respond favourably to Britain's attempts to reach agreement with Germany. Nevertheless, Simon dropped hints to the French as early as July 1934 that Britain wanted to discuss naval matters with Germany in the near future. The committee's report, which was adopted by the cabinet in late December 1934, endorsed Simon's strategy.

It was still necessary for London to co-ordinate its strategy with Paris. On 3 February the two governments published a four-point plan to promote European security. The plan included a settlement on armaments, an Eastern Locarno, Germany's return to the League and an addition to the original Locarno treaty that would prohibit the use of air power as an instrument of aggression. In response, Hitler accepted the idea of an air pact but expressed complete lack of enthusiasm for the other proposals. The British cabinet was encouraged by the apparent willingness of the French to abandon Versailles and, it seemed, the emergence of an Italian–French–British front against Germany. The cabinet felt that the time had come for Simon to visit Berlin to discuss European affairs with Hitler. The British also hinted at the desirability of talks on naval issues with Germany.

The urgency of obtaining agreement with Germany was partly propelled by difficulties with Japan. Preliminary discussions with the United States and Japan at the end of 1934 on the future of naval disarmament had proved discouraging: the Japanese would settle for nothing less than full equality with the United States and Great Britain. On 29 December 1934 Japan denounced the Washington Naval Agreement. With reports on the progress of German naval building reaching London Britain was confronted with the possibility of a renewal of the costly naval race that had preceded the First World War and that, in some eyes, made war almost inevitable. Great urgency was given to securing a deal with Germany. Simon made arrangements to go to Berlin in March to begin preliminary talks. Eden was to accompany him to Berlin and then visit East European capitals, including Moscow, on his own. By February 1935 the Admiralty was particularly insistent on the need for agreement with Germany. The Germans were already indicating that they would ask for a naval tonnage thirty-five per cent that of Britain's. Many in the British government hoped that the German demand was simply a bargaining position that could be whittled down.

Progress was seriously delayed by the publication of a British White Paper on defence on 4 March 1935. Written by a committee over MacDonald's signature, it was a fairly innocuous document that proclaimed Britain's intent to rearm as a necessary response to German rearmament. The White Paper had been issued mainly for political reasons: the government had to be seen to be doing something. On the day that the document was issued the French government announced that it was increasing the term of conscription from one year to two. Again, German rearmament was the justification.

Hitler reacted badly. He declared that he had caught a cold during the Saar celebrations and therefore could not receive Simon. What followed was even worse. First, on 9 March, Göring announced the existence of a German air force that, he claimed, was powerful enough to crush any enemy. Although Göring's boast was a wild exaggeration, it still came as a sensational shock to British public opinion. Then, on 16 March, Hitler announced that Germany had unilaterally repudiated the disarmament provisions of the Treaty of Versailles. Germany would reintroduce conscription and create an army of thirty-five divisions or half a million troops, roughly equivalent to the size of the French army. It was a brilliant stroke on Hitler's part that deprived the British of bargaining chips just before Simon's visit. No longer could the British and French agree to allow German rearmament in exchange for concessions on other issues.

Some thought was given to cancelling Simon's visit altogether. Ultimately, Simon decided that he really had no alternative but to continue the search for agreement with Germany. His reasoning was expressed as follows:

> We should not retort by saying that now we will not go to Berlin. After all, what ultimate end would that serve? It will not alter the German decision and it will break down what ever contact is left and destroy finally any prospect of agreeing about anything. It would be quite a different matter if excommunicating Germany would lead to a combination to stop her. On the contrary, it would have quite the opposite effect.[18]

The British did send a protest to Berlin, but, as was noted at the time and by historians ever since, the effect of the protest was undermined by a rather pleading enquiry as to whether or not Simon could still go and call on Hitler.

Simon's meeting with Hitler on 25 and 26 March produced little in the way of results. Hitler was evasive and absolutely refused to give any promises. He declined to commit Germany to an Eastern Locarno, would not guarantee Austrian independence and expressed no interest at all in having Germany return to the League. Although he had earlier seemed interested in an air pact, he now responded with only vague assurances and claimed that Germany had reached air parity with Britain. His only encouraging response was to a proposal for naval disarmament. Here he seemed interested in doing something. Again he mentioned a navy that would be thirty-five per cent the size of Britain's. Simon proposed a conference in London to work out the technical details, to which Hitler instantly agreed.

Simon's visit was a notable disappointment. A brief period followed during which it appeared that Simon was rethinking his policy of seeking agreement with Germany. Reflecting on his experience in Berlin, he concluded: 'all this is pretty hopeless. We may see the curious spectacle of British Tories collaborating with Russian communists while the League of Nations Union thunders applause.'[19] The next few weeks saw an acceleration of the trend towards collective security. Eden received a warm reception in Moscow and discovered considerable enthusiasm in Eastern European capitals for a policy aimed at containing Germany. A meeting was scheduled with the French and the Italians at Stresa in April to work out a common policy on Austria.

Simon soon had second thoughts. The urgency of reaching a bilateral accord with Germany continued to assert and impress itself on the cabinet. Hitler's claim that the German air force (Luftwaffe) was strong enough to challenge the RAF was soon proved false. The Germans were, however, building aircraft at an impressive rate (or so the British believed) and would soon be in a position to deliver their knock-out blow. The press expressed deep alarm at the growth of German air power by the spring of 1935. The British government hoped that a bilateral accord with Germany on naval armaments might start a process that would lead to a similar agreement on air power. That hope was held by Simon, Vansittart, Eden, the Admiralty and the cabinet.

The 'front' which resulted from the meetings at Stresa on 11–14 April 1935 was already being undermined by Britain's pursuit of a bilateral accord with Germany. At Stresa MacDonald and Simon met with Laval, the French foreign minister, and Mussolini. In a public statement they reaffirmed support for the League and Locarno. The three powers pledged to preserve Austrian independence and generally maintain the status quo in Europe. Germany's unilateral actions in overturning Versailles were criticized. Stresa was not a formal alliance, since none of the powers committed themselves to specific action if Germany should violate Locarno or commit an act of aggression, but it none the less qualifies as a major success in the French campaign to create an anti-German front. The French diplomatic offensive was furthered on 2 May with the signature of the Franco-Soviet Pact, a mutual defensive alliance. Two weeks later the Soviets signed a pact of mutual assistance with Czechoslovakia. The potency of the Soviet–Czech Pact was perhaps diminished by the fact that it would only come into effect if the Franco-Czech pact of 1925 came into effect first. At the same time the Comintern announced the new Popular Front policy. European communist parties were now to form alliances with liberals, social democrats and anyone opposed to fascism. Social democrats, previously called 'social fascists' and singled out for scorn by communists, now became potential allies for communist parties.

Simon did not like Stresa or any of these new developments, especially the Franco-Soviet pact. He feared that Britain might be dragged into giving the sort of continental commitment that every British government since 1919 had tried to avoid. Neither Simon nor Baldwin wanted Germany to feel encircled and therefore reluctant to join a European settlement. In May the British government heard rumours that Japan would be willing to attend an international naval conference if European powers could work out some sort of agreement between themselves first. In late April the German government had publicly admitted that it had started to build submarines. Hitler gave a speech in the Reichstag on 21 May 1935 in which he proposed a naval agreement that would give Germany a naval strength thirty-five per cent that of Britain's. By that point the British cabinet was ready to come to terms.

The Anglo-German Naval Agreement

The signature of the Anglo-German Naval Agreement (AGNA) on 18 June 1935 was a major blow to French diplomacy. Negotiated without the prior knowledge of their government, the AGNA came as a terrible shock to the French. Furthermore, the signing of the agreement took place, inadvertently, on the 120th anniversary of the Battle of Waterloo, prompting comment in France of 'perfidious Albion'. The AGNA allowed the Germans to build not only a navy up to thirty-five per cent the tonnage of Britain's but also a submarine fleet equal to that of Britain. The AGNA fulfilled virtually all of Britain's foreign policy aims in early 1935. It promised to head off a financially ruinous naval race, to limit German naval strength and to allow a greater concentration of force on Japan. It also promised to be the first step in a comprehensive programme of

European arms control, perhaps leading to an air pact. Finally, it gave Simon a badly needed triumph and reassured public opinion. Anti-war sentiment was running high in Britain in June 1935, with the Peace Ballot campaign (see below) about to reach a conclusion.[20]

The AGNA has been criticized on the grounds that it undermined both the Stresa front and the Treaty of Versailles, and it has occasionally been cited as a glaring example of the folly of appeasement. Versailles had placed strict limitations on the size of the German navy (no armoured ships of more than 10,000 tons) and Stresa had pledged to uphold the European status quo. The AGNA weakened both. The argument that there was nothing in Versailles or at Stresa that prohibited a bilateral arms limitation agreement seems a little too clever. However, it must also be recognized that the AGNA represented the culmination of profound currents in British foreign policy in 1934–35. Some in the Foreign Office, such as Vansittart, doubted that Hitler would keep his word but still thought it worthwhile trying to make him do so. Ultimately, Vansittart's worst fears were realized. The AGNA can perhaps be seen as a noteworthy attempt to achieve reconciliation with Germany, but eventually Hitler ignored it, as he did virtually all other agreements.

The weeks prior to the signing of the AGNA saw some reshuffling in the British cabinet. On 7 June MacDonald finally resigned as prime minister and was succeeded by Baldwin. The fiction of a National government remained, but it was almost wholly a Conservative machine, with a tiny faction of Liberals and a splinter group of former MacDonald supporters. Simon became home secretary, while Chamberlain continued as chancellor of the exchequer. The new foreign secretary was Samuel Hoare. Despite his popularity, Eden was not given serious consideration as successor to Simon.

Samuel Hoare

Born in 1880 and educated at Oxford, Hoare first won election to Parliament as a Conservative in 1910. He described his family background as typically Victorian with a strong Quaker Evangelical tradition. He had been horrified by the Great War, thought it had been the war to end all wars and claimed to subscribe to League principles. His previous cabinet posts included secretary of state for air and secretary of state for India. Short in stature, he was notorious also for his short temper. Some of his colleagues called him 'an intriguing little brute', and at least one of Baldwin's advisers feared that Hoare's appointment would cost Baldwin the next election.[21] On the positive side, Hoare was a reliable minister and a capable administrator with many political allies in spite of his personality. Since Baldwin thought Eden was still too young, Hoare succeeded to the post of foreign secretary. He soon found himself out of his depth. He had just spent four years dealing with the intricacies of the Government of India Bill and arrived at the Foreign Office with minimal briefing. He was unfamiliar with the details of the AGNA, which was then on the verge of being signed.[22] Furthermore, a crisis was brewing over Abyssinia that required attention (see below), and a few weeks after his appointment as foreign secretary he and Baldwin were confronted with the results of the League of Nations Union Peace Ballot.

The Peace Ballot

Since leaving the cabinet in 1927 Cecil had emerged as the most prominent leader of the League of Nations Union (LNU). He was the prime mover behind the Peace Ballot, officially known as 'The National Declaration on the League of Nations and Armaments'. During 1934 LNU supporters expressed deep concern about the future of the League and the depth of the British government's commitment to the League. Manchuria, the break-up of the disarmament conference, the subsequent growth of isolationism and the decline in LNU membership left LNU supporters with a sense of grim foreboding. Rothermere's press campaign in favour of air rearmament in early 1934 reinforced fears of an arms race. Cecil and others in the LNU worried that the British government might try to escape from its commitments to the League. They decided that something had to be done to show the government that the League enjoyed substantial public support. Hence the idea for a referendum, carried out by the LNU, that would demonstrate dramatically to the cabinet that they ignored League principles at their peril.[23]

The referendum consisted of five questions:

(1) Should Great Britain remain a member of the League of Nations?

(2) Are you in favour of an all-round reduction of armaments by international agreement?

(3) Are you in favour of the all-round abolition of national military and naval aircraft by international agreements?

(4) Should the manufacture and sale of armaments for private profit be prohibited by international agreement?

(5) Do you consider that, if a nation insists on attacking another, the other nations should combine to compel it to stop by (a) economic and non-military measures? (b) if necessary, military measures?

Polling began in November 1934. Almost immediately the ballot came under attack from the right-wing press and from the Conservative Party. On 8 November 1934 Simon responded to a Labour motion condemning the private arms trade (question four) by criticizing the Ballot and accusing the LNU of socialist bias. It was a remarkably inept performance which implied that Simon favoured private arms trading, although he had not actually said so, and which managed to cast further doubt on the sincerity of the government's commitment to the League. Steadily the ballot process became politicized. The attacks on the ballot brought together a previously divided peace movement split into Christian pacifists, socialist war resisters and League supporters who vaguely hoped that the League could provide an alternative to war. All now jumped at the chance to crusade against a deeply distrusted government.

The success of the ballot depended on about half a million volunteers who went from door to door distributing the forms and returning to pick them up. Many homes had to be visited five or six times. One volunteer had less than pleasant memories of the experience:

> It meant calling at houses where the house-holder shouted at you and looked as though he might throw things at you, and at houses where the people were totally indifferent and apathetic. It meant having discussions with people who had strong opinions, and giving explanations to those who were puzzled. In rural areas it meant long journeys on foot to collect forms from isolated farms and villages.[24]

The Peace Ballot campaign attracted many women volunteers who were given a rare opportunity to express their views in large numbers on international issues during the inter-war period. Many volunteers came from the left, but it should be noted that the campaign attracted many Liberals and Conservatives as well and truly qualifies as a mass-based political movement.

Balloting ended on 27 June 1935 (nine days after the signature of the AGNA) with a rally at the Royal Albert Hall in London. More than 11.6 million people had voted, accounting for approximately thirty-eight per cent of the British population over the age of eighteen. The 'yes' vote for question one was almost ninety-six per cent, ninety per cent for question two, eighty-two per cent for question three and ninety per cent for question four. Even after allowing for the fact that 'no' votes were under-represented (most 'no' voters boycotted the ballot on the advice of the press, thereby inflating the 'yes' vote), it was clear that the League of Nations and disarmament enjoyed the support of the majority of the people of Great Britain. The response to question five shows a willingness to confront aggressors primarily through the use of League economic sanctions; much less enthusiasm surfaced for the military option.[25]

The Peace Ballot demonstrated that the people of Britain still believed in 1935 that 'collective security' (a term that came into common usage after 1933, replacing 'pooled security' and 'collective defence'), embodied in the League of Nations, constituted the best method of ensuring peace. Collective security was perceived as an alternative to war and to large standing armies, and it was hoped that the combined might of peace-loving countries in the League would prevent aggression. One may note a certain degree of self-deception, as many people clearly believed that League economic sanctions alone could deter aggression. Others, ironically, hoped that collective security would keep Britain out of the sort of complications in Europe that had led to Britain's involvement in war in 1914. Harold Nicolson, campaigning for election as a National Labour candidate in 1935, told of a letter he had received from a constituent who wanted Nicolson's assurances that he favoured the League and collective security and opposed any 'entanglements' in Europe. Nicolson read the letter aloud at campaign rallies. Hardly anyone noticed the contradiction. Support for the League and collective security meant involvement in the affairs of Europe as a matter of course.[26] Confusion over international affairs in Britain was widespread among the public in 1935.

Officially, Baldwin said that he accepted the results of the Peace Ballot. Although cabinet ministers had previously disparaged the ballot, they now made a point of showing how government policy upheld the League's ideal, and the League was portrayed as the keystone of British foreign policy. The sincerity of Baldwin's commitment to the League remains one of the historical controversies that surround the 1935 election. Did Baldwin mean what he said or was he playing cynically to the wishes of the voters? Further controversy concerns the related issue of rearmament. Some historians have argued that Baldwin downplayed the need for British rearmament in the 1935 election, deliberately misleading the public, whereas others have said that he was being pragmatic in following public opinion.[27] Still others allege that Baldwin called the election on 19 October because he wanted to get it out of the way before the limitations and weaknesses of British foreign policy became apparent in the budding crisis with Italy over Ethiopia (see page 179).

The election was held on 14 November 1935 (the last in Britain for ten years) and was a great triumph for Baldwin.[28] The National government won 428 seats with more than fifty-three per cent of the popular vote. No fewer than 386 of those seats were held by Conservatives. One of the few National government losers was Ramsay MacDonald. A safe seat was later found for him to contest in a by-election and he then returned to the cabinet in a symbolic post until his death in 1937. For his part, Harold Nicolson won first time round for the National Labour Party.

Labour, under its new leader Clement Attlee, won 154 seats, a gain of almost one hundred. More impressively, Labour captured thirty-eight per cent of the popular vote, a fact that caused some discomfort in government ranks. Although he lacked charisma ('a sheep in sheep's clothing', Churchill later remarked[29]), Attlee was a skilled parliamentarian who quickly set to work uniting his notoriously fractious party. The Liberals slumped to nineteen seats and their leader Herbert Samuel lost his own constituency. The election took place during the middle of the Italian invasion of Ethiopia, when the British government was determined to assuage public opinion and demonstrate its solidarity with the League.

Ethiopia

Ethiopia was one of only two African countries to escape the onslaught of late nineteenth-century European imperialism. During the 1880s the Italians had subdued the coastal Red Sea province of Eritrea. In 1896 an Italian army invaded Ethiopia as part of an attempt to carve out an African empire for Italy. The Italians suffered a stunning defeat at the Battle of Adowa, a catastrophe that was always remembered as a major calamity for Italian nationalists. During the 1930s, as part of his quest to rebuild the Roman Empire, Mussolini decided to avenge Adowa by again invading Ethiopia. Plans for the attack were drawn up as early as 1932.

Mussolini argued that the borders of Ethiopia were ill-defined, especially that between Ethiopia and Italian Somaliland. In pursuit of their claims the Italians established a garrison at the oasis of Walwal, deep inside Ethiopian territory. In December 1934 a clash took place at Walwal between Ethiopians and Italian-backed Somalis. Mussolini now had a pretext and he demanded an apology and compensation from Ethiopia. Italian troops began to mass in Eritrea in preparation for war.

Ethiopia was a member of the League of Nations. On 3 January 1935 the Ethiopian emperor, Haile Selassie, appealed to the League for help in maintaining the peace. A formal request for League arbitration followed on 17 March in the midst of the uproar over Hitler's reintroduction of conscription. The League responded in May by setting up a Committee of Five to negotiate a solution to the dispute. The committee for its part recommended a two-month delay during which the Italians and Ethiopians were to negotiate a settlement themselves.

Mussolini believed that the agreement with France in early January 1935 had given him permission to proceed in Ethiopia (see page 168). A few weeks later he hinted that an arrangement might be made with Britain. He apparently envisaged a naval limitations agreement with Britain in exchange for Italian predominance in Ethiopia. Simon did not give an immediate reply as he was then swamped with other issues, but in early March he established a joint Foreign Office and Colonial Office committee (headed by John Maffey of the Colonial Office) to report on the implications of an Italian conquest of Ethiopia.

Astonishingly, Maffey's committee did not report back until 18 June, when it concluded simply that it did not have the qualifications to discuss the implications for Europe of an Italian absorption of Ethiopia. Regionally, however, Britain had no interests in Ethiopia. An Italian absorption of Ethiopia would not affect the British positions in Somaliland, Egypt, Sudan, Kenya or Uganda. A copy of the report was forwarded to the British embassy in Rome, where it was promptly scooped up by Italian intelligence.

The Stresa conference in April 1935 dealt mainly with German issues, but Eden urged MacDonald to confront Mussolini and warn him not to invade Ethiopia. MacDonald unaccountably neglected to do so when he arrived at Stresa. Vansittart did not want a quarrel over Ethiopia at Stresa, since his priority was to maintain Austrian independence with Italian co-operation. 'I thought', he said later, 'a better tactic might be to land Mussolini first and lecture him later.'[30] Simon also failed to raise the issue. However, the possibility of an Italian move into Ethiopia arose in a discussion between a lower-ranking member of the British Foreign Office delegation and two members of the Italian Foreign Service. The British diplomat warned his Italian counterparts not to resort to force of arms.

In addition, in a speech at Geneva on 15 April Simon called for progress in negotiations to resolve the Walwal episode. Some warnings were also delivered by the British ambassador in Rome. On a number of occasions Italian diplomats were alerted to the fact that British public opinion would not tolerate an attack on Ethiopia. Mussolini took little notice, and late in April the Italian ambassador in London informed Simon that Italy intended to 'eliminate' Ethiopia before the situation in Europe became 'acute'. In a speech to the Italian Senate in May Mussolini claimed that neither Britain nor France had raised objections over Ethiopia. He also said that he would not bow to the will of the League and that Italy would resign from the League if it made trouble for him.

During a cabinet meeting on 15 May Simon predicted that an Italian advance would begin in late September or early October, after the end of the rainy season. In his view, Britain faced two equally unpleasant alternatives. Support for Ethiopia and the League would end the Stresa front and drive Italy into the arms of Germany. Acquiescence in the Italian conquest of Ethiopia would fatally weaken the League and lead to political catastrophe at home.

Ethiopian independence was not a popular cause within the British government. Ethiopia was regarded as a primitive, autocratic state with a harsh judicial system. Slavery was still legal in Ethiopia, much to the distaste of British opinion (for instance, Lady Simon was a prominent anti-slavery activist in the mid-1930s). Ethiopia's application to join the League of Nations in 1923 had been opposed by some in the Foreign Office, although the British delegation in Geneva eventually voted in its favour. The proclamation of an Italian protectorate over Ethiopia would have met with some sympathy in Britain. An Italian protectorate, especially under a League mandate, might have been portrayed as an altruistic act of bringing the benefits of civilization to a primitive state. Humanitarianism had long served as a justification for European imperialism. Nevertheless, Ethiopia was a member of the League, and if it were attacked the British government would have to stand by League principles, especially given the popularity of the League in Britain in an election year.

A consensus in favour of a compromise with Italy emerged in the Foreign Office. Vansittart was the prime mover behind the attempt to make a deal with Italy over Ethiopia. He agreed with Simon and did not want Britain to have to choose between the League and Italy, since the choice would have unpleasant consequences either way.

By mid-June 1935 the Foreign Office had drawn up compromise proposals for Mussolini's consideration. Ethiopia was to cede the southern province of Ogaden to Italy. In exchange Ethiopia would receive a corridor of land leading to the port of Zeila, in British

Somaliland, on the Gulf of Aden. Britain would foot the bill for Italian expansion. In explaining the Zeila deal Vansittart argued that he had 'long thought the distribution of this limited globe quite untenable, and quite unjustifiable. Like fools we made it far worse at Versailles'.[31] The British Empire was 'grossly over-landed (and British Somaliland was a real debit)'. Giving up Zeila would facilitate agreement between Italy and Abyssinia:

> The position is as plain as a pikestaff. Italy will have to be bought off – let us use and face ugly words – in some form or other, or Ethiopia will eventually perish. That might in itself matter less, if it did not mean that the League would also perish (and that Italy would simultaneously perform *another* volte-face into the arms of Germany, a combination of *haute politique* and *haute cocotterie* that we can ill afford just now).

Not settling with Italy would risk a 'disastrous explosion' that would 'wreck the League and very possibly His Majesty's Government too, if the League [were] destroyed on the eve of an election'.

Fear of Germany was the decisive determinant in British policy during the Ethiopian crisis. Italy must not be allowed to slip into Germany's orbit, especially since a hostile Italy could sever Britain's tenuous links through the Mediterranean and Suez to the Far East, where the British faced a hostile Japan. But Vansittart was also aware that the League was still popular with the British public. The Peace Ballot campaign, then coming to a conclusion, was obviously making an impact. Vansittart appealed to the survival instincts of British cabinet ministers facing re-election: the government's foreign policy had to be in lock-step unison with League principles or it might not survive the wrath of the voters. The Zeila compromise would head off the need to involve the League. Without a compromise Italy would invade Ethiopia, the League would be drawn in, the British government would have to side with the League, the Stresa front would rupture and Italy would side with Germany. Vansittart's pro-active diplomacy was designed to avoid such an unpleasant scenario.

Given that Mussolini had already indicated that he would settle for nothing less than the whole of Ethiopia, the Zeila proposal stood little chance of success when Eden delivered it to him in Rome on 24 June. Mussolini, who did not like Eden as a person, accorded him a very rude reception. The Duce said that he did not want yet another semi-arid desert plain. Eden also got an earful from the French when he stopped off in Paris on the way home. The French premier, Laval, delivered the full weight of French displeasure over the AGNA. Laval went on to say that he was not inclined to do anything to stop Mussolini from moving into Ethiopia. The French and Italians were working on a plan to demilitarize the Franco-Italian border, where both sides had stationed substantial numbers of troops. A demilitarization agreement could release ten French divisions for use on the German frontier, and Laval refused to jeopardize this agreement.

Vansittart, back at square one, tried again. By August the French had recovered from the shock of the AGNA and were much more co-operative. In that month Britain and France offered Italy a privileged economic position in Ethiopia, with the right to appoint Italian advisers to the police and install an Italian-dominated military and bureaucracy. Similar actions had usually preceded the establishment of a protectorate by a European state over an African state or territory. In a brilliant display of calculated reasonableness Haile Selassie accepted the August plan, as he had accepted the Zeila proposal. Again the Duce turned down the compromise, thereby reinforcing his image of international thug. In September the Committee of Five offered him yet another variation of the August proposal. He could have gained Ethiopia by the use of patient diplomacy, but he wanted military glory for his armed forces.

Italy invaded Ethiopia on 3 October 1935. Since Italy was the obvious aggressor, public opinion was overwhelmingly sympathetic to Ethiopia. On 11 October Italy was declared an aggressor state by fifty of the fifty-four members of the League Assembly. The time had come to apply sanctions. Baldwin had already warned the cabinet that the imposition of sanctions might entail the enforcement of a naval blockade on Italy. Britain, with the world's most powerful navy, would have to take the leading role. The likely result would be war with Italy.[32] The Admiralty was confident that Britain would win a war with Italy but pointed out that a number of capital ships would be lost. Britain would be further weakened if a possible confrontation with Germany or Japan ensued. The military also worried about a 'mad dog' act by Mussolini, a suicidal attack by Italian forces that would deplete British strength.

The cabinet had previously concluded in August that if Italy invaded Ethiopia the government would have no choice but to stand by the League. On 11 September Hoare gave a stirring speech to the League in Geneva in which he restated British support for the 'collective maintenance of the League Covenant in its entirety'.[33] British naval reinforcements were sent to Gibraltar in a blaze of publicity. Hoare soon discovered that Laval favoured the application of only the mildest form of sanctions and nothing more. Medlicott argues that the 'French attitude was decisive in this matter. If Britain had been prepared to impose military sanctions, France would not have followed her; if France had been prepared to impose military sanctions, probably the British government would have done so.'[34] Baldwin was particularly determined to maintain Anglo-French unity on Ethiopia and not to repeat the mistakes of Chanak.

Immediately following the condemnation of Italian aggression the League established a Committee of Eighteen to draw up a programme of sanctions. A Committee of Thirteen was established at the same time to seek conciliation. Meanwhile Hoare had embarked on what he called a 'dual policy'. In a carrot and stick approach sanctions would be applied through the League, but a political solution would be quietly sought at the same time. On 19 October Baldwin called the election for 14 November. For all the public knew, the British government stood solidly behind the League. From Baldwin's point of view, delaying the election call posed numerous risks. A strong pro-League, anti-Italian line might well trigger war with Italy, thereby ending any chance of gaining Mussolini's co-operation against Hitler. How would pacifist opinion in Britain react to the prospect of war, even if it were waged in support of the League? What about those in Baldwin's own party who favoured closer co-operation with Italy? What about the military losses in any campaign against Mussolini? On the other hand, a weak sanctions policy would leave the government open to charges that it had betrayed the League's principles. And how would Paris react if it were revealed to all the world that the French government favoured a soft line against Mussolini? Would Britain ever regain France's trust and co-operation after an embarrassment of that magnitude? Surely it must have seemed better to Baldwin to get the election out of the way before such questions were raised.

In mid-October Mussolini signalled that he was ready for compromise. Pressed by the Vatican, he outlined his proposals for a peace settlement on 17 October. He demanded an Italian mandate over the outlying provinces of Ethiopia, while the region around the capital of Addis Ababa would come under League control but with strong Italian participation. The October proposals amounted to a retreat, to some extent, on Mussolini's part. Secret negotiations began between the British, the French and the Italians. Meanwhile the sanctions programme, the stick in Hoare's dual policy, came into effect.

The sanctions that were imposed on 18 November were of a wide-ranging economic nature and Hoare believed they would prove effective. Sanctions on industrial commodities from non-League countries, however, were not imposed, which meant that oil from the United States continued to reach Italy. In fact, American oil companies increased their exports to Italy substantially during the Ethiopian war. An oil sanction imposed earlier would undoubtedly have been effective, but the League could do little to force compliance by non-members. The League hoped to put into place as quickly as possible those sanctions that could be enforced by League powers and then negotiate with non-League powers to urge them to follow the programme of League sanctions.

The behind-the-scenes negotiations produced results in early December. The British and French worked out a scheme that would see Ethiopia hand over areas in the south and north to Italy. Ethiopia would receive Zeila in compensation, although it would not be permitted to build a railway to connect the capital to Zeila. Italian economic primacy in the south of Ethiopia would be established, albeit under League supervision. The Ethiopian army would be abolished.

Hoare informed the cabinet in advance of the plan and obtained its consent to it before leaving for Paris where he was to gain final French approval. The scheme would then be put before Mussolini and Haile Selassie. Some cabinet members later claimed that they knew nothing of what Hoare was about to do, but their claims have not withstood historical scrutiny. Vansittart and Eden both apparently approved, and Vansittart was waiting in Paris to help Hoare with the details when he arrived on 7 December.

Publicly, Hoare said that his doctor had advised him to take a rest. Accordingly he was going to have a skating holiday in Zuoz, Switzerland (near St Moritz), with a brief stopover in Paris. Hoare quickly obtained the approval of Laval for what subsequently became known as the Hoare–Laval Pact, then left for Geneva.

News of the agreement was broken by the French press on 9 December. The Hoare–Laval plan immediately met with a wave of public outrage. It was viewed as an act of the 'old diplomacy'. Baldwin's government had only just been elected on a pro-League platform. As late as 31 October Hoare had denied press rumours that a secret deal was being worked out with Italy over Ethiopia. Now the government seemed to be pursuing a policy that was completely at odds with League principles. Mussolini was to be rewarded for his aggression by receiving a third of Ethiopia. The Zeila corridor was scorned as a 'corridor for camels'. Press commentary was uniformly hostile. The cabinet decided that Hoare had to go. Hoare graciously accepted the role of sacrificial lamb and resigned when he returned to London. To add to the humiliation, Hoare (who had been a speed skater of some renown in his youth) had blacked out while skating at Zuoz, fallen and broken his nose in two places. As with many disgraced politicians, Hoare was briefly the object of public ridicule. 'No more coals to Newcastle, no more Hoares to Paris', went one popular joke. Even King George V, a man not usually noted for a robust sense of humour, thought that joke a good one. Eden, at the age of thirty-eight, succeeded Hoare as foreign secretary. Hoare's exile did not last long. In June 1936 he returned to the cabinet as First Lord of the Admiralty.

The Hoare–Laval plan was a dead letter. Mussolini loudly rejected the plan, largely in order to save face, and by May 1936 his armies had bombed, poison-gassed and strafed their way into Addis Ababa. The oil sanction was never applied. In June the cabinet decided to recommend the lifting of League sanctions on Italy. It was argued that since the victim of the Italian aggression, Ethiopia, no longer existed, there was hardly any need for sanctions.

The results of the Ethiopian war could not have been worse for Britain. Throughout the crisis London's task had been to uphold League principles in Ethiopia, thus satisfying domestic wishes while retaining Mussolini's friendship. These factors had cleared the path for the Hoare–Laval plan. Now Ethiopia was lost, the League fatally discredited and the Stresa front irretrievably broken. Another layer of mistrust was added to Britain's relations with France. The British public mood shifted away from talk of collective security in the direction of isolationism from European affairs. Isolationism was further reinforced by the events of 1936.

Notes

1 Mussolini's power in Italy was always somewhat constrained by the army and the monarchy.
2 The disarmament conference continued with efforts to lure Germany back before finally dissolving on 11 June 1934.
3 See G. Morrell, *Britain Confronts the Stalin Revolution: Anglo-Soviet Relations and the Metro-Vickers Crisis* (Waterloo, Wilfrid Laurier University Press, 1995).
4 W. N. Medlicott, 'Britain and Germany: the Search for Agreement, 1930–37', in D. Dilks (ed.), *Retreat from Power: Studies in Britain's Foreign Policy of the Twentieth Century*, volume one (London, Macmillan, 1981), pp. 78–101.
5 Medlicott, 'Britain and Germany: the Search for Agreement, 1930–37', p. 83.
6 Medlicott, 'Britain and Germany: the Search for Agreement, 1930–37', p. 94.
7 See E. Gulick, *Europe's Classical Balance of Power: A Case History of the Theory and Practise of One of the Great Concepts of European Statecraft* (Norton, New York, 1955), for a lucid introduction to balance of power theory.
8 D. Lukowitz, 'The British pacifists and appeasement: the Peace Pledge Union', *Journal of Contemporary History*, IX, 1974, pp. 115–27.
9 M. Ceadel, 'The 'King and country' debate, 1933: student politics, pacifism and the dictators', *The Historical Journal*, XXII, 1979, pp. 397–422.
10 K. Middlemas and J. Barnes, *Baldwin: A Biography* (London, Macmillan, 1969), pp. 745–6, and P. Kyba, *Covenants Without the Sword: Public Opinion and British Defence Policy, 1931–35* (Waterloo, Wilfrid Laurier University Press, 1983), *passim*.
11 R. Heller, 'East Fulham revisited', *Journal of Contemporary History*, VI, 1971, pp. 172–96, and C. Stannage, 'The East Fulham by-election, 25 October 1933', *The Historical Journal*, XIV, 1979, pp. 165–200.

12 R. A. C. Parker, *Chamberlain and Appeasement: British Policy and the Coming of the Second World War* (London, Macmillan, 1993), pp. 272–93.

13 M. Howard, *The Continental Commitment: The Dilemma of British Defence Policy in the Era of the Two World Wars* (London, Temple Smith, 1972), p. 105.

14 Lloyd George was a follower of phrenology, the pseudo-science of the time that held that the personality of an individual was revealed in the shape of their head. H. M. Hyde, *Neville Chamberlain* (London, Harford, 1976), p. 27. In his early days as an opposition MP Lloyd George had been savagely critical of Joseph Chamberlain's policies in the Boer War.

15 See more on Chamberlain in Chapter Eight.

16 Medlicott, 'The Hoare–Laval Pact Reconsidered', in Dilks (ed.), *Retreat from Power*, volume one, p. 119.

17 C. Hill, 'Great Britain and the Saar plebiscite of 13 January 1935', *Journal of Contemporary History*, IX, 1974, pp. 121–42.

18 D. Dutton, *Simon: A Political Biography of Sir John Simon* (London, Aurum, 1992), p. 198.

19 Dutton, *Simon*, p. 201.

20 H. Hines, 'The foreign policy-making process in Britain, 1934–1935, and the origins of the Anglo-German naval agreement', *The Historical Journal*, XIX, 1976, pp. 477–99.

21 Middlemas and Barnes, *Baldwin*, pp. 336 and 822.

22 Simon announced the British acceptance of German proposals on 6 June as his last act in office. Hoare signed the formal agreement on 18 June.

23 M. Ceadel, 'The first British referendum: the Peace Ballot, 1934–5', *English Historical Review*, XCV, 1980, pp. 810–39.

24 Ceadel, p. 818. Original source N. Branson and M. Heinemann, *Britain in the Nineteen Thirties* (London, 1971) p. 304.

25 Eighty-six per cent 'yes' for question 5a and fifty-eight per cent 'yes' for 5b.

26 D. Birn, 'The League of Nations Union and collective security', *Journal of Contemporary History*, IX, 1974, pp. 131–59.

27 See, for example, the divergent views presented by Kyba, Middlemas and Barnes, Ceadel, Stannage, and Robertson (see note 28 for full citation), the last three being especially critical of Baldwin.

28 J. Robertson, 'The British general election of 1935', *Journal of Contemporary History*, IX, 1974, pp. 149–64.

29 A. Partington (ed.), *The Oxford Dictionary of Quotations*, 4th edn (Oxford, Oxford University Press, 1992), p. 203.

30 Middlemas and Barnes, *Baldwin*, p. 831.

31 Medlicott, 'The Hoare–Laval Pact Reconsidered', pp. 118–38.

32 Middlemas and Barnes, *Baldwin*, p. 840.

33 Middlemas and Barnes, *Baldwin*, pp. 856–7.

34 Medlicott, 'The Hoare–Laval Pact Reconsidered', p. 129. See also R. A. C. Parker, 'Great Britain, France and the Ethiopian crisis, 1935–1936', *English Historical Review*, LXXXIX, 1974, pp. 293–332, which stresses the importance, for the British, of maintaining unity with the French.

CHAPTER EIGHT

THE RHINELAND AND THE IMPACT OF THE SPANISH CIVIL WAR, 1936

Unlike the Ethiopian crisis, which built up slowly and stayed in the public view for a relatively long period, the Rhineland crisis of 1936 erupted suddenly on the European scene and then faded with the abruptness of a *fait accompli*.[1] The British cabinet had secretly suspected as early as January 1935 that an attempt by Germany to remilitarize the Rhineland might be forthcoming, but it was not until December of that year that the German press began to hint that Hitler was seriously considering the possibility. Stresemann had promised in 1925 to leave the Rhineland demilitarized as a gesture of German goodwill. If Hitler sent in the troops he would strike a fatal blow at both Locarno and whatever remained of the Versailles system. In mid-February 1936 Hitler decided to use the approaching ratification of the Franco-Soviet Pact by the French parliament as a pretext for remilitarizing the Rhineland.

British policy towards the Rhineland was influenced by several factors. Eden believed that France would not fight over the Rhineland and that French troops would remain strictly on the defensive if Hitler attempted remilitarization. A defensive posture had been enshrined in French military policy ever since work began on the construction of the Maginot line. In any event, the last French intervention on German soil, the Ruhr occupation of 1923–24, had ended in ignominious failure. If France did not intervene, Britain could hardly be expected to do anything by itself.

In February 1936 Eden approved an elaborate Foreign Office plan whereby Britain would accede to German remilitarization of the

Rhineland and, in exchange, Germany would promise not to change the status quo by force. Germany would also agree to begin negotiations for an air pact. Eden hoped to use the Rhineland as a bargaining chip and did not want to give it up for nothing. The cabinet took up discussion of the plan in early March.

The advice that Eden received from the Foreign Office emphasized the necessity of doing something to come to grips with Germany. Various ideas were advanced. One line of thinking advocated negotiations with Germany as a means of gaining time for rearmament. When rearmament was at a more advanced stage Britain could then negotiate from a position of strength. Others in the Economic Relations Section of the Foreign Office argued in favour of economic aid to Germany. A weak, heavily armed Germany was dangerous to European peace. The return of economic prosperity might undermine the appeal of Nazism. The use of economic aid to restore stability in Europe is known to historians as 'economic appeasement'. Vansittart, for his part, took up the idea of returning Germany's former African colonies in exchange for a German return to the League. As usual, Vansittart was enthusiastic, but Hitler saw little value in any colonial settlement.

Broadly, the Foreign Office in 1936 believed that Britain faced three alternatives in its dealings with Hitler. The first, inaction, or 'drift', was rejected out of hand. The second, forging alliances with Germany's potential enemies was dismissed as 'encirclement'. Britain might 'become the centre force in a great anti-revisionist block dressed in the cloak of collective security... In reality this block would differ little from the old pre-war defensive alliances'. The lesson of 1914 had of course been that defensive alliances led to war. The only alternative was the third: to 'come to terms with Germany in order to remove grievances by friendly arrangement and by the process of give and take, before Germany once again [took] the law into her own hands'.[2] Such reasoning formed a fundamental component of appeasement. An agreement with Germany would secure British and imperial security, head off a financially ruinous arms race and thereby maintain domestic harmony.

On 6 March Eden received permission from the cabinet to approach Hitler with the offer of an air pact. Achieving such a pact had been a long-standing goal in British foreign policy and one that would have alleviated public fears about the consequences of air power in the next war. Certainly the timing seemed propitious. In February Hitler had given the interviews to the French journalist Bertrand de Jouvenel and the British historian Professor Arnold Toynbee in which he had indicated a willingness to 'correct certain pages' in *Mein Kampf* and come to an agreement with Britain (see Chapter Seven). Eden was also advised by the cabinet to begin talks soon, before Hitler took unilateral action. Unfortunately, Hitler had already set the wheels in motion.

Hitler's troops entered the Rhineland during the early hours of Saturday 7 March 1936. Most British government officials and ministers had left London for their weekend houses in the country. The Germans used surprisingly small numbers of troops to carry out the remilitarization operation. Twelve infantry battalions numbering ten thousand troops were accompanied by eight artillery groups and 22,700 armed police. Initially only three battalions crossed the Rhine river. Behind them lay the rest of the German army, which in March 1936 could muster twenty-four infantry and three panzer divisions. However, the German army was nowhere near fully equipped, and the Luftwaffe lacked modern aircraft. In public, Hitler justified his action on the grounds that the 27 February ratification of the Franco-Soviet Pact by the French parliament had nullified the Locarno pact.

At one time it was fashionable to think that if the French and British had attacked the Germans in March 1936, the latter would have been forced to retreat and Hitler would have suffered his first defeat. The army might then have overthrown Hitler. It is an argument that ignores the essentially defensive stance of the French army. Furthermore, although Hitler had given orders to his forces to retreat if they met resistance, such a withdrawal would only have been the prelude to a renewed offensive and a general war. War in 1936 might have begun on marginally more favourable terms for Britain and France than it did in 1939, but the whole point of British foreign policy was to avoid war in the first place.

For the most part, public opinion in Britain seemed to accept the German action. Hitler's move was easily rationalized as a normal act of a sovereign power. After all, how could Britain object to German troops being stationed in German cities such as Köln? Shortly after the remilitarization Eden climbed into a London taxi and asked the driver what he thought of Germany's action. The driver replied simply: 'I suppose Jerry can do what he likes in his own back garden, can't he?'[3] The reaction of the press on Sunday and Monday was far from hostile to Hitler. Garvin of the *Observer* seemed generally sympathetic, while *The Times* attributed the German action to fears of encirclement. *The Times* went on to argue that Britain now had a chance to 'rebuild' the peace with Germany. Other leading dailies shared similar sentiments, including the *Daily Herald*. In the House of Commons Eden spoke of the need to 'appease' Europe.

The Rhineland remilitarization deprived Eden of a much valued bargaining chip. It was a tactic Hitler had used before, most recently with Simon in 1935, and he would use it again in the future. Hitler confused matters further by lavish promises of a deal with the Western powers, again repeating his method of the previous year. In the same statement as that given to Eden in which he announced the German move Hitler also proposed 25-year non-aggression pacts with France and Belgium, an air pact, non-aggression pacts in the East and a demilitarized zone along the French–German border (which would have required a dismantling of the Maginot line). Of course nothing came of these proposals and Hitler had not intended them to be serious. Some advantage was gained for Nazi propagandists, who portrayed the Western powers as obstructionist.

Since the remilitarization of the Rhineland violated the terms of Locarno, Britain and Italy, as the guarantors of Locarno, were obliged to consult together. By March 1936 Britain's relations with Italy were at a low point as a result of all that had gone wrong during the previous few months over Ethiopia. A few messages were exchanged. Mussolini for once kept his temper and simply 'reserved' Italy's position. The Duce was still uneasy about the German threat to Austria. The League Council condemned Germany's action but did not pursue the matter further.

Arguably, it was France's Eastern European allies who felt the consequences of the Rhineland episode most keenly. Following the remilitarization of the Rhineland the Germans quickly began to fortify the region. Once they had completed their fortifications they could stand on the defensive in the West (the French were not going to go over to the offensive) and pick off Poland and Czechoslovakia. Since the political leaders of Czechoslovakia had always looked to the West for security, the future for that state looked grim indeed.

Even if the French had decided to take action in March 1936 it is debatable whether Britain could have done anything. British defences were in no condition to allow the country to embark on war. The Royal Navy had deployed the bulk of its strength in the Mediterranean to guard against a 'mad dog' attack by Mussolini. The navy had three antiquated capital ships available in home waters, but no one was sure how they would perform against the new 'pocket' battleships that the Germans were bringing into service. The Germans had three pocket battleships in March 1936 – the *Deutschland*, the *Admiral Graf Spee* and the *Admiral Scheer*, while two larger battle-cruisers – the *Scharnhorst* and *Gniesenau* – were under construction.[4] Neither the British army nor the Royal Air Force had the capabilities needed for a major European undertaking. The army reported that it could muster only twenty battalions, none with modern equipment.

During January and February 1936 the cabinet debated further measures to upgrade British defences.[5] The new Defence Policy Requirements Committee, chaired by Baldwin (who actually attended only the first session), met nine times in January to debate rearmament. Chamberlain continued to oppose spending on the army, arguing that a more effective defence could be purchased by investing in the air force. The second White Paper on defence, which was presented to Parliament on 3 March 1936, proposed modest spending increases for the air force (mainly on bombers to deter Germany) and the navy while keeping the army in third place. The programme would cost £400 million over five years. The cabinet also decided to implement a 'shadow factory' scheme – though it was not made public at the time – whereby the government would provide funding to contractors to purchase additional equipment and set up production lines that could quickly convert to the production of war material in a national emergency. Finally, it should be noted that the cabinet decided in February, after severe criticism in the House (led by Austen Chamberlain) to create a Ministry for the Coordination of Defence to supervise rearmament plans. After considerable delay and hand-wringing Baldwin decided to appoint Thomas Inskip as the first holder of the new portfolio. Inskip was a lawyer with no background in defence matters, but he was politically unobjectionable and soon proved to be quite competent at his new job.

From the time of the remilitarization of the Rhineland until late 1937 relations between Britain and France on the one hand and Italy and Germany on the other can be described as watchful and suspicious but relatively calm. International attention focused instead on Spain, which descended into a bloody civil war in July 1936. The Spanish Civil War provided an opening for German and Italian ambitions while posing an awkward dilemma for Britain and France.

The Spanish Civil War

The history of the Spanish Civil War has faded from our collective memory. From the distance of sixty years students often approach the events of the Spanish Civil War with a sense of incomprehension. Why did Spain capture the imagination of people all over the world in the late 1930s? Forty thousand volunteers felt strongly enough about the issues at stake to fight and die in the Spanish war. For those on the left in Britain, the defence of the Spanish Republic against the forces of General Franco seemed to offer a real opportunity to stop the growth of fascism. George Orwell, for example, felt certain that at long last the British government would be compelled to take action against fascist aggression. Philip Toynbee, the writer and intellectual, thought that 'at last the gloves were off in the struggle against Fascism'.[6] For the government and the Foreign Office, however, the Spanish Civil War offered no obvious contrast between the forces of good and evil.

The long, slow decline of the Spanish Empire from its position of strength in the fifteenth century need not concern us here. The defeat of Spain at the hands of the United States in 1898, with the loss of Spain's last significant possessions in the Philippines and

Cuba, marked the end of Spain as a power of any significance. The early twentieth century found Spain to be an isolated, backward country dominated by the monarchy, a land-owning aristocracy and the Roman Catholic Church. A powerful anarchist movement, based in the countryside and among the members of Spain's embryonic working class, posed the main challenge to the established order.

In the 1920s the monarchy ruled through a military dictatorship, but popular discontent soon surfaced. The urban middle class was losing patience with the slow progress towards liberal democracy. Separatist challenges gained ground in Mediterranean province of Catalonia and in the northern Basque region. The country suffered grievously under the Depression and the monarchy was unable to cope. In 1931 the monarchy was ended and the Spanish Republic proclaimed.

Initially the Republic was governed by a middle-class liberal party that unfortunately failed to enact any substantial reforms. In the elections of November 1933 the right was returned to power. The next two years witnessed increasing tension leading to open class warfare. An uprising of miners in the north, supported by strikes in Madrid and Barcelona, was savagely suppressed by the army and thousands were killed. In January 1936 a liberal–leftist coalition called the Popular Front was formed. It included liberals, socialists, anarchists and a tiny communist party. In the elections of February 1936 the Popular Front swept to power.

The Spanish right never accepted the victory of the Popular Front. On 17 July 1936 the army attempted a coup d'état. The coup was quickly defeated in Madrid and Barcelona, where the government had had the foresight to arm trade union workers. Most of the centre and the south of Spain, as well as the Basque region in the north, remained under government control, but large areas of the north and west fell to the army.

The government forces, known as the Loyalists, possessed some notable advantages. They held the capital city, Madrid, formed the legitimate government of Spain, controlled the Treasury and could legally buy weapons abroad. But the rebels – known as Nationalists, under the leadership of General Francisco Franco – controlled the bulk of the Spanish army. The uprising had also succeeded in

Spanish Morocco, where the best units of the army were stationed, engaged in a war against a local Arab insurgency. The Spanish army in Morocco immediately returned to the mainland to launch an offensive on Madrid. The initial drive to take Madrid failed and the war degenerated into a bloody stalemate.

Foreign intervention in the war began almost immediately. German aircraft played a critical role in transporting Spanish army units from Morocco to the mainland. Hitler subsequently sent more aircraft, plus tanks, weapons and equipment, to Franco. The German experimental tank and aircraft contingent in Spain was known as the Condor Legion. At the peak of the war the Condor Legion fielded 200 tanks and 600 aircraft, backed by 10,000 support personnel. The Italians also came to the aid of Franco. At their maximum, Italian forces in Spain numbered between 40,000 and 50,000 troops, backed by 660 aircraft and 150 tanks.

Italy and Germany had common interests in Spain. Ideological affinities between Franco and his fascist mentors were strong and cannot be overlooked. Practical reasons also existed why Hitler should support Franco. A Spain dominated by Franco could threaten the British base at Gibraltar and serve as a second front against France. The taking of Gibraltar could unhinge Britain's entire position in the Mediterranean and sever the lifeline to India. Germany hoped to establish submarine bases in Spain that could threaten British shipping routes in the North Atlantic, while Mussolini wanted naval bases in the Balearic Islands. In addition, both Germany and Italy wanted to test new weapons, gain combat experience and win glory for their armies. Furthermore, Hitler needed access to Spanish supplies of iron and copper, both of which were valuable war materials. The Germans intended to barter for Spanish iron and copper by offering other war materials in exchange, thus saving Germany's scarce foreign reserves. Finally, the Spanish Civil War had a certain diversionary effect in that it drew the world's attention away from German rearmament.

The British government greeted the war with dismay and quickly decided to support a French proposal for a policy of nonintervention, which meant that all powers should stay out of Spain. Immediately after the outbreak of war Eden placed an embargo on

British arms shipments to Spain. He did so on his own initiative and apparently had some difficulty persuading the prime minister to pay attention to the issue.[7] Baldwin then told Eden that nothing should be done to help communism. In August 1936 the French government closed its border with Spain to arms trafficking and declared that it would not interfere in the war. The French Popular Front government that had come to power in May should have been sympathetic to its counterpart in Madrid, but it feared that active support of the Spanish Republic might provoke the French right and the Catholic Church. The French government had no intention of sparking a civil war in France along the lines of that in Spain.

The idea of non-intervention caught on and within one month twenty-six nations had issued statements of non-involvement, including Germany and Italy (despite having already violated non-intervention), Britain and the Soviet Union. Unfortunately, non-intervention was not a formal treaty but rather a mere declaration of intent and thus easily violated.

On 9 September 1936 a Non-intervention Committee was set up in London to monitor compliance with the policy of non-intervention. It soon became a symbol of hypocrisy since it was unable to do anything to stop Hitler and Mussolini from supporting Franco. Mussolini took great offence at non-intervention as it implied disapproval of his support for the Spanish fascists. The Spanish Civil War widened the breach between the Italians and the British and French, to the eventual benefit of Hitler. In Britain writers on the left and those most sympathetic to the Spanish Republic charged that non-intervention was a policy hatched by the Foreign Office to encourage a fascist victory in Spain and derail a leftist revolution. Such criticisms were valid to the extent that the immediate effect of non-intervention was to cut off support to the Republic while failing to stop support going to Franco. But as far as the British government was concerned, the objective of non-intervention was to localize and contain a conflict that might quickly escalate and draw in all the great powers, as had happened in 1914. Eden argued that a leaky dam was better than no dam at all.

Overall, British policy in the Spanish Civil War was guided by a determination to be on good terms with whichever side won the war. A Foreign Office memorandum of 1 September 1936 stated: 'It is highly desirable in either event that the government which does emerge should not enter upon its inheritance with any serious grudge against His Majesty's Government.' Strategically, the concern was to maintain the base at Gibraltar, which was very vulnerable to overland attack. The Chiefs of Staff pointed out in late August that a threat to Gibraltar carried with it a threat to Britain's whole position in the Mediterranean. As a result the Chiefs advised that one of Britain's major objectives must be to maintain 'such relations with any Spanish government that may emerge from the conflict as will ensure benevolent neutrality in the event of our being engaged in any European war'.[8]

The British government also worried that the war might heighten tensions between left and right in France, Britain's main European friend. French support for the Loyalists might prolong the war, intensify hostility between Italy and France and make any *rapprochement* between Britain and Italy impossible. For all these reasons, non-intervention seemed the logical policy for the British government to pursue. Spain posed a further danger, perhaps best explained by Neville Chamberlain in a speech to the House of Commons shortly after he took over as prime minister in May 1937. The Spanish war, he argued, was a struggle between two great ideologies with passionate supporters. Each side regarded the war as decisive to the cause:

> if some country or Government representing one of these two ideas attempts to intervene beyond a certain point, then some other country taking the opposite view may find if difficult, if not impossible to refrain from joining in, and a conflict may be started of which no man can see the end.[9]

After all, that was the lesson of 1914. An obscure struggle in the Balkans had drawn in the two great alliance systems and resulted in the horrors of the First World War.

Many on the right in Britain obviously hated the Spanish Republic and made no secret of it. Substantial evidence can be found of anti-republican, pro-Franco sentiment in governmental bodies as well. Ramsay MacDonald noted in August that 'enthusiasm for Franco [was] growing in Tory breasts', and that cabinet members

198

had absolutely no understanding of the differences between Socialism, Bolshevism and Nazism.[10] At least one member of the Foreign Office rebuked colleagues who, 'as Conservatives first and Englishmen after', preferred fascism in Spain as an 'antidote to Communism'.[11] A victory for the Republic was equated by some to a victory for Soviet communism. Many in the Foreign Office suspected that the Comintern was responsible for provoking the Civil War and accused it of having engaged in subversion for some time prior to the outbreak of the war. The Admiralty, mindful of the vulnerability of Gibraltar, was particularly hostile to the Republic. Admiralty officials feared that the Soviets would intervene in the war to support the Communist Party in Spain and then embark on a long-term programme of subversion in the region. In a Foreign Office memorandum dated 5 August Hoare, at that time First Lord of the Admiralty, argued:

> On no account must we do anything to bolster up Communism in Spain, particularly when it is remembered that Communism in Portugal, to which it would probably spread, and particularly in Lisbon, would be a grave danger to the British Empire.[12]

Such apprehensions also reflected traditional Admiralty fears, dating back to the 1820s, of any Russian influence in the Mediterranean that might threaten the British lifeline. Baldwin was characteristically dismissive: Britain must certainly not make a Soviet victory in Spain more likely, but he would not mind if Fascism and Bolshevism bled each other to death.

It should be remembered that in spite of widespread pro-Franco sympathy no British politician ever advocated involvement in the Spanish Civil War. The Conservative Party's hostility to the Republic was based, as MacDonald realized, not on emergent pro-fascism but on 'traditional Tory obscurantism' and reflex hostility to Soviet communism. The objective of the government was to prevent the balance of power in the Mediterranean from tilting against British interests, and that aim was ultimately realized.[13]

The involvement of the Soviets in the Spanish Civil War was substantial and it occasioned enormous controversy. They shipped about 1000 aircraft and 900 tanks to the Republic in addition to supplies, ammunition and advisers. The support of the Soviets for the Spanish Republic was consistent with their support for the united front strategy. The Civil War, however, was certainly not provoked by Soviet subversion. Similarly, the Republican government was never a Soviet puppet, although the malignant influence of the Spanish Communist Party had grown substantially by the end of the war. In fact, the Spanish communists did much – through factional infighting and the relentless purging of allies (and potential rivals to power, such as the anarchists) – to undermine the anti-fascist war effort.

During the course of the conflict the anti-fascist forces in Spain sank into a squalid civil war of their own, fought in parallel with the war against Franco. The divisions in the Republican ranks are vividly portrayed in George Orwell's *Homage to Catalonia*. Orwell fought for the anarchist militia in Catalonia (the POUM) and was shocked and dismayed when the communists turned on their anarchist allies in Barcelona in 1938. Anarchists were arrested, shot and imprisoned, their reputations blackened by groundless accusations of treason.

The infighting on the Republican side was glossed over by leftists in Britain who viewed the war as a simplistic battle of light against dark. The struggle of the Republic to hold Madrid captured the imaginations of thousands in Britain who wanted to stop fascism. Volunteers for the Republican cause were recruited, largely by the Comintern, into the International Brigades, which numbered 18,000 at the peak of their strength. A total of perhaps 40,000 volunteers from fifty nations served with the International Brigades in Spain at one time or another. About 2000 volunteers came from Britain, 500 of whom were killed and another 1200 wounded. The International Brigades were disbanded by the Republic in 1938 as part of an unsuccessful attempt to persuade Hitler and Mussolini to withdraw their forces.

The British Labour Party sympathized strongly with the Republic. It officially favoured non-intervention but also thought that the Republic should be able to buy weapons in Britain. The leader of the Labour Party, Clement Attlee, visited the Republic and expressed support for the cause, as did many other Labourites. The Spanish Civil War mobilized and inspired the British left, forcing many to re-examine and eventually abandon the pacifism of the 1920s and early 1930s. W. H. Auden's famous poem 'Spain 1937' voiced the sense of exhilaration experienced by many after they discovered that they could take action against the fascist threat.

The Spanish Civil War quickly became a topic of public debate. It reawakened a sense of purpose in politics and the conviction that the cause of the Republic was just. Arguments, pamphlets and speeches about the war poured forth, mostly outside the House of Commons, which seemed hopelessly irrelevant to the issue. In 1937 the periodical *Left Review* polled one hundred British writers on their views of the war. The results were instructive. Five writers, including Edmund Blunden and Evelyn Waugh, supported Franco. Sixteen expressed neutrality, including H. G. Wells, T. S. Eliot and Ezra Pound. The remainder sided with the Republic, among them W. H. Auden, Cyril Connolly, Aleister Crowley, Ford Madox Ford, Aldous Huxley, V. S. Pritchett, Stephen Spender and Rebecca West. Among the major newspapers opinion was more evenly divided. The *Observer* and the *Daily Mail* gave their backing to Franco, while *The Times* and the *Daily Telegraph* stayed neutral. Supporters of the Republic included the *Daily Mirror*, the *Manchester Guardian* and the *News Chronicle*.

Perhaps the most ghastly and sensational episode of the Spanish Civil War was the bombing of the Basque town of Guernica on 27 April 1937. Guernica, near the Basque capital of Bilbao, was a spiritual centre for the Basque people, who had lived in the region since prehistoric times. New Spanish kings traditionally took oaths in Guernica as a mark of respect for Basque culture and traditions. During a Nationalist offensive in April 1937 the German Condor Legion bombed Guernica, a defenceless town of no military importance, in order to test the effectiveness of mass aerial bombardment of civilian targets. About one-third of the population of seven thousand was killed or wounded. News of the bombing was received with shock, horror and the utmost indignation. For supporters of the Republic, Guernica was further proof of the ruthlessness of the fascists. Among the general population in Britain the effect may have been more subtle. Coverage of the Guernica bombing rekindled the fear in Britain that 'the bomber [would] always get through'[14] and that an adequate defence against air attack did not exist. A reinforced horror of war and the fear that the next war would be much worse than the last in turn helped to support Chamberlain and his brand of active appeasement.

The Spanish Civil War also gave rise to an incident that, for critics, has shown what the British government might have been capable of if it had been willing to stand up to the dictators. Beginning in August 1937 random acts of 'piracy' occurred in the Mediterranean in which unknown submarines fired torpedoes at Republican Spanish, Soviet and British merchant ships. Several vessels were sunk. The pirate submarines were assumed to be Italian, but Mussolini admitted nothing. On 6 September the British and French governments, under enormous pressure to do something to protect their own citizens, called an international conference at Nyon, Switzerland, to discuss the matter. Hitler and Mussolini refused to attend, while the Soviets were kept out of the proceedings, largely at Eden's behest. The conference agreed to divide the Mediterranean into zones that would be patrolled by the British and the French. The piracy ceased almost immediately, which has led some commentators to interpret the Nyon conference as evidence of what the British and the French could have accomplished against the dictators had they been so inclined. Such a judgement stretches the evidence, since Mussolini was much easier to intimidate than Hitler. The Nyon conference also had a bizarre after-effect. Mussolini protested at having been excluded from patrolling the Mediterranean. After some consideration of the matter the Italian navy was granted an area of the Mediterranean to guard against its own submarines.

After the withdrawal of the International Brigades in 1938 the Republic was unable to withstand the combined military might of Franco, Hitler and Mussolini, and Madrid fell in March 1939. The British government's policy of keeping on good terms with the winner ultimately proved successful.[15] Spain remained neutral during the Second World War, Gibraltar was never threatened, and neither Hitler nor Mussolini gained a dutiful ally in Madrid. Franco did send troops to fight on the Eastern front during the Second World War, but ultimately he emerged as more of a nationalist authoritarian than a fascist and he refused to grant bases in Spain to the Axis powers. As far as Britain was concerned, the Spanish Civil War had two main consequences: it mobilized the liberal left and shook many people out of a somnolence induced by Baldwin's style of leadership,[16] but probably for most people it provided a reminder, through Guernica, of the importance of preventing another war from ever taking place.

Exit Baldwin

How strong were British fears of aerial attack in 1936–37? Historians such as Correlli Barnett and Uri Bialer maintain that the fear of a German attack from the air was an overriding concern of British policy makers in the late 1930s. Certainly, the RAF and those who favoured British rearmament had an interest in stirring up the spectre of a knock-out blow on Britain as a means of gaining scarce funds for rearmament. Churchill speculated in 1934 that the Germans could kill or maim 30,000 to 40,000 people in the first week to ten days of war. Three to four million could then be expected to flee London.[17] Separate estimates by RAF planners showed that the Germans could drop more than 2,000 tons of bombs on London on the first day of war and inflict 50,000 casualties. No one thought to ask if the Germans had the capability or the numbers and types of aircraft to undertake operations on the scale that was being proposed.[18]

Similarly, pacifists, who felt they needed to convince people of the horrors of the next war, drew the most lurid conclusions possible. In 1936 Bertrand Russell published *Which Way to Peace?*, a collection of quotations from government officials and experts on aerial warfare that showed that the next war would reduce Britain to stone-age rubble. The use of poison gas by aircraft was particularly terrifying. Tanks would only add to the carnage on the new Western front. One of the more popular films of 1936 was *Things to Come*, based on a novel by H. G. Wells, which portrayed the progressive collapse of British society as a result of air raids that would begin on the first day of war. Although it is easy for historians to overestimate the role such fears played in the formulation of British foreign policy, both Baldwin and Chamberlain used the public's dread of aerial bombardment to justify their foreign policies. Chamberlain spoke at one point of deaths from aerial bombardment in the next war numbering in the 'hundreds of millions'.

As the Spanish Civil War settled into stalemate during the autumn of 1936 attention in Britain turned to domestic issues. Some observers noted that Baldwin appeared visibly tired. Speculation grew that the prime minister might soon announce his retirement. If thoughts of retirement did cross his mind, Baldwin kept them to himself. At any event he soon found himself completely preoccupied with a national melodrama of unparalleled proportions. At issue was King Edward VIII's relationship with Wallis Simpson, the wife of an American businessman. Rumours of their affair surfaced in October, but a general news blackout held in the national press until early December, when the *Yorkshire Post* printed the story. By the standards of the time Edward could not be allowed to continue to reign, so he abdicated on 10 December. George VI was proclaimed king the next day, the third British king in the space of one year. The abdication crisis had several implications for foreign policy. It rivetted the public's attention on a fairly inconsequential domestic matter at a time when the situation in Europe continued to deteriorate. On 1 November 1936, for example, Mussolini proclaimed the existence of the Rome–Berlin Axis. According to Mussolini, Rome and Berlin formed the axis around which the future of Europe would revolve. Mussolini also dropped his objections to a German absorption of an independent Austrian state. On 25 November 1936 Germany and Japan signed the Anti-Comintern Pact, ostensibly an anti-Soviet alliance. In reality Hitler now stood at the centre of a diplomatic network that brought Britain's three potential enemies solidly into line. Italy's joining of the Anti-Comintern Pact in November 1937 only confirmed what was an ominous scenario for British military planners.

Many in Britain doubtless welcomed the diversion provided by the spectacle of the abdication, but precious months were lost. In December Baldwin decided that he would not resign until the coronation of the new monarch in May. He wanted to see George VI firmly installed as king before retiring. Once again a politician had convinced himself of his own indispensability. Baldwin put in five full months in 1937 as little more than a caretaker prime minister. Britain could scarcely afford such luxuries of time.

Eden did manage one step forward in January 1937 with the signature in Rome of the so-called Gentleman's Agreement. Eden still distrusted Mussolini deeply, but the Chiefs of Staff insisted that every possible avenue be explored in order to remove Italy from the list of Britain's potential enemies. The Gentleman's Agreement was simply an exchange of notes in which both powers recognized the Mediterranean as an area of vital interest. They would respect each other's rights and interests and agree not to alter the status quo. Mussolini promised to end Italy's intervention in the Spanish Civil War. No sooner was the agreement was signed and Eden on his way back to London than the Duce despatched another three thousand troops to Spain and boasted publicly of Italian victories in Spain.

In his last act as prime minister Baldwin presided over the Imperial conference of May 1937 (the first Imperial conference since 1931), where he gave a pessimistic speech on the European situation. Chamberlain was sworn in as prime minister on 28 May 1937. A few days later he was proclaimed leader of the Conservative Party. A minor cabinet shuffle followed, in which Simon went from home secretary to exchequer, Leslie Hore-Belisha took the place of Duff Cooper at the War Office, Cooper was moved to the Admiralty and Hoare left the Admiralty to take Simon's place as home secretary. Finally, Lord Halifax (Edward Wood) was made Lord President with special duties to assist Eden, who continued as foreign secretary.

War in the Far East

During his first nine months in office Chamberlain did not have to confront any major crises in Europe. The situation in the Far East was rather different. After a confrontation at the Marco Polo bridge (near Peking) on 7 July 1937 the Japanese renewed war against China.[19] Japanese armies burst out of their strongholds in northern China[20] and captured Peking in July. In August the Japanese unleashed a savage attack on the Chinese coastal city of Shanghai as a prelude to a drive on Nanking, 170 miles further up the

Yangtze valley. The Japanese aerial bombardments of Chinese civilian targets, coming only a few weeks after Guernica, received extensive coverage in the West. For the people of China and Japan the Second World War began in 1937. Japanese troops soon conquered large areas of China, despite desperate resistance from the Chinese. Nanking fell in the second week of December. The British had substantial economic investments in Shanghai and the Yangtze valley region and a large number of British citizens resided in the International Settlement in Shanghai. Both the Foreign Office and Chamberlain concluded that little could be done to protect British lives or interests in China. Chamberlain in particular argued that picking a fight with Japan in the Far East would 'tempt' the dictators to strike in either Spain or Eastern Europe, or both.

In October, in response to continued Japanese aggression in China, President Roosevelt suggested that the international community should place a 'quarantine' on aggressor states. Eden thought that Roosevelt's offer was worthy of consideration; any opportunity to bring the United States out of isolationism should be explored. Chamberlain flatly rejected the idea. He felt that the Americans were unreliable and untrustworthy, that Roosevelt was all talk and no action and that the United States would pull out at the last moment, leaving Britain holding the baby, as had happened in 1919. The long history of Anglo-American recrimination exacted a steep price.

In the last weeks of 1937 events in the Far East took a turn for the worst. A British gunboat, the *Ladybird*, was shelled by Japanese artillery on 11 December while it was evacuating refugees up the Yangtze from Nanking. The next day an American gunboat, the *Panay*, was sunk by Japanese aircraft. In response the Americans sent a senior naval officer, Captain Royal Ingersoll, to London in January 1938 to discuss possible defensive counter-measures in the event of further Japanese attack. Eden was enthusiastic about Ingersoll's visit and hoped that it would lead to closer Anglo-American co-operation in the Far East. Some talks did take place between Ingersoll and the Admiralty, and although Eden seems to have been disappointed with the results, others in the British government were much more optimistic and felt that co-operation with the United States was within the realm of possibility.[21]

Chamberlain as prime minister

Chamberlain's first few months in power showed that he approved of the essential direction of British foreign policy since 1919 and that he had his own personal accents, many of which were widely shared by his countrymen. At no time over the next two and a half years did Chamberlain lack public support.[22] He disliked alliances and was convinced that they had been the main cause of the First World War. He had a deeply felt revulsion towards war and a determination that it must never happen again, although (contrary to popular perception) he never advocated peace at any price.[23] He shared the sense that bombers would always get through and inflict massive civilian casualties in the next war. During a flight to meet Hitler in 1938 Chamberlain recalled looking out the window of his aircraft and seeing the vast expanse of London below as completely defenceless and vulnerable to attack.

Chamberlain thought that the League was a nice idea but that it was essentially impractical. Neither the United States nor the Soviet Union could be counted on to help with Britain's difficulties. The United States was in the grip of isolationism and the USSR could not be trusted while it was in turmoil as a result of Stalin's purges. Instead, Chamberlain favoured a four-power pact (Britain, Germany, France and Italy) to solve Europe's problems and, indeed, put his ideas into action at the Munich conference of 1938. He persisted in his belief that a deal with Hitler could be achieved and thought that if only he could sit down with Hitler and run through all his grievances with a blue pencil, peace would then follow. Mussolini was a nuisance, but some kind of agreement had to be worked out with him as long as Germany posed a threat. Chamberlain was also an advocate of accommodation with Japan, although the resumption of the Japanese offensive against China in July 1937 minimized his hopes for a reconciliation in the Far East.

In terms of his style of governing, Chamberlain preferred to conduct his own diplomacy, largely bypassing the Foreign Office, which he dismissed as too slow-moving and stuck in its ways to serve as an effective instrument for his ideas. He expressed a desire to 'stir up' the Foreign Office with 'a long pole'; under his government the Foreign Office sank to its lowest level of prestige since the days of Lloyd George. During Chamberlain's tenure the Foreign Policy Committee of the cabinet emerged as the main forum for the discussion of foreign policy issues. This committee consisted of a small group of key cabinet ministers. Occasionally, senior civil servants and military experts would be called on for their advice. Chamberlain and Halifax invariably took the lead in discussions. The full cabinet then ratified the recommendations made by the committee.

Like all prime ministers, Chamberlain relied on a close circle of advisers. Horace Wilson, his chief 'industrial adviser', seconded from the Treasury, was foremost among that inner circle. He accompanied the prime minister on daily walks from Downing Street to St. James's Park. David Margesson, Conservative parliamentary whip, maintained discipline and unity within the party. Joseph Ball headed the Conservative Research Department and controlled *Truth*, an ostensibly independent journal that in reality existed to propagate the Conservative Party line. He could always be counted on to take the government line in editorials. Philip Kerr, now Lord Lothian, also advised Chamberlain and was appointed ambassador to the United States in 1939.

Chamberlain was a skilled politician and an exemplary administrator, but many of his colleagues found him aloof, vain and stubborn. He did not tolerate criticism, either from the opposition or from within the ranks of the Conservative Party. He avoided the London clubland, where politicians met out of hours to socialize, and preferred luncheon engagements to dinners because he had too much work to do in the evenings.[24]

In appearance Chamberlain was tall, gaunt and austere. He had considerable personal wealth and never had to worry about money. Widely read and cultured, he was an enthusiastic follower of the arts and admired traditional English painting but hated modernism. He frequently attended piano recitals and occasionally saw films, but did not care for the opera. Even in 1939 he found time for leisure reading, favouring literary criticism, biographies (especially one of Jane Austen) and history. He was also an amateur horticulturist and naturalist. After moving in to 11 Downing Street (the official residence of the chancellor of the exchequer) he had a bird feeder and nesting box set up in the back garden. He had a dog named Spot, loved to go hunting and fishing and was once so proud of a five and three-quarter pound trout he caught on a trip with Joseph Ball that he called the press on his return to London.

Much of the advice Chamberlain received during his first months in office tended to reinforce his basic assumptions about the direction British foreign policy should take. A well-known (to historians) report by the Chiefs of Staff in November 1937 concluded in the following terms:

> We cannot foresee when our defence forces will be strong enough to safeguard our territory, trade and vital interests against Germany, Italy and Japan simultaneously. We cannot therefore exaggerate the importance, from the point of view of Imperial Defence, of any political or international action that can be taken to reduce the numbers of our potential enemies and to gain the support of great allies.[25]

Chamberlain spoke constantly of the limits of British power. In a private letter written shortly after he came to office, he said that ideally Britain should be able to fight Germany, Italy and Japan simultaneously. Unfortunately, 'that was a limit of perfection which it was impossible to follow. There were limits to [Britain's] resources, both physical and financial, and it was vain to contemplate fighting single-handed the three strongest powers in combination.'

At the end of 1937 Chamberlain's government rated Britain's strategic priorities as follows. The first priority was to protect the home base – the British Isles – especially against air attack. Since Britain was so heavily dependent on seaborne trade, the second priority was to protect the trading routes that led to Britain. The third was to safeguard the British Empire. The final and lowest priority was the defence of Allied territories. The ranking of those priorities was given urgency by the Treasury, which continued to give warnings during 1937 that Britain's financial situation imposed sharp limits on the funds available for rearmament. In April 1937 Chamberlain set aside his anxieties about deficit spending and proposed a National Defence Loan of £80 million for rearmament.

Late in 1937 the cabinet decided that, given the strategic priorities outlined above, funding for rearmament would continue along previously established lines. However, a fundamental shift was to take place in RAF planning. Up to 1937 most of the money had been spent on building an RAF bomber fleet to serve as a deterrent to the Luftwaffe. Now a much more defensive mind-set took over. The RAF was to concentrate on building fighters, which were much cheaper and easier to produce. In 1937 the RAF deployed the first Hurricanes, the promising new high-speed fighters. The Spitfire followed in June 1938. Both aircraft were initially produced in very small numbers. Moreover, the development of radio direction-finding technology (radar) by Henry Tizard and Robert Watson-Watt promised to be a great advantage for defensive air forces in the next war. By 1939 a chain of twenty radar stations had been built in southern England.

Charged with defending trade routes and the Empire, the Royal Navy came next in line. Obsolete battleships and battle-cruisers from the First World War had to be modernized and new designs of cruisers and destroyers needed to be built.

Last in line was the army. Much of the minimal funding the army received was allotted to anti-aircraft defence (anti-aircraft guns and crew and air-raid precautions), which fell under the army's purview. Accordingly, the cabinet decided in March 1938 to inform the French that only two British divisions could be spared for action on the continent. 'Limited liability' was the order of the day. Chamberlain, supported by Hore-Belisha (and many prominent defence commentators, such as Basil Liddell Hart of *The Times*), believed that one of the worst mistakes Britain ever made was to send a mass conscript army to Europe in the First World War. In the next war Britain would use its greatest asset, naval power, to blockade the enemy into submission.

Neville Chamberlain took office in 1937 with strong views on the direction of British foreign policy and rearmament. He felt a sense of mission and had a determination to resolve differences with Hitler, and he enjoyed solid support from his advisers, from the press and from public opinion. A collision with his own foreign minister must have seemed the least of his worries.

Notes

1   J. Emmerson, *The Rhineland Crisis, 7 March 1936: A Study in Multilateral Diplomacy* (Iowa, Iowa State University Press, 1977).

2   W. N. Medlicott, 'Britain and Germany: the Search for Agreement', in D. Dilks (ed.), *Retreat from Power: Studies in Britain's Foreign Policy of the Twentieth Century*, volume one (London, Macmillan, 1981), p. 91.

3   This story has also been attributed to Philip Kerr and Baldwin. Perhaps all three shared the same driver.

4   The British also had three battle-cruisers that could theoretically catch and sink the 'pocket' battleships, but one was being refitted and modernized while a second was stationed in the Mediterranean for most of the 1935–36 period.

5   G. C. Peden, *British Rearmament and the Treasury, 1932–1939* (Edinburgh, Scottish Academic Press, 1979), *passim*.

6   British opinion on the Spanish Civil War is surveyed in K. Watkins, *Britain Divided: The Effect of the Spanish Civil War on British Political Opinion* (London, Thomas Nelson, 1963).

7   Baldwin was already preoccupied with 'the King's matter', or the affair between King Edward VIII and Mrs Simpson that culminated in the abdication crisis of December 1936.

8   J. Edwards, *The British Government and the Spanish Civil War, 1936–1939* (London, Macmillan, 1979), chapters one and two.

9   L. Fuchser, *Neville Chamberlain and Appeasement: A Study in the Politics of Appeasement* (New York, Norton, 1982), p. 81

10   D. Marquand, *Ramsay MacDonald* (London, Jonathan Cape, 1977), pp. 787–8.

11   Edwards, *The British Government and the Spanish Civil War*, pp. 136–7.

12   G. Stone, 'The European Great Powers and the Spanish Civil War, 1936–1939', in R. Boyce and E. Robertson (eds), *Paths to War: New Essays on the Origins of the Second World War* (New York, St. Martin's Press, 1989), pp. 199–232.

13   See Edwards, *The British Government and the Spanish Civil War*; L. Pratt, *East of Malta, West of Suez: Britain's Mediterranean Crisis, 1936–1939* (Cambridge, Cambridge University Press, 1975); and D. Smythe, *Diplomacy and the Strategy of Survival: British Policy Towards Franco's Spain, 1940–41* (Cambridge, Cambridge University Press, 1986).

14   A phrase first used by Baldwin in a speech to the House of Commons on 10 November 1932.

15   On 25 March 1997 *The Times* published details of Spanish plans to attack Gibraltar in 1939 and 1940.

16   As Eric Hobsbawm recalls, the war gave people a chance to participate in the anti-fascist struggle 'as individuals, if not in uniform, then by collecting money, by helping refugees, and by the never-ending campaigns to put pressure on our chicken-hearted governments'. When writing of those who served with the International Brigades he notes that they 'were neither mercenaries, nor, except in a very few cases, adventurers. They went to fight for a cause'. E. Hobsbawm, *Age of Extremes: The Short Twentieth Century, 1914–1991* (New York, Vintage, 1995), p. 160.

17   Speech to the House of Commons, 28 November 1934.

18   Unless one counts some members of the air staff who, by September 1938, seem

to have been aware that the Germans would have difficulty bombing London from bases in Germany.

19 Unlike the Mukden incident, the Marco Polo episode was not staged. The Japanese evidently wanted to force the Chinese to the bargaining table, so that Japan could focus on other areas.

20 Northern Manchuria was fully occupied in 1932. In 1933 the Japanese went on to occupy the province of Jehol, which bordered Manchuria to the south-west. Jehol brought them within striking range of Peking. Inner Mongolia was occupied in 1935. Their control of Inner Mongolia and Manchuria brought the Japanese in face-to-face contact with Soviet forces in Mongolia and the Soviet Far Eastern province, thus setting the stage for border clashes in the late 1930s.

21 See M. Murfett, *Fool Proof Relations: Anglo-American Naval Co-operation During the Chamberlain Years, 1937–1940* (Singapore, University of Singapore Press, 1984), chapter eight. For the course of Anglo-American relations in general, see D. Reynolds, *The Creation of the Anglo-American Alliance, 1937–41: A Study in Competitive Co-operation* (University of North Carolina Press, 1981).

22 Admittedly the prime minister used a considerable amount of news management. Editors of national newspapers were asked to provide favourable coverage, as were the BBC and newsreel producers. For Chamberlain's manipulation of the press, see R. Cockett, *The Twilight of Truth: Chamberlain, Appeasement and the Manipulation of the Press* (London, Weidenfeld and Nicolson, 1989).

23 Chamberlain supported the proposed defence loan of 1937 and also proposed a tax on business that raised howls of outrage from the City.

24 Biographies of Chamberlain include K. Feiling, *The Life of Neville Chamberlain* (London, Macmillan, 1976); D. Dilks, *Neville Chamberlain, volume one* (Cambridge, Cambridge University Press, 1984); Fuchser, *Neville Chamberlain and Appeasement*; R. A. C. Parker, *Chamberlain and Appeasement: British Policy and the Coming of the Second World War* (London, Macmillan, 1993). Chamberlain receives sympathetic treatment from Feiling and Dilks, but Fuchser's portrayal is much less attractive.

25 I. Colvin, *The Chamberlain Cabinet* (London, Gollancz, 1971), p. 64.

CHAPTER NINE

ACTIVE APPEASEMENT, 1938

Shortly after Chamberlain took office as prime minister it became evident that he and the foreign secretary, Anthony Eden, were at odds on several issues. Both men agreed on the fundamental need to appease Germany, but problems between them arose over British policy towards Italy and the United States, together with a more wide-ranging dispute concerning the general conduct and formulation of British foreign policy. Critics have always pointed to Eden's resignation in February 1938 as an example of the manner in which Chamberlain 'purged' his government of all opposition to his policies.[1] However, for most of 1937 neither Chamberlain nor Eden thought that their differences were so serious as to justify Eden's resignation.

The main problem concerned Britain's policy towards Italy. Chamberlain favoured closer relations with Italy in order to keep Mussolini away from Hitler. Ever since the final stage of Italian unification in 1870 Italy had enjoyed generally good relations with Britain. Italy had ignored its alliance with Germany and Austria–Hungary in 1914 to enter the war in 1915 alongside Britain and France. Mussolini had been co-operative during the period that led up to 1935, signing the Locarno treaty, enlisting in the Stresa front and supporting Austrian independence. Given the long history of Anglo-Italian amity and the mutual interest in Austria, Chamberlain felt certain that it would be possible to overcome the legacy of the Ethiopian and Spanish disasters. He was not discouraged by the proclamation of the Axis in 1936 or by the meagre results of the Gentleman's Agreement. He argued that Mussolini could be won over by granting to Italy *de jure* recognition of its conquest of Ethiopia. Eden was by no means convinced and preferred a much harsher line. He flatly opposed *de jure* recognition and viewed Mussolini as unstable and untrustworthy, especially after the Gentleman's Agreement. Eden should probably have resigned over the issue when this difference of opinion with Chamberlain first surfaced in July 1937.

Chamberlain convinced himself that the Foreign Office supported Eden's intransigence, although evidence suggests that Vansittart actually took Chamberlain's side. The prime minister decided to make personal contact with Mussolini, much to the annoyance of Eden. Chamberlain always assumed, when dealing with Hitler or Mussolini, that personal contact was the key to diplomatic success.

On 27 July 1937 Chamberlain held an interview with Count Dino Grandi, the popular Anglophile Italian ambassador to Britain. Grandi passed on a message from Mussolini in which he asked for *de jure* recognition of Ethiopia as part of the Italian empire. Grandi also expressed some anxiety over British naval power in the Mediterranean. Chamberlain said that Britain had no aggressive designs on Italy and asked Grandi whether he ought perhaps to write personally to the Duce to assure him of Britain's peaceful intentions. Grandi agreed that it would be a good idea, so Chamberlain pulled out a pen and some paper and apparently drafted a letter on the spot, in which he offered to meet Mussolini in person and also recalled that Austen Chamberlain (who had recently died) had held the Duce in 'the highest regard'.

Chamberlain later claimed that he was trying to impress both Grandi and Mussolini by showing them that he was a strong leader who could take initiatives without constantly consulting his advisers. Chamberlain also admitted that he had not shown the letter to Eden because he knew Eden would object. Eden did indeed make clear his displeasure over the episode.

Mussolini replied to Chamberlain's letter favourably but vaguely. The Italian 'pirate' submarine campaign and the Nyon conference derailed further progress in the late summer and autumn of 1937, but Chamberlain had no intention of giving up. In mid-October Eden was scheduled to give a foreign policy speech to an audience estimated at 18,000 at Llandudno in Wales. Chamberlain asked that the speech be postponed, fearing Eden might further offend Mussolini during the course of his speech. Eden refused, and a meeting between Eden and Chamberlain in November resulted in a serious argument over rearmament. The discussion ended abruptly when Chamberlain, thinking his excitable foreign secretary was acting too feverishly over the issue, told him to go home and take an aspirin.

In December Chamberlain renewed unofficial contacts with Italy, again through a roundabout route. Ivy Chamberlain, the widow of Austen, visited Rome in December 1937.[2] She held informal conversations with both Count Ciano, the Italian foreign minister, and Mussolini himself and then told her brother-in-law that Mussolini wanted better relations with Britain. Mussolini could not understand what was taking so long and blamed Eden for slowing things down on the British side. At one point Ivy Chamberlain showed Mussolini a private letter that she had received from Neville in which he expressed a desire to improve relations with Italy. Ivy continued to act as a mediator well into January, relaying messages from Mussolini to Chamberlain and back again. Chamberlain repeatedly offered Mussolini *de jure* recognition of Ethiopia in exchange for a general settlement of other issues between the two countries.[3] Eden objected strongly to Ivy Chamberlain's role; and most historians would agree that to conduct a foreign policy without the input of the foreign secretary is problematical. The prime minister, for his part, did not think that Ivy had done any real harm.

Halifax visits Hitler

Chamberlain's efforts to conduct personal diplomacy also extended to Germany. In October 1937 Erhard Milch, second in command of the Luftwaffe, paid an unofficial visit to London. The visit went well and, on Milch's return to Berlin, Halifax, as Master of the Middleton Hounds, received an invitation to visit Göring, the *Reichsjägermeister* at the International Hunting Exhibition in Berlin. The trip was a ruse under cover of which Chamberlain hoped Halifax would be able unofficially to discuss the state of Anglo-German relations. Eden was not impressed and instructed Halifax to spend most of his time listening rather than talking.[4] Chamberlain hoped for much more.

Halifax arrived in Berlin on 17 November. Two days later he journeyed by automobile to meet Hitler at the Führer's Berchtesgaden retreat in Bavaria. Stepping out of his vehicle on arrival, Halifax nearly committed a major gaffe. He took off his hat and was about to hand it to an ordinary-looking footman dressed in a brown coat, black trousers and black leather shoes, when Baron von Neurath, the German foreign minister who had accompanied Halifax on his trip, excitedly began to shout '*Der Führer, der Führer*' and to point at the 'footman', who was Adolf Hitler.

Halifax soon discovered that Hitler was in a foul mood. It is unlikely that this was due to the *faux pas* concerning the footman, as Hitler's testiness seemed to have had deeper roots. Hitler said that his intentions in Europe were entirely peaceful and that Germany wanted better relations with Britain, but British press criticisms of Germany were making that impossible. The British government, he said, should do more to control the press, in the same way that he had brought the German press into line. He added that a 'colonial settlement' would do much to improve Anglo-German relations.

Halifax's remarks to Hitler have been much criticized.

> I said that there were no doubt other questions arising out of the Versailles settlement which seemed to us capable of causing trouble if they were unwisely handled, e.g., Danzig, Austria, Czechoslovakia. On all these matters we were not necessarily concerned to stand up for the status quo as to-day, but we were concerned to avoid such treatment of them as would be likely to cause trouble. If reasonable settlements could be reached with the free assent and goodwill of those primarily concerned, we certainly had no desire to block.[5]

Critics have alleged that by those comments Halifax was effectively inviting Hitler to expand into Eastern Europe since, by implication, Britain would stand aside and do nothing. It seems more probable that Halifax was simply trying to make the point that Britain would help to negotiate a solution to the injustices of Versailles, provided that Germany refrain from the use of force.

Lunch was a painful ordeal. Hitler's black mood worsened as he attacked his vegetarian meal. Small talk proved impossible. When Ivone Kirkpatrick, a British embassy official who was accompanying

Halifax, tried to initiate a conversation about the weather, Hitler practically bit his head off. 'The weather?', Hitler snarled. 'The weather prophets are idiots; when they say it is going to be fine it always rains and when they foretell bad weather, it's fine.' Someone asked cautiously if Hitler enjoyed flying. Hitler immediately snapped back: 'Only a fool will fly if he can go by train or road.' Hunting was tried next:

> I can't see what there is in shooting; you go out armed with a highly perfected modern weapon and without risk to yourself kill a defence-less animal. Of course Göring tells me that the pleasure lies not in the killing, but in the comradely expedition in the open air. Very well. I merely reply: 'If that's the case let's spare ourselves all bother and make a comradely expedition to a slaughter-house where in the greatest comradeship we can together kill a cow in the open air.

Somehow the topic of India came up. Hitler said that the British should shoot Gandhi and his followers in increments of two hundred. The trouble would soon stop. By that point, Halifax was speechless.

After taking leave of Hitler Halifax turned to Kirkpatrick and remarked, in typically understated fashion, that he and Hitler seemed to have totally different values. Von Neurath said it was too bad that Hitler was so grouchy, but all the same it was good that he should come into contact with the outside world. Kirkpatrick sensed that Hitler's raw temper could be attributed to the fact that he had already lost all interest in negotiation. Hitler 'felt he was wasting his time and showed that he resented it'.[6]

Back in London Chamberlain, in one of his less astute judgements, thought that Halifax's visit had been a great success. Halifax told the cabinet that the Germans desired good relations with Britain and that there was no evidence to suggest that Hitler was about to embark on foreign adventures. From Berlin the British ambassador, Nevile Henderson, reported that Halifax's sincerity must have made a wonderful impression on Hitler.

The prime minister immediately set to work devising a plan for the return to Germany of its former colonies. Chamberlain knew the Germans wanted Togoland and the Cameroons and possibly

South-West Africa. He was unsure of Tanganyika. He briefly entertained the idea of a joint European condominium over all Central
Africa in which Germany would participate. The Portuguese would
have to be persuaded to part with Angola, Belgium would have to
part with the Congo (now the Democratic Republic of the Congo)
and France would have to give up some territory, but Chamberlain
did not think that was much of a problem as they could be given
compensation elsewhere. The prime minister then considered the
need for reforming the League and restarting disarmament talks.
Most of Chamberlain's hopes were fantasy. As Henderson discovered later, Hitler was never serious about recovering Germany's
colonies. Eden expressed reservations about many aspects of
Halifax's visit and complained of excessive press coverage, but he
still seems to have agreed with the prime minister that it was essential to seek agreement with Germany. Disagreements between the
two men over Italy and a couple of other issues had surfaced, but
not to such a degree that Eden's departure was seen as imminent.

Vansittart out, Cadogan in

In December Chamberlain used his 'long pole' to stir up the Foreign
Office. Vansittart was relieved of his duties as permanent under-
secretary and given the newly created post of chief diplomatic
adviser to the foreign secretary on 1 January 1938. Chamberlain had
complained for some time that Vansittart's 'instincts' were against
his policy. He also felt that Vansittart was responsible for 'multi-
plying' Eden's 'natural vibrations'.[7] Eden supported the move,
feeling that Vansittart was blocking an agreement with Germany.
Observers at the time were uncertain what to make of the appointment. Did the new post represent a triumph for Vansittart? He had
a high public profile and was known for his anti-German stance. Did
his 'promotion' mean that Britain would take a much stronger line
against Germany? Or was he actually being 'kicked upstairs'? As it
turned out, the last interpretation was the correct one. In his new
post Vansittart exercised no control over the formulation of foreign
policy and in subsequent years he churned out lengthy, obtuse memoranda that were seldom read or understood by cabinet ministers.

Vansittart's replacement as permanent under-secretary was Alexander Cadogan, a hard-working and efficient administrator who did not suffer fools gladly. For the time being Cadogan was a solid supporter of Chamberlain's policies. His relations with Vansittart proved thorny. In April Cadogan complained:

> Van is being tiresome – developing the technique of writing minutes on every paper he can lay his hands on and thus trying to become a super Permanent U[nder] S[ecretary]. Afraid the time has come for a remonstrance, which I shall make to H[alifax] on Monday. It's a great bore – why will Van be such an ass, and put me in the tiresome case of talking about one's 'position', like a housemaid? But there it is, and I must do it.[8]

In Germany the weary von Neurath was replaced as foreign minister in early February by Joachim von Ribbentrop in a move that Vansittart believed heralded the beginning of a much more aggressive phase in German foreign policy. According to Vansittart, von Neurath represented the last of the 'moderates' in the German government, whereas von Ribbentrop typified the more extremist wing of the Nazi movement. Göring was given the newly created title of Reichsmarschall while Hitler took over the supreme control of the German armed forces.

Eden resigns

The breach between Eden and Chamberlain widened considerably in the first weeks of 1938. In January Roosevelt sent a message to the British government informing it of a plan to convene an international conference to discuss methods of resolving world tensions. Both Chamberlain and Cadogan rejected the idea for reasons similar to those advanced by Chamberlain at the time of Roosevelt's 'quarantine' speech in October 1937 (see Chapter Eight). Eden, who had just returned from holiday in France on 14 January, again welcomed the chance to lure the United States back into the world arena. He was dismayed by Chamberlain's opposition and even more upset when he discovered that Roosevelt's message had been kept secret from him for two days while he was on the continent.

In his reply to Roosevelt Chamberlain said the proposed conference should be delayed for the time being as it might pre-empt important developments in the direction of peace that were about to unfold in Europe. Roosevelt's plan lapsed into obscurity.

The important developments to which Chamberlain referred concerned Mussolini. The early weeks of 1938 had seen a number of signals from Rome. Some came via Ivy Chamberlain, whom Cadogan privately denounced as 'that jackass'.[9] As before, Mussolini hinted at an agreement with Britain in exchange for *de jure* recognition of Ethiopia. He wanted to draw closer to Britain not because of Chamberlain's diplomacy but because Hitler was about to pounce on Austria and Mussolini would have to decide how closely to Hitler he wanted to be linked. Eden's resignation in 1938 was finally provoked by the issue of an appropriate response to Mussolini's latest initiative. Chamberlain thought that Italy could serve as a reliable and trustworthy friend for Britain; Eden thought that would be impossible as long as Mussolini ruled. At a meeting between Grandi, Chamberlain and Eden on 19 February 1938 (arranged by Chamberlain through the office of Joseph Ball) the disagreements between the prime minister and his foreign secretary flared out into the open, much to Grandi's surprise. Eden's resignation was announced the next day and he was succeeded by Halifax. Within three weeks Hitler's troops had occupied the whole of Austria.

Anschluss

The fact that two events occur in sequence does not necessarily imply a causal link between them. With that caution in mind, most historians have wondered whether Eden's resignation, following as it did on Halifax's visit and Vansittart's 'promotion', unintentionally sent the wrong message to Hitler. On the other hand, given the nature of his long-term plans, one might ask whether Hitler would have gone ahead with the *Anschluss* regardless of Eden's position. Perhaps Eden's resignation effected only the timing of Hitler's move. If nothing else, Hitler was a clever opportunist. Some of Chamberlain's defenders, on the other hand, have argued that Eden's dismissal convinced Hitler that Italy and Britain were on the verge of a reconciliation, and that he had to strike against Austria immediately.[10]

German threats against Austria and Nazi subversion within the country had built up steadily throughout 1937. On 12 February 1938 the Austrian chancellor, Kurt von Schuschnigg, had a meeting with Hitler in Berchtesgaden. Schuschnigg was bullied and intimidated into accepting Hitler's demand that prominent Austrian Nazis be included in the Austrian cabinet. On returning to Vienna Schuschnigg discovered that the Austrian Nazis were interested not in governing the country but rather in destabilizing it. Schuschnigg decided to call Hitler's bluff. On 9 March he announced that a plebiscite would be held on 13 March in which Austrians would be asked if they wanted to join Germany.

If a plebiscite had been held in 1919, the overwhelming majority of Austrians would have voted to join Germany. By 1938, however, a sense of Austrian nationalism was emerging and many Austrians were leery of joining Hitler's Germany. To avoid a possible serious embarrassment if the plebiscite went ahead Hitler decided to strike first and ordered his army to march.

The order to invade was characteristically impulsive and took the German generals by surprise. An invasion force was hastily assembled and entered Austria on 12 March. The Austrian army decided not to resist – a particularly fortuitous decision from the German point of view. Large numbers of German vehicles broke down or ran out of fuel on the road to Vienna. Some German officers had to purchase maps from roadside garages to find their way around Austria. Nevertheless, Hitler's triumph was assured within hours.

The British government had never indicated that it was willing to fight for the independence of Austria. Moreover, as it pointed out during the crisis, Britain was not bound to Austria by any treaty obligations. A French proposal on 18 February to forward a joint Anglo-French warning to Germany not to change the status quo in Europe aroused suspicions in the Foreign Office. If the French army had not marched to prevent the Rhineland remilitarization, it could hardly be expected to fight for Austria now. In any event, the French government was in the midst of another cabinet crisis. The French, it was argued, made unrealistic proposals in the full knowledge that the British would turn them down so that Paris could then pin the responsibility for inaction on London. The post-Versailles Anglo-French rancour now exacted a steep price, a trend that had been apparent for some time. In December 1937 the Chiefs of Staff had rejected a proposal for Anglo-French staff talks on the grounds that if news of the talks leaked out, it would incur the irreconcilable hostility and suspicion of Germany.

Practical considerations also prohibited an Anglo-French defence of Austria. A look at a map shows that neither Britain nor France had contiguous borders with Austria. Italy did, but unfortunately Mussolini had agreed to the *Anschluss* during a dramatic telephone call to Hitler on the evening of 11 March. Hitler pledged eternal gratitude and support for Mussolini, who had now cast his lot. A British and French defence of Austria would also have meant fighting for the odious and discredited Treaty of Versailles. Public support for such a war simply did not exist. Finally, as in the case of the Rhineland, the German move could be rationalized as a fulfilment of German national self-determination.

Chamberlain's first reaction was to assure the cabinet that Britain could not have done anything to prevent the *Anschluss*. Indeed, the *Anschluss* proved that Eden was wrong: a reconciliation with Mussolini would have forestalled Hitler's move. Schuschnigg's decision to order a plebiscite had been an act of folly. On the down side, Chamberlain feared that the *Anschluss* may have strengthened the hand of those who wanted to take a harder line with the dictators. In a letter to his sister Chamberlain still felt compelled to deny that the League could have been of any use in preventing the *Anschluss*. He argued that to be persuasive, collective security required overwhelming military force. For his part, Cadogan argued that encouraging the Austrians to resist when Britain could do nothing to help would be an act of criminal irresponsibility.

In spite of Austria's disappearance from the map, the new team of Halifax and Chamberlain remained optimistic about the chances of agreement with Hitler. Chamberlain expressed gratitude at having an unflappable and supportive foreign minister. Naturally, Europe remained the focus of British diplomacy. With regard to the Far East Chamberlain and Halifax hoped for a stalemate in the Sino-Japanese war, after which a ceasefire could be negotiated. The British showed some sympathy for the plight of the Chinese government. A proposal, endorsed by Halifax, to lend money to China was rejected by the Treasury and the cabinet in 1938, but the British did support a plan to construct a road (later known as the Burma road) to link China with the outside world. Since China's coastline was under the control of Japan an overland link was of vital strategic importance. On the other hand, the British had to avoid incurring Japanese hostility, and the British ambassador in Tokyo, Robert Craigie, emerged as a strong advocate of Anglo-Japanese hostility. Britain's position was complicated further by the government of the United States, which itself was strongly pro-Chinese and anti-Japanese and liable to view an Anglo-Japanese *rapprochement* with suspicion and hostility. The British could not do anything to alienate the United States, but nor could the United States be counted on to take action in a crisis.

Once the dust from the *Anschluss* had settled Chamberlain and Halifax resumed contact with Mussolini. On 16 April 1938 Britain and Italy signed the so-called Easter Agreement, designed to reduce tensions between the two countries. Britain promised to grant *de jure* recognition to the Italian empire in Ethiopia once the League's permission had been gained and Italian forces had begun to leave Spain. In return, Mussolini promised to reduce Italian troop levels in Libya (at that time an Italian colony and too close to Suez for British comfort) and curtail the anti-British propaganda of Radio Bari. Mussolini denied that he had any territorial ambitions in Spain and promised to respect the status quo in the Mediterranean. The two countries also promised to exchange information on troop movements in the Mediterranean and northwest Africa. The agreement did not come into force until November 1938, when the first Italian troops were withdrawn from Spain. At that time the British ambassador in Rome, Lord Perth, was required to present his credentials anew to the 'King of Italy and Emperor of Ethiopia'.

Czechoslovakia

During the summer of 1938 attention in Europe turned to Czechoslovakia. A creation of Versailles, the Czechoslovakian state contained large numbers of minority populations. The Czechs, numbering 6.5 million, dominated the government and bureaucracy and were concentrated in Bohemia and Moravia. Some three million Slovaks lived in the eastern half of the country. About 700,000 Hungarians lived along the southern border with Hungary and thus served as a focus of Hungarian territorial ambition. The Ruthenes, numbering 400,000, were concentrated in the far eastern tip of Czechoslovakia. Poland eyed the city of Teschen, which had a population of 70,000 Poles. The most problematical minority were the 3.5 million Germans who lived mainly in Sudetenland, a horse-shoe-shaped territory along Czechoslovakia's borders with Germany and Austria.

By 1938 the main political vehicle of the Sudeten Germans was the Sudeten Deutsche Partei, led by Konrad Henlein. His job, as outlined by Hitler in late March, was to keep raising the level of demands and to avoid a compromise settlement at all costs. The secession of Sudetenland was to serve as a pretext for the occupa-tion of the whole of Czechoslovakia. At a major rally in Karlsbad on 24 April Henlein took the first step by demanding self-government for Sudetenland and the 'full freedom to profess membership in the German race'.[11] Hitler had already given speech-es threatening grave consequences should Prague fail to resolve the alleged grievances of the Sudeten Germans.

Naturally the Czech government could not agree to Henlein's wishes. Prague needed Sudetenland as a key strategic barrier against Germany and feared, rightly, that to grant autonomy of the region to Germany, or even cede it altogether, would open the floodgates for similar irredentist demands from Poland and Hungary. The ironic result was that Prague was seen increasingly as the obstacle to a peaceful resolution of the Sudeten issue.

By 1938 Czechoslovakia was a reasonably prosperous state with a functional democratic system despite some discontent among the minorities. The Sudeten Germans had certain grievances but were never the persecuted minority that Hitler made them out to be. Czechoslovakia also had a strong armament industry, the Skoda works, located in Sudetenland. In peacetime the Czech army consisted of twenty-one divisions (seventeen infantry and four cavalry) that were reasonably well equipped, supported by four hundred aircraft. Two additional infantry divisions were added in 1938, while mobilization of reserves was supposed to provide a total strength of more than thirty divisions. Some progress had been made in fortifying the Czech–German frontier, which was longer than France's border with Germany, although German experts who later inspected the Czech lines were not impressed. Unfortunately, Czech defences were rendered useless after the *Anschluss* left Czechoslovakia's entire southern frontier – which was practically devoid of natural obstacles – open to attack. The worst miscalculation made by the inter-war Czechoslovakian leadership, however, was that it pinned all its hopes for security on the Western powers.

Following the Rhineland episode and the *Anschluss* Czechoslovakia's alliance with France was strategically useless. The Czech–Soviet pact was scarcely of much value either since it depended on the Franco-Czech pact coming into force first. In July 1938, in the midst of threats from Hitler, France informed Prague that it could not meet its alliance commitments. No great surprise was registered on the Czech side. Hitler knew that his new alignments with Japan and Italy could be counted on to keep France and Britain in check. Poland and Belgium, two of Germany's neighbours, were neutral. Czechoslovakia's partners in the Little Entente, Yugoslavia and Romania, did not share borders with Czechoslovakia. Neither state was considered a military powerhouse. In any event, by 1938 both Romania and, especially, Yugoslavia were cowed by German economic pressure. Germany was a major importer of resources from both countries (oil from Romania and wheat from Yugoslavia), and Hitler used his position to force unfavourable barter arrangements on both countries. Hitler's position was further enhanced by the fact that the bulk of Czechoslovakia's export trade was carried over German territory.

From the point of view of Chamberlain and Halifax, the principal danger in the Sudeten issue was the Franco-Czech alliance, which carried the theoretical risk of dragging Britain into a war with Germany over France's commitments to Czechoslovakia. The obvious course of action was for Britain to mediate an agreement between Czechoslovakia and Germany that might lead to a general

European settlement. Hitler had to be kept guessing what Britain might do, while France and Czechoslovakia had to be restrained by the knowledge that Britain would not fight.[12] In March 1938 Chamberlain was sure that Hitler did not mean to destroy all of Czechoslovakia and that Henlein was still willing to sign an agreement of some sort with Prague. Halifax seemed to envisage a kind of federal arrangement for Czechoslovakia along the lines of the Swiss cantonal system. In March Chamberlain mused to a group of journalists about the possibility of Sudetenland being ceded to Germany.

For their part the British had long since concluded that a guarantee of Czech independence was out of the question. A report by the Chiefs of Staff in late March argued that France and Britain would not be able to prevent the Germans from quickly conquering Czechoslovakia, which could then only be restored at the end of a long and costly war. The report also raised the possibility of a German aerial knock-out blow against London in the opening phase of war and the likelihood that Japan and Italy would enter the war on the side of Germany. Chamberlain and Halifax used the report as a means of persuading government members and ministers to support their policy of appeasing Hitler over Sudetenland. Between 20 and 24 March Chamberlain outlined his position both to the House of Commons and in private correspondence: 'You only have to look at the map to see that nothing France or we could do could possibly save Czechoslovakia from being overrun by the Germans'.[13] Czechoslovakia would only be a pretext for war with Germany and war was justifiable only if Germany could be beaten in a reasonably short length of time. British interests in the area were negligible and did not require a guarantee to Czechoslovakia. At the same time, the prime minister warned Hitler publicly that if war were started, 'it would be quite impossible to say where it would end and what Governments might become involved'. The 'inexorable pressure' of events might well outrun formal pronouncements.[14]

The French were brought into line at a meeting in London on 28 April. The French premier, Édouard Daladier, warned that Hitler intended to destroy Czechoslovakia and subdue the whole of Eastern Europe. He argued eloquently against Chamberlain's policy of appeasement, yet when the conference ended he fell in meekly behind Chamberlain's lead. Why? Undoubtedly Daladier was aware of France's military and economic weakness and of the left–right polarization in French society that could lead to a disastrous split in the event of war. Anti-war sentiment was as strong in France as in Britain. Given France's weakness, Daladier had to do all he could to maintain the goodwill and friendship of the British. He may also have been speaking to posterity, hoping to shift the blame for appeasement on to Chamberlain. Or he may have been hoping that his tough talking would galvanize the British into seeking a solution of the Sudeten problem.

In early May the Germans scored yet another brilliant propaganda victory when Konrad Henlein visited London. Henlein had previously come to London in 1935 and addressed the prestigious Royal Institute of International Affairs. Then, and again in May 1938, Henlein charmed everyone he met. He followed a script carefully outlined for him by Ribbentrop, Germany's former ambassador to Britain. Henlein proclaimed his peaceful intentions and argued that if a settlement were not achieved soon, it might be difficult to restrain his more radical followers. Vansittart, Churchill and the editors of *The Times* all felt reassured that Henlein was a reasonable man with moderate views. The Prague government, by contrast, looked downright obstructionist.

Meanwhile, in Czechoslovakia Henlein's Karlsbad demands had provoked a state of crisis and imminent showdown. Municipal elections in Sudetenland had been scheduled for Sunday 22 May. Rumours swirled through the Sudeten community that Hitler would strike on that date. Other rumours, beginning on 19 May, suggested that the German army had mobilized troops along Germany's northern border with Czechoslovakia. Two days before the election two Sudeten German farmers were shot dead by Czech police at Eger. Fearing that Hitler might use the shootings as a pretext, the Czech government started calling up reservists on 21 May. The Germans protested at the Czech action and used threatening language. Ribbentrop complained to Henderson that one hundred Germans had been killed or wounded in the Sudeten region. Halifax, through Henderson, warned Ribbentrop that if war started over Czechoslovakia France would support Prague and Britain could well

227

become involved. Despite the gravity of the situation the municipal elections proceeded as normal and Henlein's party won decisively. Hitler was furious that the world might conclude that he had backed down in the face of Czech resolve.

The rumours of German military movements were probably started as a result of the German army's attempts to consolidate positions in Austria. Germany's protestations only lent force to the rumours; similar reports and denials had preceded the *Anschluss* only two months earlier. The British military attachés stationed in Prague did not detect anything unusual on the northern border and were mystified by the reports of German troop movements. The British attaché in Berlin later concluded that the Germans had not been preparing a strike against Czechoslovakia, and that seems to have been the truth of the matter. Hitler was simply not yet ready to launch a war.

What prompted the Czech government to call up the troops? At the time the Czechs were accused of provocation. Was Prague responding to a perceived, if mistaken, threat? Or were the Czechs taking a tough stand in order to discredit Chamberlain's policy of appeasement? One might argue that the real lesson of the May crisis was that Hitler would have backed down if he had been confronted by a will to resist[15] – which is precisely what he feared people at the time would conclude. For Chamberlain, however, the real lesson was that Europe stood on the brink of war and that efforts had to be redoubled to seek a peaceful solution before it was too late.

The road to Munich

In the week following the May crisis Hitler repeatedly proclaimed his peaceful intentions to all who would listen, as did Henlein. Privately, Hitler told his generals that his 'unalterable decision' was to 'smash Czechoslovakia by military action in the near future'. The army was to be ready to move by 1 October. In June and July Hitler issued a series of public threats against Czechoslovakia. Mass rallies in Germany and by Germans in Sudetenland escalated the tension, as did continuing rumours of German troop movements. Talks between Henlein and Prague failed repeatedly as Henlein rejected whatever concessions the Czechs offered.

In spite of the hostility towards Czechoslovakia Hitler continued to send signals to London indicating that he favoured a peaceful solution. On 18 July one of Hitler's wartime buddies and close associates, Captain Wiedemann, arrived in London for a chat with Halifax. Wiedemann said that Hitler wanted the friendship of Britain and that Hitler had no plans to resort to force over the Sudetenland dispute, provided unforeseen or serious incidents did not occur, and he suggested that perhaps Göring should come to London to discuss matters. Chamberlain took heart from Wiedemann's visit.

The summer of 1938 also saw a scheme floated by Halifax and the Foreign Office to counter the growing economic power of Germany in Eastern Europe and the Balkans. The idea was to combine the strength of the Balkan states in a Danubian federation. Nothing ever came of the plan and Chamberlain seems to have been lukewarm at best. He argued that German economic dominance in the east and southeast of Europe was natural and that it was in Britain's interests to encourage German economic prosperity. Surely a prosperous Germany would be more stable than a Germany in economic crisis?

By late July tension over Czechoslovakia had reached such a peak that the prime minister decided to take action. It was time, he argued, to send an independent mediator to Czechoslovakia to work out a deal between Henlein and Prague. The Czechs were initially hesitant, but Prague eventually decided that it could not afford to lose Chamberlain's goodwill and therefore agreed to the proposal. Chamberlain and Halifax chose Lord Runciman, a relatively obscure former Liberal cabinet minister, for the task. Officially, Runciman was to act purely as an independent mediator, not as an agent of the British government. Unofficially, his mission was to persuade Prague to agree to as many of Henlein's demands as possible.

Runciman and his staff arrived in Czechoslovakia on 3 August and set to work. Runciman met all the leading Czech politicians and compiled masses of statistical information. He soon developed a strong sympathy for Henlein, the Sudeten Germans and their myriad difficulties. Henlein remained his charming self, even though he avoided meeting Runciman for one full week. Runciman blamed the Czech president, Eduard Beneš, for all the problems of the preceding five months. Henderson wrote from Berlin that 'the Czechs are a pig-headed race and Beneš not the least pig-headed among them'. Eventually Runciman produced a lengthy report in mid-September that recommended autonomy for Sudetenland along the lines of the Swiss cantons, preserving Czechoslovakia's existing boundaries. By that time, however, such a solution had been overtaken by events.

By the end of August it was apparent to Chamberlain that the turning point was at hand. Hitler had scheduled a Nazi Party rally at Nuremberg on 12 September, when it was expected that he would announce his intentions. Chamberlain told his cabinet that a blunt warning from Britain to Germany might push Hitler over the edge and provoke him into declaring war, a fear shared by Henderson. Furthermore, support from the Dominions for a strong stand might not be forthcoming. On 1 September the prime ministers of Australia and South Africa had told Chamberlain that they would not support war over Czechoslovakia. Finally, the British military was unprepared for war. In such circumstances, Chamberlain thought that the best course of action would be to keep Hitler guessing about Britain's intentions. In case a last-ditch effort were needed, the prime minister came up with 'plan Z': he would fly to Germany and attempt to negotiate a solution with Hitler face to face. Chamberlain first raised the idea in a late-night meeting with Horace Wilson at the end of August. It has often been noted that Chamberlain possessed a sense of self-confidence reminiscent of that of a nineteenth-century missionary. If so, the prime minister's self-confidence certainly played its role in generating plan Z. Chamberlain next talked it over with Nevile Henderson when he paid a brief visit to London on 28 August. Henderson supported plan Z enthusiastically. By 8 September Chamberlain had gained the backing of Halifax, of Simon and Hoare (both former foreign secretaries) and of Cadogan and Inskip. Vansittart strongly disapproved of the idea. Two days earlier final negotiations between Henlein and Prague had broken down, despite the fact that Beneš had conceded to all of Henlein's demands.

In his speech at the 12 September rally Hitler rejected autonomy and called for full self-determination for Sudetenland. On the other hand, he did not threaten imminent war. As Cadogan noted, Hitler's speech 'pulled no triggers'. A slim opportunity for peace remained. A soon-to-be notorious editorial in *The Times* by the newspaper's editor, Geoffrey Dawson, on 7 September had already called for Sudetenland to be handed over to Germany. Since the writer was so closely connected to Chamberlain, it has often been assumed that the editorial was instigated by Chamberlain. No proof has been found to support such an accusation, but certainly a consensus had emerged in London by the first week of September that Sudetenland would have to be turned over to Germany. Although Hitler's speech of 12 September did not threaten immediate invasion, it did succeed in prompting riots in certain areas of Sudetenland. Agents from the SS had been infiltrating Sudetenland for weeks. The Czechs had little trouble containing the riots, but some Sudeten Germans were killed and Henlein fled to Germany. On 14 September Chamberlain gained the approval of the full cabinet for plan Z. In fact the prime minister had already sent a message to Hitler asking for an immediate meeting, but no one in cabinet objected to his taking the bull by the horns. The French had not been forewarned of Chamberlain's intentions either. Hitler replied that he was at the full disposal of Chamberlain.

The prime minister flew to Munich on Thursday 15 September, accompanied by Horace Wilson and William Strang, a Foreign Office official. It was the first time in his life that Chamberlain had flown in an aeroplane. From Munich the prime minister continued by train and automobile to Hitler's Berchtesgaden retreat. The meeting was conducted in the same room where Halifax had encountered Hitler the year before. Recounting the events to his sister later, Chamberlain felt compelled to point out that at first glance Hitler looked 'entirely undistinguished' and 'ordinary'. At the meeting Chamberlain received Hitler's demands but had to listen to a long diatribe from Hitler outlining the grievances of the Sudeten Germans and the efforts that he himself had made to preserve the peace. Hitler said that he wanted to 'settle it', and that he would risk war rather than have events continue to drag on. He did promise that if the British government agreed to the secession of Sudetenland, and said so publicly, there was a chance of maintaining peace. Chamberlain said that he had to gain the agreement of his cabinet and of France. As many historians have noted, Prague's role or assent was not mentioned by either leader.[16]

Chamberlain arrived back in London on Friday 16 September determined to settle matters quickly. He recounted his meeting with Hitler in a letter to his sister and noted: '[despite the] hardness and ruthlessness I thought I saw in his face I got the impression that here was a man who could be relied upon when he had given his word'.[17] Hitler had not shown any signs of insanity, although he did become extremely agitated when discussing the attitude of the Czech government. Chamberlain felt he had gained Hitler's confidence, and that had been his aim. Some of Hitler's subordinates told Wilson that Chamberlain had made a great impression on Hitler. Chamberlain was sure that Hitler's objectives were 'strictly limited' and that he wanted a solution of the Sudeten problem.[18]

The prime minister won the approval of his cabinet on Saturday, 18 September. Serious opposition to his course did not surface. Runciman attended the Saturday meeting and told the cabinet that Prague was responsible for 'most of the present trouble', and Chamberlain argued that it was wrong to start a war in order to stop national self-determination.[19] Public backing for the prime minister was building up and his office was flooded with messages of support.

The next step was to win over the French. A delegation from Paris arrived on Sunday, consisting of Daladier, Bonnet (the foreign minister) and their 'circus', as Cadogan called their entourage. After a day-long wrangle the French agreed to the transfer of Sudetenland, provided that Britain join with France in guaranteeing the remainder of Czechoslovakia. Chamberlain agreed. The new guarantee was to supersede the treaties that France and the USSR had signed with Czechoslovakia.

The final step was to convince the Czechs. This proved very much harder, and the Czechs held out for two full days. Prague conceded only when the British threatened to end mediative efforts and the French indicated that they would not fight in support of Czechoslovakia if Germany invaded it.

Chamberlain then flew to Godesberg, on the Rhine, to meet Hitler on the afternoon of 22 September. He received a nasty shock. Hitler was in a black mood and rejected his own solution: it was no longer good enough. The Poles wanted Teschen and the Hungarians wanted areas of southern Slovakia, and their grievances had to be resolved. German troops would march on 28 September. The meeting was, according to Chamberlain in a classic understatement, 'very unsatisfactory'.[20]

The next morning Hitler and Chamberlain remained in their respective hotels on opposite sides of the Rhine. Chamberlain sent Hitler two messages that were ferried across the river on a launch especially provided by the Germans. The first stated that Hitler's demands of the previous day – in particular, a military occupation of Sudetenland – were unacceptable to the British government and the British public. The second, carried personally by Wilson, asked Hitler to set out his proposals in full in a written document. At half past ten that evening Hitler replied that the document was ready.

On this occasion Hitler was in a rare good mood, 'making an obvious effort to be pleasant', according to Kirkpatrick.[21] But his demands had not changed. Chamberlain persuaded Hitler to tone down some of the language in the document and Hitler moved the deadline for the invasion back to 1 October. The meeting broke up at two o'clock in the morning with Chamberlain promising to pass Hitler's demands on to Prague.

Chamberlain returned to London later that day, on 24 September. Hitler's Godesberg demands caused some in London to have second thoughts. Cadogan, in particular, was appalled. At the cabinet meeting that afternoon Cadogan was 'completely horrified' by Hitler's demands and by the fact that Chamberlain appeared to be 'quite calmly for total surrender'. He was 'more horrified to find that Hitler [had] evidently hypnotised him to a point'. Chamberlain said that he still thought that Hitler was telling 'the truth' when he claimed to want only the unification of all Germans and not domination over all of Europe. Chamberlain argued that he had established a degree of personal influence over Hitler, 'and that the latter trusted him and was willing to work with him'. Cadogan decided to speak to Halifax.[22]

The week that followed was one of unbearable international tension. The Czechs had ordered a general mobilization on 23 September. The French government started to marshall troops as well. The Royal Navy was mobilized on 27 September. Gas masks were distributed to the civilian population of Great Britain and trenches for air-raid shelters were dug in public parks right across the country. A handbook on air-raid precautions was mailed to every household in Britain, and searchlights and anti-aircraft guns were set up in London. Daladier and Bonnet arrived in London on 25 September for emergency consultations, followed the next day by General Gamelin, head of French national defence.

In the meantime Cadogan had succeeded in planting doubts in Halifax's mind. At a cabinet meeting on 25 September Halifax said that Britain must reject Hitler's Godesberg demands. The foreign secretary's change of course came as 'a horrible blow' to Chamberlain.[23] Halifax succeeded in rallying a number of other cabinet ministers, including Duff Cooper, secretary of the Admiralty, to his side. Chamberlain suggested sending Wilson to Berlin with one last message for Hitler. The Führer would be asked to agree to an international commission that would supervise the orderly transfer of the Sudeten areas to Germany. If Hitler rejected this offer, Wilson was to warn him verbally that if Germany were to invade Czechoslovakia, France would support the Czechs and Britain would stand by France. Wilson left the next morning.

Halifax then took an initiative of his own. Gamelin had left the British with the impression that France would do something to support the Czechs. Halifax telegraphed Wilson as follows:

since you left the French have definitely stated their intention of supporting Czechoslovakia by offensive measure if latter is attacked. This would bring us in: and it should be made plain to Chancellor that this is inevitable alternative to a peaceful solution.

Halifax instructed the News Department of the Foreign Office to issue a communiqué stating that if Germany were to attack Czechoslovakia, 'the immediate result must be that France [would] be bound to come to her assistance, and Great Britain and Russia [would] certainly stand by France'.[24]

Wilson arrived in Berlin late in the afternoon of Monday 26 September. His first interview with Hitler went badly. Hitler was in yet another of his foul moods. He demanded that the Czechs agree to the Godesberg memorandum in full. Kirkpatrick noted that whenever Wilson mentioned Chamberlain's desire for peace Hitler simply 'pushed back his chair and smote his thigh in a gesture of frustrated rage'. Hitler constantly interrupted Wilson with long tirades so that Wilson was unable to deliver his verbal message. Wilson and Kirkpatrick obtained a second meeting the next day. Yet again 'Hitler looked black as thunder'. He threatened to 'smash the Czechs' and was fairly 'itching to drop a bomb on Prague'. Wilson delivered his message in measured tones, but Hitler showed 'signs of exasperation, wriggling in his seat, slapping his knee, drumming on the floor with his heel'. When Wilson finished speaking Hitler exploded in rage and screamed that the world would be at war in six days.[25]

On the evening of Tuesday 27 September Chamberlain addressed the nation in a radio broadcast:

> How horrible, fantastic, incredible it is that we should be digging trenches and trying on gas masks here because of a quarrel in a far-away country between people of whom we know nothing. It seems still more impossible that a quarrel which has already been settled in principle should be the subject of war...

No matter how much Britain sympathized with 'a small nation confronted by a big powerful neighbour', Chamberlain continued, 'we cannot in all circumstances undertake to involve the whole British Empire in war simply on her account'. He had to be sure that 'the great issues' were at stake.

Later that same evening Chamberlain received a letter from Hitler saying that German troops would only occupy the Sudeten areas of Czechoslovakia, that a free plebiscite would be carried out and that Germany would join in an international guarantee of Czechoslovakia. Chamberlain replied the next morning by saying that he was prepared to make a third trip to Germany, if necessary. Chamberlain also appealed to Mussolini and asked him to intercede. Mussolini replied a few hours later by saying that he had achieved a twenty-four hour postponement of the German deadline. Chamberlain then went to address the House of Commons. In his speech he stressed the numerous efforts that the British government had made to resolve the dispute. During the speech Cadogan received a call from Henderson: Hitler had just invited Chamberlain, Mussolini and Daladier to a conference at Munich. Cadogan wrote out the message 'and ran with it to House. Fished H. out of Peers' Gallery and we went along to behind Speaker's Chair and sent it to P.M., who was still speaking'. Chamberlain read out the message to a breathless House and concluded with the words: 'I need not say what my answer will be'. The House exploded in cheers of joy and relief. Members rushed to Chamberlain with tears streaming down their faces. The opposition joined in wishing Chamberlain the best.[26]

Why did Hitler back down from a war he so desperately wanted and agree to a conference? Although the order for the mobilization of the Royal Navy was issued on 27 September, it was not publicized until the next day, by which time Hitler may already have decided to hold a conference. Wilson's warning to Hitler on the morning of 27 September might well have been the cause of Hitler's hesitation. The French mobilization could have had an effect. Mussolini may also have played a role in pulling Hitler back from the brink; the Italian leader argued strongly against unleashing war in 1938. The German generals were also unenthusiastic about the idea of war, as was the mass of the German population. Kirkpatrick and other British diplomats in Germany noted that the crowds milling around in the streets of Godesberg and Berlin seemed apathetic and downcast. Even members of Hitler's entourage at the meeting with Wilson looked depressed and anxious. Hitler undoubtedly decided that more propaganda was necessary to fire up the masses for war.

Chamberlain flew to Munich on 29 September and, in the early hours of 30 September, signed an agreement with Hitler, Daladier and Mussolini that provided for the transfer of Sudetenland from Czechoslovakia to Germany. A referendum would be held to fix the frontiers in the disputed areas. The final borders would be delineated by an international commission. Sudetenland was to be evacuated by the Czechs during the period beginning on 1 October and ending on 10 October. The region would subsequently be occupied by the Germans in four phases. Britain and France would guarantee the remainder of Czechoslovakia, and Germany and Italy would do the same after Polish and Hungarian claims against Czechoslovakia had been settled. The Czech leaders, who had been excluded from the conference at Hitler's insistence and kept waiting at a nearby hotel, were given the text of the agreement and told to sign. Abandoned by France and confronted by a war that could not be won, the Czechs were too stunned to resist. Throughout the conference proceedings Mussolini and Göring strutted around in high spirits while Hitler sulked in a corner. Hitler regarded Munich as a defeat, since it deprived him of the opportunity to wage a glorious war of vengeance on Czechoslovakia.

The next morning Chamberlain held a private interview with Hitler. Chamberlain reviewed the course of Anglo-German relations in some detail and asked Hitler to sign the following statement, which is worth reproducing in full.

> We, the German Fuehrer and Chancellor, and the British Prime Minister, have had a further meeting today, and are agreed in recognising that the question of Anglo-German relations is of the first importance for the two countries and for Europe.
>
> We regard the agreement signed last night and the Anglo-German Naval Agreement as symbolic of the desire of our two peoples never to go to war with one another again.
>
> We are resolved that the method of consultation shall be the method adopted to deal with any other questions that may concern our two countries, and we are determined to continue our efforts to remove possible sources of differences and thus to contribute to assuring the peace of Europe.[27]

Chamberlain returned to a rapturous welcome in London. To the crowd at Heston airport he expressed his hope that the Munich agreement was the prelude to a 'larger settlement' that would achieve peace for all Europe. He read aloud the contents of the recently signed paper and waved it around for all to see. Chamberlain and Halifax were then driven to Buckingham Palace, cheered all the way by adoring crowds. At one point Chamberlain turned to Halifax and remarked cryptically, 'All this will be over in three months'. After an interview with King George VI Chamberlain appeared on the balcony of the palace and was cheered again. He finally returned to his Downing Street residence where he spoke to the crowds: '[This is] the second time in our history that there has come back from Germany to Downing Street peace with honour. I believe it is peace for our time'.[28] In the next few days tens of thousands of gifts and letters of congratulations poured into the prime minister's office as a grateful nation gave thanks to its leader.

Notes

1 L. Fuchser, *Neville Chamberlain and Appeasement: A Study in the Politics of Appeasement* (New York, Norton, 1982).
2 Ivy and Austen Chamberlain had befriended Mussolini at Locarno in 1925.
3 This was as far as matters got before Eden's resignation and the Anschluss.
4 It was on 16 November that Eden and Chamberlain had the 'aspirin' argument.
5 Quoted in C. Barnett, *The Collapse of British Power* (London, Methuen, 1972), p. 467.
6 I. Kirkpatrick, *The Inner Circle: The Memoirs of Ivone Kirkpatrick* (London, Macmillan, 1959), pp. 94–8.
7 R. Douglas, 'Chamberlain and Eden, 1937–38', *Journal of Contemporary History*, XIII, 1978, pp. 97–116.
8 D. Dilks (ed.), *The Diaries of Sir Alexander Cadogan, 1938–1945* (London, Cassell, 1971), p. 67.
9 Dilks (ed.), *The Diaries of Sir Alexander Cadogan*, p. 50.
10 See the essay by R. Douglas in W. Mommsen and L. Kettenacker (eds), *The Fascist Challenge and the Policy of Appeasement* (London, George Allen and Unwin, 1983), pp. 79–88.
11 C. Thorne, *The Approach of War, 1938–1939* (London, Macmillan, 1968), p. 57.
12 R. A. C. Parker, *Chamberlain and Appeasement: British Policy and the Coming of the Second World War* (London, Macmillan, 1993), p. 140.
13 K. Feiling, *The Life of Neville Chamberlain* (London, Macmillan, 1947), pp. 347–8.
14 Dilks (ed.), *The Diaries of Sir Alexander Cadogan*, p. 66.
15 The same argument can be made about Mussolini and the Nyon conference.
16 Parker, *Chamberlain and Appeasement*, pp. 162–3, an account based on cabinet documents.
17 Parker, *Chamberlain and Appeasement*, pp. 162–3.
18 Parker, *Chamberlain and Appeasement*, p. 164.
19 Parker, *Chamberlain and Appeasement*, p. 164.
20 Dilks (ed.), *The Diaries of Sir Alexander Cadogan*, p. 102.
21 Kirkpatrick, *The Inner Circle*, pp. 122–6.
22 Dilks (ed.), *The Diaries of Sir Alexander Cadogan*, pp. 103–4.
23 Dilks (ed.), *The Diaries of Sir Alexander Cadogan*, p. 105.
24 Dilks (ed.), *The Diaries of Sir Alexander Cadogan*, p. 106.
25 Kirkpatrick, *The Inner Circle*, pp. 122–6.
26 Dilks (ed.), *The Diaries of Sir Alexander Cadogan*, p. 107–9.
27 Feiling, *The Life of Neville Chamberlain*, p. 381.
28 The first occasion was when Disraeli returned from the Berlin Conference in 1878. The phrase 'peace with honour' was used by Disraeli and his foreign secretary to describe the results of the conference, which had been called to deal with a crisis in the Balkans.

CHAPTER TEN

THE END OF APPEASEMENT AND THE RISE OF CONTAINMENT, 1939

The Munich agreement had immediate and disastrous consequences for Czechoslovakia and, in the long run, for all the states of eastern and southeastern Europe. The promised plebiscites for the disputed areas of Sudetenland never took place. Poland seized Teschen in October, and in November, under the terms of the so-called Vienna award, Hitler granted Hungary a large area of southern Czechoslovakia. The international guarantee of Czechoslovakia, which was supposed to be given after the resolution of Polish and Hungarian claims, likewise never materialized. The federal system of Czechoslovakia was overhauled and the country was split into three autonomous regions: Bohemia–Moravia, Slovakia and Ruthenia. The latter two provinces quickly fell under the control of anti-democratic authoritarians agitating for their own state. The post-Munich state was called Czecho-Slovakia, the hyphenation reflecting the new balance of power.

Munich failed to prompt any changes in Nazi foreign policy and Hitler continued to behave as obnoxiously as ever. He plainly regarded Munich as a defeat and vowed that next time he would have his war. Within weeks of signing the 30 September note with Chamberlain he was giving violent anti-British speeches. In the Far East, the Munich agreement encouraged the Japanese to place further pressure on British interests in China, culminating in the Japanese blockade of the Tientsin concession on 14 June 1939.

To the states of eastern and southeastern Europe Munich came as a terrible shock: France had apparently just thrown its strongest ally to the wolves and the leaders of those states drew their own conclusions. Bulgaria, Romania, Yugoslavia and Hungary all soon orientated their foreign policies away from Paris and towards Berlin.

On 6 November a German diplomat in Paris was assassinated by a young Jewish student named Herschel Grynszpan. Grynszpan was distressed at the expulsion of thirteen thousand Polish Jews from Germany. Among those who were expelled and subjected to brutal treatment by the Nazis were members of Grynszpan's family. The assassination provided the Nazis with an excuse for a mass pogrom against the Jewish population of Germany, and on 9 November Jewish shops, homes and synagogues were burned and looted. Thirty thousand Jews were arrested, hundreds beaten and one hundred murdered. The pogrom soon became known as the *Kristallnacht*, or night of the broken glass. Hitler imposed a fine of one billion marks on the Jewish community for allegedly provoking the *Kristallnacht*. Insurance payments to Jewish citizens were seized by the state. The *Kristallnacht* triggered a wave of Jewish emigration from Germany, but the fleeing Jews had to leave all their possessions behind and were often unable to find another country in which to take refuge. The British newspapers universally condemned the Nazi actions, and Chamberlain and Halifax both expressed their horror.

In the Foreign Office the post-Munich mood was one of despair, unease and a sense that Britain had been deeply humiliated. Leading Foreign Office officials circulated a series of memoranda in November analysing Britain's position in the immediate post-Munich era. According to these documents, the guiding principle in British foreign policy was the British empirical tradition, which eschewed ideology for 'realism'. Some members of the Foreign Office concluded that Germany's expansion into eastern and south-eastern Europe was unstoppable. The demise of the Versailles system was greeted with relief. The League was seen as admirable but unrealistic and unworkable. Britain's room for manoeuvre in the future was limited by the low state of readiness of the armed forces for war. Generally the consensus was to concede, continue appeasing and hope for the best.[1]

If supporters of the National government expected a political pay-off from Munich they were soon disappointed. A by-election loss at

Bridgwater late in 1938 led Joseph Ball to recommend that a general election be postponed, but Chamberlain's morale was buoyed in December by a victory at Kinross and West Perthshire. Here the Conservative incumbent, the Duchess of Atholl, had resigned her seat in order to run as an independent. The Duchess decided to make the conduct of Chamberlain's foreign policy her main platform. Her defeat left Chamberlain in high spirits at the year's end.

Following the Munich agreement Chamberlain intensified efforts to draw closer to Mussolini. The latter's efforts as peacemaking at Munich led Chamberlain to believe that relations with Italy could be improved. Soon afterwards Mussolini announced that he was about to withdraw ten thousand Italian troops from Spain. Franco stood on the verge of victory and needed less foreign assistance. Chamberlain quickly announced to the House of Commons that he was about to enact the Easter Agreement.[2] A deterioration in Franco-Italian relations in November brought about by Italian threats to seize Tunis, Djibouti and Corsica prompted a warning from Britain, which Chamberlain and Halifax followed up with a visit to Rome in early January 1939. Chamberlain urged Mussolini to use his best efforts to restrain Hitler, but nothing was accomplished other than exchanges of warm feelings.

Post-Munich Europe was also punctuated by a series of war scares. One historian has calculated that no fewer than twenty reports of impending German, Italian or Japanese attacks reached London between December 1938 and April 1939.[3] The most serious scare in January 1939 involved rumours of a German assault on Holland. Additional intelligence reports that originated from within Germany itself confirmed suspicions that Hitler was not open to moderate influence and that Nazism was a dynamic, expansionist ideology.[4]

The rumours of an attack on Holland were particularly unnerving for British military planners. For once, Hitler was not threatening a distant East European state but rather a country very close to home. Historically, the British had always been sensitive about the neutrality of the 'low countries'. Ports in Belgium and Holland could serve as ideal bases for an invasion of Britain. By 1939 the British also had to worry about a hostile power setting up air bases in

Belgium and Holland. The war scare of January quickly faded away, but it did leave a number of important after-effects. Although it was not made public, the British cabinet decided on 2 February that Britain would declare war against Germany if Hitler attacked Holland. It also decided to extend military assistance to France if Franco and Mussolini challenged France's southern frontier with Spain. Chamberlain told the House of Commons on 6 February that 'any threat to the vital interests of France from whatever quarter it came must evoke the immediate co-operation of this country'.[5] The doctrine of limited liability, or any avoidance of a continental commitment, was now on the way out.

The month of February was comparatively quiet, but Cadogan was not fooled. In his diary he took note of 'a curious lull in Germany' and speculated on the cause. Was it due to an internal power struggle in Germany? Was Hitler perhaps preparing some 'awful devilment'?[6] Or was it possible that Chamberlain's warning of 6 February had paid off? Henderson reported on 13 February that Hitler was not about to embark on any immediate adventures and that German policy was headed towards peace. Henderson's report, together with the lull from Germany, raised Chamberlain's hopes. Perhaps the Munich payoff had finally arrived.

The end of Czechoslovakia

Of course it was too good to last. A flurry of SIS (Secret Intelligence Service) reports on the weekend of 11–12 March indicated that a German strike on Czechoslovakia was imminent. Henderson discounted the rumours, as did Chamberlain. Halifax was more wary. On Wednesday 15 March German troops poured over the border and occupied Prague, Bohemia and Moravia without resistance. Slovakia was set up as an independent state heavily dependent on German patronage. The German action violated the Munich accord, but Britain, France and Italy did nothing to help the Czechs. Indeed, Mussolini, determined not to be outdone, occupied Albania three weeks later.

The occupation of Prague was an act of blatant aggression and could not be justified on the grounds of national self-determination, as had happened in the cases of the Rhineland, Austria and Sudetenland. British press reaction was uniformly hostile to Hitler's move. Even *The Times* abandoned appeasement. Chamberlain's immediate reaction was to tell the House of Commons that he would continue with his current policy and that he would not be deflected from his course. He went on to explain that the promised guarantee to Czechoslovakia had lapsed because the state of Czechoslovakia no longer existed and hence could not be guaranteed.

Two days later, in a speech to the Birmingham Conservative Association, Chamberlain apparently did change course. He asked if the occupation of Prague signalled 'the end of an old adventure, or the beginning of a new' and whether the seizure of Czechoslovakia was 'a first step in the direction of an attempt to dominate the world by force'. He gave the following warning:

> no greater mistake could be made than to suppose that, because it believes war to be a senseless and cruel thing, this nation has so lost its fibre that it will not take part to the utmost of its power in resisting such a challenge if it ever were made.[7]

It could be argued that Chamberlain had miscalculated the mood of the British public after Prague and that his change of tack between 15 and 17 March was forced on him by public outrage over Hitler's actions. The prime minister obviously wanted to deflect criticism over his own tepid response to Hitler's aggression, but it is worth remembering that the government had already accepted a renewed continental commitment and that he may well have been trying to mobilize public support for an even stronger stand.

The guarantee to Poland

The occupation of Prague sparked another round of rumours about Hitler's next move. Poland was the obvious target. With the break up of Czechoslovakia Hitler's Germany now outflanked Poland to the south, just as Czechoslovakia had been outflanked after the *Anschluss*. In the case of Poland Hitler revived all the old grievances about the loss of German land as a result of the Versailles Treaty, especially the city of Danzig. Hitler's agenda dictated that

243

Poland had to be dealt with, ideally by September 1939, before any move against France. The immediate cause of Hitler's wrath was Warsaw's refusal to join the Anti-Comintern Pact. Poland had co-operated with Hitler in the past – signing a treaty with him in 1934 (see above, p. 167) and seizing Teschen from Czechoslovakia after Munich – but Polish national pride imposed limits on how far co-operation with Germany could proceed. To turn over control of Poland's foreign policy to Hitler was simply not on the cards.

Rumours about a possible German attack on Romania also abounded, encouraged by the Romanian ambassador in London who obviously wanted to force London to extend help to his country. For the time being, however, Hitler had a more immediate target. On 20 March (less than a week after German troops entered Prague) the Germans presented an ultimatum to Lithuania demanding the return of the city of Memel, which had been given to Lithuania in 1919 but was populated mainly by Germans. The Lithuanian government immediately capitulated. Taking everything into consideration, Cadogan concluded: '[the] crisis is worse, really, than last September, but the public don't know it'.[8] For its part, British intelligence failed to detect any evidence of an imminent German attack on either Poland or Romania. Nevertheless, the rumours had made their mark, and on 31 March (a few days after Franco entered Madrid) Chamberlain rose to his feet in the House of Commons to make a major announcement.

The strain of recent events had taken its toll on the prime minister. Nicolson thought he looked gaunt and ill. According to observers, Chamberlain read his statement slowly and quietly, with his head bent:

> in the event of resort by the German government to any action which the Polish government feels obliged to regard as a threat to their independence and accordingly to resist, His Majesty's Government will at once lend the Polish government all support in their power.[9]

Britain had guaranteed the territorial integrity of Poland against German attack. Wild applause greeted Chamberlain's speech. On 13 April 1939 the British government extended a similar guarantee to Romania.

How did the British government reach its decision to extend this guarantee? After his Birmingham speech of 17 March Chamberlain came under intense pressure, both in the press and in the House of Commons, to do something specific to back up his words. Originally he had proposed that Britain, France, Poland and the Soviet Union issue declarations pledging that they would consult together in any case of future aggression. The French rejected the idea on the grounds that a pledge merely to talk about future aggression would only encourage Hitler. Poland objected to any association with Russia, its historical enemy, and argued that an alignment with Moscow might actually provoke Hitler. Moreover, during March Polish diplomats astutely manipulated British fears about a Polish–German deal. Perhaps Warsaw might cave in to Hitler's demands, thereby dealing another crushing blow to the West. In the British cabinet Halifax emerged as the main advocate in favour of guaranteeing Poland against German aggression; he encountered little resistance. A guarantee also represented a chance to confront Germany with the possibility of a war on two fronts.

On the face of it, the guarantees marked a major transformation of British foreign policy. A strong sense of moral outrage had gripped the country, together with a determination never to be fooled again. Britain was now firmly committed to preventing further German expansionism by constructing a 'dam' in Eastern Europe. A 'peace front' of Eastern European states would deter Hitler from further aggression. Militarily, the scheme did not make sense since Britain could do little to defend Eastern Europe, and over the next few months London failed utterly to provide any substantial military or economic aid to Poland. The guarantees served largely as a psychological gesture and as a deterrent for further aggression.

Chamberlain, however, apparently had not fully grasped the likely consequences of what he had done[10] and was soon trying to wriggle out of the implications of the guarantee. Evidently the prime minister did not share the resurgent determination to resist Hitler that had swept over the public, the opposition, the government backbenches and even members of his own cabinet. He hinted that the guarantee committed Britain to maintaining only the independence of Poland, not every square inch of the territorial status quo.

He clearly hoped that the guarantee would spark another round of negotiations with Hitler. Chamberlain was not going to sacrifice Britain's vital security interests, but nor had he given up the possibility of negotiation.[11] For the most part he could not express such views publicly, since feeling against Hitler was running high, but he made his hopes known in private correspondence and in remarks to colleagues. Appeasement was not necessarily dead by the end of March 1939, but it was certainly on life support.

It is crucial to note also that by March 1939 British military leaders were feeling increasingly confident about the readiness of the country for war. The production of aircraft had increased dramatically and was drawing level with that of Germany. The new fighters had exceeded all expectations and work was proceeding rapidly on radar stations. The long-dreaded possibility of a knock-out blow was receding. Reports from the Chiefs of Staff showed a new and perceptive awareness of German military weaknesses. In early 1939 the Chiefs had expressed cautious optimism about Britain's ability to prevail in a long war with Germany.

Dealing with the Soviets

By April it was also abundantly clear that Britain would at long last have to deal seriously with the Soviets. Chamberlain's preference during his first two years as prime minister had been to keep the Soviets well in the background, excluded from European affairs. But if the Eastern front was to be given any credibility at all, some kind of arrangement had to be made with the Soviet régime, if only to head off the possibility of a German–Soviet deal.

For their part, the Soviets now had to choose between two foreign policy options. Since the rise of Hitler they had pursued a policy of attempted collaboration with the Western democracies, supporting the popular fronts, collective security and adherence to the League's principles. The Soviet foreign minister, Maxim Litvinov, was the main proponent of the pro-League tradition. He spent a considerable amount of time at Geneva between 1934 and 1938 proclaiming Soviet loyalty to League ideals. Unfortunately, it was a policy that had produced few results by 1939. Soviet offers of collaboration with the West after the *Anschluss* and at the time of the Munich agreement had been politely but firmly rejected by Chamberlain, who noted on both occasions that the offers were vague and unconvincing. The popular fronts only seemed to stir up increasing suspicion of Soviet motives among European conservatives and nationalists. Immediately after Munich rumours began to circulate in European capitals that Litvinov was on the way out.

One alternative open to Stalin was the Rapallo policy of collaboration with Germany. Stalin certainly had many reasons to fear Hitler, but given the paucity of results from Litvinov's policy, perhaps the best course was to seek an accommodation with Hitler. On 10 March 1939 Stalin addressed the Eighteenth Congress of the Communist Party of the Soviet Union. During his oft-quoted speech Stalin warned his colleagues 'to be cautious and not allow [their] country to be drawn into conflicts by warmongers who [were] accustomed to having others pull the chestnuts out of the fire for them'.[12] It has been suggested that Stalin was actually hinting that he would welcome an approach from Hitler, but the idea of Stalin courting Hitler in 1939 remains speculation. A more likely explanation is that Stalin was simply declaring Soviet non-involvement in 'inter-capitalist' quarrels. If Stalin lost interest in collective security after Munich, he still had not decided to cast his lot firmly with Hitler.

Did the Foreign Office think that a Soviet–German *rapprochement* was on the cards? The Foreign Office Northern Department had long been monitoring relations between the Germans and Soviets and watching carefully for any tell-tale signs. For the most part the Foreign Office was inclined to discount the possibility of a deal between the two bitter enemies, mainly because of Hitler's fanatical anti-communism. A major part of Hitler's political success had been built on anti-communism. He could hardly be expected suddenly to make a deal with the devil after years of anti-communist rhetoric. On the other hand, the Foreign Office suspected that if Hitler overcame his anti-communism, Stalin, a supreme realist, would have little hesitation in accepting a deal with him.

In Britain the 'Soviet experiment' evoked a variety of responses. The Labour Party leadership frequently denounced Stalinism and expelled pro-Soviet groupings (such as Stafford Cripps' Socialist

League) from the Party. On the other hand, Labour leaders had to take into account the idealism of their supporters as well as the fact that Soviet support for the Spanish Republic had given an enormous boost to Soviet prestige. Members of all three political parties recognized that it was necessary to deal with the USSR because it was a great state in the European state system.

Anti-communist and anti-Soviet sentiments were strongest on the right. Tories of all persuasions disliked the Soviet system, but the depth of their antipathy varied from the fanatical anti-communism of those who felt genuinely threatened by Soviet power to the more moderate views of those who cultivated anti-communism mainly for political purposes. No Conservative politician could admit to being 'soft' on communism and expect to last.

Anti-Russian sentiment in Britain had deep historical roots. Fear of Russian power and the potential for a Russian threat to the British Empire in India had been dominant strains in nineteenth-century British foreign policy. In 1854 Britain went to war with Russia in the Crimea largely to roll back the growth of Russian power in the Balkans. At the end of the century Britain cultivated close links with Japan to contain Russian influence in the Far East. The Anglo-Russian entente of 1907 settled many outstanding differences between the two countries, but the Foreign Office remained deeply suspicious of Russian intentions and expressed fears about the growth of Russian influence in Persia and Afghanistan.

Prior to 1914 the Russian army expanded and Russian industrialization proceeded apace. Great hopes arose in Britain that the 'Russian steamroller' might overpower the Germans. Instead, the apocalyptic collapse of the Russian Empire in 1917 left many in Britain deeply disappointed and anxious about the future of the war. The rise of the Bolsheviks and the proclamation of world revolution sparked a wave of anti-communist hysteria. Anxiety focused on Comintern attempts to foment revolution in India and in Britain itself. The failure of the Soviet government to keep repeated promises to curtail Comintern anti-British propaganda raised questions about the trustworthiness of the Soviets, and some feared that Russian Imperialism was about to be resurrected in the guise of Soviet Communism, a potentially more appealing and therefore more dangerous method of expansion. The difficult course of Anglo-Soviet relations in the 1920s has already been recounted. The nature of the Stalinist régime and events in the USSR in the mid- to late 1930s raised further questions about the desirability of the USSR as an ally. Stalinist tyranny, collectivization and forced industrialization aroused genuine disgust among many in Britain, and the great purges of 1937–38 reinforced such feelings. The Moscow show trials of those years, in which prominent Communists confessed to spectacular crimes of treason and sabotage, showed either that the régime was ridden with traitors or that Stalin was hopelessly paranoid and ruthless. According to the British embassy in Moscow, the constant purging of the country's élite was leading to chaos and disorganization in industry. The Soviets could hardly be expected to maintain a solid war industry if all the leading figures in industry were shot or jailed every few months.

Worst of all, however, was Stalin's purge of the Red Army officer corps in June 1937. Before the purge was over the Red Army had lost three of its five marshals, all eleven deputy commissars of defence, seventy-five out of eighty members of the Military Soviet, all its Military district commanders, thirteen out of fifteen army commanders, fifty-seven out of eighty-five corps commanders, 110 out of 195 divisional commanders and 186 of its 406 brigade commanders. Among the casualties were innovative and forward-looking generals, such as Marshal Tukhachevsky who had been experimenting with the combined use of tanks and aircraft in offensives. Also victimized were the heads of the naval and air forces and their Chiefs of Staff, as well as builders and designers. A full eighty per cent of the staff of the Far Eastern army were arrested. Overall, anywhere between twenty-five and fifty per cent of the members of the Red Army officer corps met some sort of personal disaster during the purge, amounting to between 20,000 and 25,000 individuals. Not all were shot, but few were ever rehabilitated.[13]

British military experts had never held a particularly high opinion of the USSR's military capability, even before the purges. After witnessing Red Army manoeuvres in 1936 British military observers concluded that the Soviet Red Army had made improvements over its tzarist predecessor but still had a long way to go. Although the

Soviet air force was impressively equipped with vast numbers of aircraft, their quality was suspect. The Red Army possessed some very good tanks and the infantry was lavishly equipped, but the tactics of both were clumsy and lacked imagination. Officers showed little originality or initiative. Moreover, the Soviet railway system was overloaded and prone to breakdown. One observer compared the Red Army to a 'bludgeon, quite incapable of rapier work'.[14] British observers concluded that the Red Army would prove formidable in the defence of Soviet territory – and any invader would soon have his hands full – but that its offensive capabilities were severely limited. The purges of June 1937 merely reinforced those conclusions.

Some historians have charged that the British vastly underestimated the military potential of the Soviets in the late 1930s, largely for ideological reasons. Rabid anti-communism, it is argued, blinded Britain to the true strength of the Soviet system, and the Red Army's ability to withstand the Nazi attack of 1941–42 is adduced as proof. Others point to the poor performance of the Red Army offensive in Finland in 1939–40 as evidence that British military assessments were correct.[15] British military officers were of course anti-communist, and it is pointless to pretend otherwise. Whether or not anti-communism warped professional judgement is another question. In the late 1930s the British were most interested in the Soviet Red Army's offensive capabilities. Could it undertake an offensive to come to the aid of Czechoslovakia? The British seemed to have good reasons for doubting the Soviets on that count.

On the other hand, one should question the political uses to which military assessments were put. For those most strongly opposed to closer relations with the USSR the military reports from Moscow were a gift: doubts about the military reliability of the Soviets could always be used to quash calls for closer relations with the USSR. Thus, when the Chiefs of Staff apparently changed their minds in May 1939 and called for alliance with the Soviets,[16] a major step towards initiating talks with Moscow was taken.

Chamberlain in particular had reservations about drawing closer to the USSR, basically viewing it as an unreliable and untrustworthy ally. He resented the espionage and propaganda activities of the Soviets and feared that they wanted to embroil Britain and Germany in a war from which the USSR would emerge as the dominant power in Europe. Closer relations with the Soviets might alienate small East European states such as Poland and drive them over to Germany.

Initiating negotiations

By the spring of 1939 pressure was growing daily on the government to improve relations with the Soviets. The signals from the Soviet side were apparently unmistakable. For instance, a lunch reception given by Ivan Maisky, the Soviet ambassador to Britain, on 7 February 1939 was attended by Harold Nicolson, who was accompanied by fellow MP Robert Boothby. As Nicolson noted,

> [Maisky said] that Russia was obviously much wounded by Munich and that we can expect no advances from her side. But (and here he became serious) if *we* made approaches, we should not find Russia as aloof or offended as we might have supposed. Bob Boothby and I have an eye-meet like a tennis-ball across a net.[17]

Members of the opposition and Churchill called for an alliance with the USSR. A few weeks later the prime minister himself attended a reception at the Soviet embassy. As an apparently flabbergasted Maisky noted, 'not one British Premier – either Conservative or even Labour – has ever before crossed the threshold of the Soviet embassy'. Maisky thought Chamberlain's step was motivated by a desire to 'give the German a fright' and to stymie opposition criticism. During the course of the evening Chamberlain asked Maisky what the USSR did with its massive gold output. Maisky jokingly replied that it was being saved for a 'rainy day'. Chamberlain 'shook his head woefully and rapped, "that's what everyone is doing now; they think of nothing but war".' The conversation then turned to more ethereal matters:

> Chamberlain recalled his father, and emphasized with particular feeling that he was carrying out his programme (the unification and strengthening of the Empire through a customs system) and so forth. This part of the conversation left me with the impression that Chamberlain sincerely regards himself as a 'man of destiny' called upon to fulfill a 'sacred mission'.[18]

Pressure for closer relations with Moscow intensified after 31 March. Following the announcement of the guarantee to Poland at least five British newspapers (the *News Chronicle*, *Daily Worker*, *Manchester Guardian*, *Daily Mirror* and *Daily Herald*) issued calls for an Anglo-Soviet alliance in order to put teeth into the guarantee. In addition, Churchill renewed a call for a full-blown Anglo-Soviet alliance in the House of Commons on 3 April, on which occasion he was supported by Anthony Eden.

One by one over the next few weeks British cabinet ministers convinced themselves of the need for a closer link with the USSR. In September 1938 Hoare and Halifax had favoured including the USSR in the proposed Munich guarantee to Czechoslovakia and therefore had little difficulty in urging better relations with the Soviets in the early months of 1939. Halifax had already ordered a Foreign Office review of Anglo-Soviet relations in January. On the other hand, both were willing to go along with the idea of reducing the USSR's role to a supporting one when the British offered the guarantee to Poland at the end of March.

On 18 April 1939 the Soviets took the initiative and offered a full-blown pact of mutual assistance between Britain, France and the USSR, together with a guarantee of all states on the Soviet border from the Black Sea to the Baltic, complemented by an agreement on military assistance. A 'no separate peace' clause was also included. Over the next several months the Soviets did not vary substantially from their April proposals.

The Soviet initiative was prompted by a variety of considerations, none of them apparent to London at the time. Stalin was rapidly running out of patience with Litvinov's policy of collective security and the 18 April offer was a last-ditch attempt by Litvinov to encourage what he thought were positive signals emanating from London. Stalin undoubtedly saw the offer as a test on which he would base further decisions.

The offer was also instructive because it illustrated exactly what the Soviets wanted as security on their western frontiers. They demanded a classic defensive alliance with precisely laid out obligations, both political and military. The British, as always, wanted a much looser, more flexible arrangement. The two visions were not compatible, and that is essentially why the two sides failed to reach agreement. From the British point of view, a host of practical objections surfaced. For example, Cadogan argued that acceptance of the Soviet offer would risk alienating Britain's new-found friends in Eastern Europe and would give substance to German propaganda that accused the British of trying to encircle Germany. Cadogan also feared that the Soviets would not be able to offer the East European states much in the way of practical aid. In the longer term, Poland's refusal to allow Soviet troops to cross Polish territory proved impossible to overcome.

The British did not refuse the Soviet offer outright and in fact took a considerable time to reply. On 3 May, however, Litvinov was dismissed as Soviet foreign minister. He was replaced by Vyacheslav Molotov, a long-time colleague of Stalin and a man much more devoted to the thinking of his boss. Molotov was soon found to be very much the opposite of Litvinov: stubborn, suspicious and ignorant of foreign languages and culture. Rumours immediately started circulating in European diplomatic circles to the effect that a major change in Soviet foreign policy was imminent. For the time being, however, Molotov was waiting for an answer from London.

On 6 May the cabinet finally decided on its response to the Soviet offer made three weeks earlier. In their reply, which was largely Chamberlain's doing, the British suggested merely that the Soviets should make a declaration stating that if Britain and France found themselves at war as a result of their Eastern European obligations, Soviet assistance 'would be immediately available, if desired, and would be afforded in such manner and on such terms as might be agreed'.[19] The Soviets rejected the proposal almost immediately and said that they wanted a pact of mutual assistance, guarantees of the Baltic states and Finland and a supplementary military agreement. Declarations of intent were no longer sufficient.

The government now came under heavy criticism in the House of Commons for its handling of relations with Moscow. On 10 May, and again on the fifteenth, the government fielded a dozen hostile questions, many of which came from backbench Tories. An opinion poll taken by the Institute of Public Opinion found that eighty-seven per cent of respondents favoured alliance with the

USSR, while Ivan Maisky was an embarrassingly popular figure in London journalistic circles. In addition, the French government urged London to speed up talks with the Soviets. Finally, on 16 May the Chiefs of Staff recommended alliance with the USSR as it would 'present a solid front of formidable proportions against aggression'.[20] Failure to achieve agreement with the USSR would be regarded as a major diplomatic defeat for Britain and might well drive the USSR over to Germany's side. Britain also needed more than the 'bare neutrality' of the USSR since Soviet resources and supplies could be used to sustain Polish and Romanian resistance.

The report of the Chiefs of Staff overcame the last reservations of cabinet ministers who were still hesitant about entering into talks with the USSR, though Chamberlain resisted the idea of alliance to the end. In the House of Commons on 19 May he said that obstacles to an agreement arose 'solely out of policy and have nothing to do with internal political doctrine or what is called ideology'. But one member of the parliamentary press lobby recalls Chamberlain telling reporters at this time that 'the real threat to European civilization came from Russian Communism'.[21] In a private letter on 21 May Chamberlain again vented his mistrust of the Soviets: 'I cannot rid myself of the suspicion that they are chiefly concerned to see the "capitalist" powers tear each other to pieces while they stay out themselves'.[22]

Nevertheless, the prime minister was clearly on the defensive. According to Cadogan, Chamberlain actually threatened to resign on 20 May rather than initiate talks with Moscow. A cabinet meeting on 24 May, however, saw the formulation of a new set of proposals, and on that basis the British government embarked on the long, frustrating search for agreement with the Soviets.

Talks in Moscow

The talks took place in Moscow between Molotov and the British and French ambassadors. Progress quickly became bogged down on key issues, and it was soon evident that the gaps between the Soviets and the Western powers would not be bridged easily. The Soviets wanted to guarantee the Baltic states against German aggression directed ultimately at the USSR. The British were reluctant to under-take further guarantees. Molotov also hinted at the issue of 'indirect aggression', by which he meant an internal coup d'état, or Czech-style capitulation, that would put a pro-German government in power in any or all of the Baltic states. The Soviets wanted the right to intervene in the Baltic states to head off such a development – a demand that the British found disturbing and unacceptable.

The British were frustrated by the fact that their guarantees to Poland and Romania had effectively safeguarded the western border of the USSR, without the Soviets having to give anything in return. The Soviets could afford to procrastinate indefinitely. It also emerged during the course of the summer that it would be impossible to establish a degree of co-operation between Poland and the USSR. The Soviets wanted 'transit rights', which meant the right to send Red Army troops across Polish territory during a war with Germany. The Polish government refused to grant them such rights, fearing that once the Red Army had entered Poland it might never leave. The impasse between Warsaw and Moscow on the issue was the result of centuries of Russo-Polish acrimony, and the British and French were not able to paper over such a long legacy of mistrust in a matter of weeks.

In late June the British decided to send a special plenipotentiary to Moscow with the aim of trying to speed up the talks. It was a well-intentioned idea, but the British inadvertently offended the Soviets when they decided to send William Strang, head of the Foreign Office Central Department. Strang was a highly competent negotiator with considerable experience in diplomacy. He had been stationed at the British embassy in Moscow between 1930 and 1933 and played a role in the negotiations for resolving the Metro-Vickers crisis. Unfortunately, the Soviets regarded Strang as a minor personage, a 'political shrimp',[23] and seemed to have expected a more senior figure, perhaps even Halifax himself.

In a memoir written some time later Strang commented on the circumstances in which the Moscow talks were conducted:

Molotov sat at a large desk in the right-hand corner of the room (as you entered), with the windows on his left. His desk was raised from the floor on a dais, and we sat in a semi-circle below him, Sir William Seeds on the left, then myself, then the French ambassador, then Potemkin, the Deputy Commissar for Foreign Affairs. No one else was present. We had to nurse our papers on our knees and make our notes as best we could. There was a conference table away to our left, but no one ventured to suggest that it would be convenient if we could use it. Behind the table on our left front was an always open door which I found faintly disturbing, as though there was somebody listening. Neither Molotov nor Potemkin took any record of the proceedings, but Molotov fiddled from time to time with what I took to be a switch under the desk-top at his left hand, and I assumed that this was relaying those parts of our talk which he wished to have taken down for record. Potemkin did the interpreting.[24]

Chamberlain had agreed to the talks in May with the greatest reluctance. During June he expressed his suspicion of the Soviets at every turn. On 9 June he told the Foreign Policy Committee that he could not decide whether 'the Bolshies' were 'double crossing' the British and 'trying to make difficulties' or whether they were 'only showing the cunning and suspicion of the peasant'. In late June he complained that the British 'were nothing like as expert in this bazaar haggling as M[onsieur] Molotov'.

The complex trading of legal formulae and the refusal of the Soviets to budge from their demands left Cadogan completely frustrated by late June. According to Strang, Molotov's 'technique [was] stubbornly and woodenly to repeat his own point of view and to ask innumerable questions of his interlocutors'. Cadogan cursed Molotov as 'an ignorant and suspicious peasant'.[25]

Halifax was a little more reflective. At the end of June he told the Foreign Policy Committee,

the Soviets were extremely suspicious and feared our real object was to trap them into commitments and then leave them in the lurch. They suffered acutely from inferiority complex and considered that ever since the Great War the Western Powers had treated Russia with haughtiness and contempt. He suspected that the Soviet government were anxious to secure the Treaty but were in no hurry to reach agreement and were content to go on bargaining so as to secure the highest terms possible.[26]

By July the press was pessimistic while Chamberlain was contemplating the course of the negotiations. 'If we do get an agreement, as I rather think we shall, I am afraid I shall not regard it as a triumph. I put as little value on Russia's military capacity as I believe the Germans do. I think they would fail us in an extremity'.[27] Later he added that the Soviets would do whatever suited their interest in war, regardless of what they had previously signed.

In July Molotov demanded that military talks begin and that a military agreement should enter into force at the same time as a political agreement. Reluctantly the British agreed, especially after the French applied considerable pressure, much to Chamberlain's displeasure. At this point Strang complained that the talks had been a humiliating experience. 'Time after time', he reported, 'we have taken up a position and a week later abandoned it'.[28]

The military mission

The subsequent selection, assembly and despatching of the British military delegation to Moscow was ridden with errors. Strang had already warned his government that the Soviets were expecting a high-ranking figure, but the British were unable to find a senior military officer to send to Moscow. With war imminent, all army generals and Royal Navy officers had opted for posts that would put them in the front lines of the fighting. Instead the government selected Admiral Sir Reginald Aylmer Ranfurly Plunkett-Ernle-Erle-Drax, a highly competent officer with a splendid name and an illustrious career, but not the senior officer that the Soviets had been hoping for. The British thus repeated the mistake they had made with Strang only a few weeks earlier.

Furthermore, what would the Soviets make of the method by which Drax's delegation was transported to Moscow? The cabinet decided that a journey by rail across Germany was out of the question, for obvious reasons. The Royal Air Force found two old transport aircraft, but they would have to land in Berlin to refuel. All other service aircraft were needed for military duties. Some Wellington bombers were available, but they were rejected as being too uncomfortable for long-distance travel. There were no commercial air links between Britain and the USSR, and the Soviets used the wrong kind of aviation fuel. The Royal Navy had a high-speed cruiser available that could have reached Leningrad in three days, but Halifax rejected the idea on the grounds that sending a British warship into the Baltic might be regarded by the Germans as too provocative. Instead, a merchant ship was chartered that would take five or six days to reach Leningrad. Chamberlain said that he did not think that a couple of extra days would make much difference.

In briefings prior to his departure Drax was instructed to proceed slowly and not to give away any confidential information. He for his part was to gain as much information from the Soviets as possible. He was told:

> the British Government is unwilling to enter into any detailed commitments which are likely to tie our hands in all circumstances. Endeavours should therefore be made to confine the agreement to the broadest possible terms. Something along the lines of an agreed statement of policy may meet the case.[29]

Drax was advised that the Russians were suspicious by nature and hard bargainers. He was also warned to be on guard against attempts to spy on the delegation, as the Soviets could be expected to install recording devices, to search baggage and to root through waste-paper baskets. Drax's ship left Britain on 5 August. It was caught in a fog and Drax did not reach Moscow until the evening of 11 August. A welcoming banquet given by the Soviets went well, but Drax was unsettled by the fact that the Soviets expected him to pay for his own lodging.

Drax's first meeting with the Soviet military delegation on 12 August was a disaster. Marshal Voroshilov, the head of the Soviet delegation, produced Soviet government documents appointing him plenipotentiary with power to sign an agreement. He said that he hoped the French and British delegates carried equivalent papers. Doumenc, head of the French delegation, replied that he had authority to discuss but not sign an agreement. Everyone turned to look at Drax, who shuffled uncomfortably and said that he had no written credentials whatsoever. The British embassy quickly wired home for the appropriate documents, but again the British reinforced the perception that they attached little value to serious negotiations with the Soviets. After all, Chamberlain had gone to see Hitler personally three times in September 1938. In his memoirs Voroshilov attributed the failure of the talks to British procrastination.

The first few meetings were confined to vague generalities. The crunch came on 17 August when Voroshilov asked if Soviet forces would be allowed to cross Polish territory in the event of German aggression. Without a straightforward answer, he said, continued talks would be useless. The British and French immediately initiated a futile attempt to persuade the Polish government to allow Soviet troops to enter Polish territory. Meanwhile, the military talks went on spinning in circles. Finally, on 22 August the Soviet press announced that the German foreign minister, Joachim Ribbentrop, was coming to Moscow to sign an agreement with Stalin.

The Nazi–Soviet Pact

The Nazi–Soviet Pact was made public on 23 August. It was a pact of mutual non-aggression, accompanied by a secret protocol providing for the division of Poland between Germany and the USSR. Poland was thus about to be partitioned by its neighbours for the fourth time in its history. Other provisions in the protocol delimited the spheres of influence the two signatories were to receive in Eastern Europe. The USSR was to dominate the Baltic states and Finland,[30] and the Soviet claim to the eastern Romanian province of Bessarabia (now Moldova) was recognized. Hitler granted Stalin what the British could not: the lost territories of the old tsarist empire.

Prestige in regaining these territories undoubtedly counted for Stalin, but strategic factors also entered into the equation. The eastern half of Poland contained large numbers of Russians. The area had been conquered by the Poles in 1920, and Warsaw had advanced its eastern border much further into Russia than the Allies had originally intended it to do. The Soviets probably could not understand why the British and French were now so scrupulous about maintaining Poland's borders. Militarily, if Germany did conquer all of Poland, as seemed probable, German armies would be in a position to launch an attack on Moscow from close to

Minsk. To push the border west by dividing Poland would give Stalin some space in which to build defences.

Stalin had other reasons for signing with Hitler. As noted above, a German attack on Poland would result in a German war with France and Britain. The USSR could stand aside and strengthen its military. Serious fighting had taken place between Japanese and Soviet forces at Nomonhan in Mongolia in August. It was therefore in Stalin's interests to guard against a two-front war. In the long run Stalin was probably banking on a prolonged war of attrition in the West, at the end of which he could intervene from a position of strength, much as the United States did in 1917. If the Allies were conniving to direct German expansion east, as Stalin may have suspected, then the pact with Hitler turned the tables back again.

Stalin's decision to sign the pact with Hitler was a disastrous mistake. Many historians remain puzzled as to how the most paranoid dictator of the twentieth century could accept the word of Adolf Hitler, whose reputation for keeping promises was a little tattered by 1939. Exactly why Stalin decided to sign with anyone in 1939 is something of an enigma. His best option – to do nothing – seems never to have crossed his mind. The Nazi–Soviet Pact gained Stalin some territory, but it came as a terrible shock to Western public opinion and dissipated much of the goodwill that had built up from the Soviet support of the Spanish Republic.

The fact that secret talks had taken place between the Germans and Soviets during the spring and summer of 1939 has led to suggestions that the Soviets were never sincere in their desire to secure agreement with the British and French. Most of these talks consisted of occasional meetings between Soviet embassy officials in Berlin and low-level members of the German foreign ministry. None of the meetings led to anything much until a dinner at the Ewest restaurant in Berlin on 26 July, when the Soviet chargé Georgi Astakhov declared that a German–Soviet *rapprochement* was in the vital interests of the two countries. Even so, he said, the tempo in reaching agreement must be very slow and gradual. As late as 4 August the German ambassador in Moscow, Schulenburg, got into a shouting match with Molotov. A distraught Schulenburg informed Berlin that the Soviets were determined to sign with Britain and France.

Some historians argue that Stalin made his choice in early August. Others plug for early May, with the dismissal of Litvinov, whereas a third group insists that Stalin had hankered after agreement with Hitler since 1933.[31] However, one curious cloak-and-dagger episode in the British Foreign Office may shed some light on Soviet intentions. Sometime in the early months of 1939 the Soviets reactivated an agent in Britain whom they had originally recruited in 1935. This was John Herbert King, a Foreign Office Communications Department cipher clerk. King, together with Donald Maclean, was one of the first in a long string of Soviet agents recruited in the British Foreign Office. From 1935 until 1937 King supplied Moscow with numerous secret documents, some of which were seen by Stalin himself. They included transcripts of interviews between British diplomats stationed at the embassy in Berlin and senior Nazi officials, including Hitler. In 1937 King's controller was recalled and King was left in the lurch until 1939. The documents obtained from King that related to the Anglo-French–Soviet talks were quickly edited in such a way as to make the British appear anxious for an agreement while the Soviets were hesitant. The edited documents were then passed to the German embassy in London. On some occasions the turn-around time was as little as five hours. The objective was clearly to distract Germany's attention from any possible deals with Britain and solicit German offers to the USSR. The first of King's documents reached the German embassy on 19 April. King's activities continued through the summer.

Obviously the King episode casts doubt on Soviet sincerity, but does it prove that the Soviets were never interested in a deal with Britain and France? Such a conclusion seems unfounded. Molotov and Stalin committed enormous time and energy to the talks with the British and French; it is difficult to believe that was this all done for the sake of an intelligence ruse that could easily have been handled by the Soviet secret services. It is most likely that Stalin spent the summer holding his cards close to his chest, keeping the alternatives open and playing for time. The decisive move was made when Hitler decided to go ahead with the attack on Poland and therefore needed Soviet neutrality. This produced a high enough bid for Stalin's satisfaction.

Rumours of a German–Soviet *rapprochement* began to circulate in Europe following Munich and reached a peak in May with the dismissal of Litvinov. Most of these rumours, however, were utterly fantastic in content and easily discredited. Several stories emanating from Germany or Italy in early May suggested that Hitler and Stalin were within days of finalizing an agreement. The Foreign Office concluded on 9 May that the Germans and Italians had 'every interest in putting such stories about and the Russians might not be over-hasty to contradict them as they might enhance the value of the Soviet connexion' in the eyes of the British.[32]

Criticism has been levelled at the Foreign Office for ignoring the revelations of a Soviet defector, Walter Krivitsky, in the summer of 1939.[33] Krivitsky published articles in the *Baltimore Sun* and the *Saturday Evening Post* alleging that Stalin had been working towards an understanding with Hitler since 1934; but his warnings were dismissed by the Foreign Office as 'twaddle' and 'nonsense'. The fact remains, however, that Krivitsky was an unknown who had defected two years earlier and could only provide 'past history'. His news was not up to date and historians have found grounds to dispute the overall accuracy of his assertions.[34] His claim to have been a 'general' of the NKVD (the Stalinist secret police) was quickly punctured.

The Foreign Office was unable to gain any reliable, concrete evidence of an imminent German–Soviet *rapprochement* prior to August because little was happening in German–Soviet relations until the infamous dinner at the Ewest restaurant. Even then, matters proceeded relatively slowly. The Nazi–Soviet pact only became a certainty in mid-August when Hitler decided to drop ideological objections in order to gain Soviet neutrality.

Nevertheless, the British received at least one very serious warning. On 17 August Ronald Lindsay, the British ambassador to the United States, met the under secretary of state, Sumner Welles, who divulged, with impressive accuracy, the contents of a recent talk between Molotov and Schulenburg. Welles' source was Laurence Steinhardt, the American ambassador to Moscow, and Steinhardt's source was Hans von Herwarth, an anti-Nazi contact on the staff of the German embassy.[35] Lindsay's telegram reporting the warning from Welles was sent as a cipher to London, where it was not decoded in the Foreign Office until 22 August. It is possible that the telegram was intercepted by King, who was arrested on 27 September, but there is no conclusive proof.[36] By mid-August 1939 the Communications Department was responsible not only for the vast flow of Foreign Office ciphers but for four other governmental departments as well (the Ministries of Information, Economic Warfare, Food and Mines). Some of these were new departments that were supposed to set up their own cipher services but failed to do so. Instead, the Foreign Office Communications Department was authorized to take on a large increase of new staff. Apparently, many of those who were hired were not up to the mark. Lindsay's telegram lay on someone's desk for four full days.

What would have happened if Lindsay's telegram had been decoded the day after it was sent? Would it have jolted Chamberlain and his cabinet into making one last effort in Moscow? Possibly, but could the British ever have offered Stalin more than Hitler was able to?

There still remained a Foreign Office post-mortem on the nature of its intelligence-gathering in the affair. The confidential Foreign Office report from later in September began by noting that British secret information on German–Soviet relations came from four sources: direct German sources, direct Soviet sources, third parties in touch with German sources, and third parties in touch with Soviet sources. In assessing their respective worth, the report stated: 'we find ourselves somewhat in the position of the Captain of the Forty Thieves when, having put a chalk mark on Ali Baba's door, he found that Morgana had put a similar chalk mark on all the other doors in the street'.[37]

Owing to the efficiency of the NKVD, information from Soviet sources was notoriously difficult to obtain. What little information did seep through indicated that a German–Soviet *rapprochement* was highly unlikely.[38] Information from German sources was contradictory: the Foreign Office knew that some sections of German opinion favoured a deal, but Hitler himself remained adamantly opposed. Third-party reports usually came from persons of questionable reliability. Moreover, the Foreign Office also believed that it was in the interests of both the Russians and the Germans 'to spread rumours of a Russo-German *rapprochement* for purposes of blackmail in their dealings with [the British]'. Additional problems were caused by the fact that Soviet–German commercial negotiations were used to mask political contacts. The position

> was, therefore, that [the British] knew of a desire on the German side for a political *rapprochement*, which, however, was reliably reported to be completely at variance with Herr Hitler's own views and intentions, but had no reliable evidence of a corresponding desire on the Soviet side.[39]

The Foreign Office concluded that the Soviets would act in their own vital interests, and that 'any positive encouragement of German ambitions would not be compatible with them'.[40] Commenting on the report, one senior member of the Foreign Office noted: 'we were never told that the Germans and Russians had started negotiations with one another – which was the only thing that mattered'.[41]

The Nazi–Soviet Pact allowed the German invasion of Poland to begin on 1 September. Chamberlain decided that the British and French declarations of war must be co-ordinated. The resulting confusion and delays left some members of the cabinet convinced that Chamberlain was trying to wriggle out of the guarantee to Poland. A cabinet mutiny, spearheaded by Simon, nearly resulted. The prime minister announced the British declaration of war with great sadness: 'Everything that I have worked for, everything that I have hoped for, everything that I have believed in during my public life has crashed into ruins.'[42]

Perhaps, but historians have identified some unintentional benefits of appeasement. Britain entered the war united and convinced that it had done all that could have been done to prevent war. There was no question in 1939, unlike 1914, that Britain had made its position clear. Britain also entered the war with the sympathy – albeit not yet active – of the United States, an especially valuable trump card. Admittedly, however, none of these were primary goals of appeasement.

Notes

1 D. Lammers, 'From Whitehall after Munich: the future course of British policy', *The Historical Journal*, XVI, 1973, pp. 831–56.

2 See above, page 223. This was the occasion when, following ratification of the agreement, the British ambassador to Rome, Lord Perth, presented new credentials to 'The King of Italy and Ethiopia'.

3 C. Andrew, *Her Majesty's Secret Service* (New York, Viking, 1986), p. 414.

4 W. Wark, 'Something very stern: British political intelligence, moralism and grand strategy in 1939', *Intelligence and National Security*, V, 1990, pp. 150–70.

5 D. Dilks (ed.), *The Diaries of Sir Alexander Cadogan, 1938–1945* (London, Cassell, 1971), p. 147.

6 Dilks (ed.), *The Diaries of Sir Alexander Cadogan*, p. 148.

7 K. Feiling, *The Life of Neville Chamberlain* (London, Macmillan, 1947), p. 400.

8 Dilks (ed.), *The Diaries of Sir Alexander Cadogan*, p. 160.

9 Feiling, *The Life of Neville Chamberlain*, p. 403.

10 D. C. Watt, *How War Came: The Immediate Origins of the Second World War, 1938–1939* (New York, Pantheon, 1989), pp. 162–87.

11 R. A. C. Parker, *Chamberlain and Appeasement: British Policy and the Coming of the Second World War* (London, Macmillan, 1993), pp. 216–18, 260–71, 325–7, 347.

12 J. Degras (ed.), *Soviet Documents on Foreign Policy, 1917–1941*, volume three (London, Oxford University Press, 1953), pp. 315–22.

13 J. Erickson, *The Soviet High Command, 1918–1941* (London, Macmillan, 1962).

14 Foreign Office document no. FO 371 20352 N5048/1298/38, 9 October 1936.

15 See J. Herndon, 'British perceptions of Soviet military capability, 1935–39', in W. Mommsen and L. Kettenacker (eds), *The Fascist Challenge and the Policy of Appeasement* (London, George Allen and Unwin, 1983), pp. 483–505, and F. S. Northedge and A. Wells, *Britain and Soviet Communism: The Impact of a Revolution* (London, Macmillan, 1982).

16 I say apparent change because the COS staff had never before been consulted on the desirability of alliance with the USSR.

17 Nigel Nicolson (ed.), *Harold Nicolson: Diaries and Letters, 1930–1939* (London, Collins, 1966), p. 391.

18 A. Gromyko, V. Falin *et al.* (eds), *Soviet Peace Efforts on the Eve of World War Two* (Moscow, Novosti, 1973), no. 140.

19 L. Woodward and R. Butler (eds), *Documents on British Foreign Policy* (Norwich, The Stationery Office), Third Series, volume five, nos. 389 and 397, pp. 443 and 450

20 British Cabinet document CAB 27/625 FP(36), Fourth meeting, 16 May 1939.

21 J. Margach, *The Abuse of Power* (London, W. H. Allen, 1978), p. 59.

22 S. Aster, *1939: The Making of the Second World War* (London, André Deutsch, 1973), p. 179.

23 Watt, *How War Came*, p. 362.

24 Lord Strang, *Home and Abroad* (London, André Deutsch, 1956), p. 175.

25 Dilks (ed.), *The Diaries of Sir Alexander Cadogan*, p. 189.

26 British Cabinet document CAB 27/625 FPC, Fifty-fourth meeting, 26 June 1939.
27 Parker, *Chamberlain and Appeasement*, pp. 239–40.
28 Woodward and Butler (eds), *Documents on British Foreign Policy*, Third Series, volume six, no. 376, p. 422.
29 Woodward and Butler (eds), *Documents on British Foreign Policy*, Third Series, volume six, Appendix 5, p. 763.
30 The Baltic states were occupied by the USSR in 1940. Finland lost a hard-fought war with Stalin the same year but remained independent.
31 See the views expressed in J. Hochman, *The Soviet Union and the Failure of Collective Security* (Ithaca, Cornell University Press, 1984); S. Aster, *1939*, and Watt, *How War Came*.
32 Woodward and Butler (eds), *Documents on British Foreign Policy*, Third Series, volume five, no. 413, p. 463, note 2.
33 See Aster, *1939*, pp. 314–15, and D. C. Watt, 'An intelligence surprise: the failure of the Foreign Office to anticipate the Nazi–Soviet pact', *Intelligence and National Security*, IV, 1989, pp. 512–34.
34 Andrew, *Her Majesty's Secret Service*, p. 423.
35 Why did Steinhardt not deliver his warning directly to Seeds, the British ambassador in Moscow?
36 King was charged with treason and sentenced to ten years in jail. His activities following his release are unknown and there is no death record in his name.
37 See note 41.
38 The nature of the Soviet sources was left unspecified, but the British had been unable to read Soviet codes since 1927. The British did have an informant on the staff of the German embassy earlier in the period. See Hans von Herwarth, *Against Two Evils* (New York, Rawson Wade, 1981), pp. 126–7.
39 See note 41.
40 This accorded well with Chamberlain's belief that the USSR and Germany would never ally.
41 The author of the report was Collier, while the commentator was Sargent (see Chapter Six). Quotes from Foreign Office document no. FO 371 23686 N4146/243/38, 25 August 1939. See also Aster, *1939*, pp. 314–16.
42 Feiling, *The Life of Neville Chamberlain*, p. 416.

CHAPTER ELEVEN

THE APPEASEMENT ANALOGY

Hitler's armies encountered little difficulty in conquering Poland. The valiant but outgunned Polish army proved ineffective against the new blitzkrieg style of warfare perfected by the German army. The rapid advances of German armoured forces, closely supported by aircraft, soon put Warsaw in peril. On 17 September Soviet troops moved into eastern Poland to occupy territory assigned to the USSR under the secret terms of the Nazi–Soviet Pact. Polish resistance finally collapsed on 5 October. There followed on the Western front a prolonged period of inactivity, known rather contemptuously as the 'Phoney War', in which there was little or no fighting on land and only desultory combat in the air and at sea. Hitler made a couple of vague 'peace offers' in October, both of which were rejected by Britain and France. It was a curious, unreal phase of the war, and it was not destined to last.

British strategy during the Phoney War was dictated by a determination to avoid the futile, bloody frontal offensives of the First World War. Instead, the British and French opted for a defensive posture behind the Maginot line, combined with the hope that an economic blockade would take a toll on Germany. Once the German people realized that they had been hoodwinked into another total war, perhaps Hitler might be forced to the bargaining table.

Eventually, however, circumstances dictated that the British take some form of offensive action. At the end of November 1939 the Soviets, determined to strengthen defences around Leningrad, attacked Finland. The Finns fought back brilliantly and initially held the Red Army at bay. The Finnish cause proved enormously popular in Britain and public opinion demanded that the small, independent state be supported in its struggle against totalitarian oppression.

Already a guilt complex about Munich had engrained itself in the British consciousness. But the Soviet invasion of Finland prompted a further cause for alarm, beyond purely the destruction of Finland.

Germany had partially evaded the British blockade by drawing supplies of iron ore from neutral Sweden. The ore was transported by rail from mines located around Gällivare in northern Sweden to the port of Luleå. It was then shipped by sea through the Gulf of Bothnia and the Baltic Sea to Germany. The Soviet invasion of Finland raised the possibility of a German–Soviet partition of the whole of Scandinavia. To enforce a blockade under such circumstances would have been impossible. Instead, British military planners cooked up a scheme whereby a British expedition would cross neutral Norway (with the permission of the Norwegian government) and occupy the iron mines of northern Sweden under the guise of extending aid to Finland. Some volunteers and supplies would be sent to Finland, but the main purpose of the expedition was to seize the mines and deny supplies of iron ore to the German war machine. Planning, however, was haphazard and desultory and, as usual, Hitler struck first. On 8 April 1940 German forces attacked Denmark and Norway. The British attempted to defend Norway and succeeded in sinking a large portion of Hitler's modest surface fleet at Narvik, but ultimately the Germans prevailed and nothing could conceal the fact that the fall of Norway signified a major defeat for the British. The Finns, for their part, had concluded peace with Stalin on 12 March 1940.

On 10 May 1940 the German armies in the West unleashed their long-awaited offensive. Holland was rapidly overrun, while the combined armies of Belgium, Britain and France were hurled back in disarray. The German offensive coincided with an acrimonious debate in the House of Commons on the conduct and progress of the war. A division on 8 May saw thirty-three Conservatives voting against the government while sixty others abstained. Two days later Chamberlain resigned as prime minister.

He was succeeded by Winston Churchill, who formed a reconstructed cabinet that included prominent members of the Labour Party. At long last Britain had a truly national government. In the short term Britain's fortunes failed to improve. The French were defeated and surrendered on 22 June. The evacuation of British and French troops from Dunkirk has since been portrayed as an heroic miracle, but at the time there could be little doubt that Britain had suffered yet another devastating defeat. Such were the circumstances under which 'Cato' sat down to work. One of the more prolific and prestigious historians of the inter-war period, D. C. Watt, remembers that news of Dunkirk sparked a lifelong interest in history and a determination to find out how Britain had been brought so low.

Churchill quickly rallied the morale of the nation. The combination of radar and high-speed fighters – both of which had been developed during Chamberlain's tenure – blunted the German air offensive during the Battle of Britain in the late summer and early autumn of 1940. From the time of the French surrender until Hitler's attack on Yugoslavia and Greece in April 1941, Britain and the Empire stood alone against Germany. That isolation came to a true end only when Hitler attacked the USSR on 22 June 1941. The Japanese attack on Pearl Harbor brought the United States into the war in December 1941. The European war of September 1939 had now developed into a Second World War.

Chamberlain developed throat cancer in July 1940, shortly after his resignation, and he died in November. He is still remembered primarily as the architect of appeasement and the Munich agreement. He remains one of the more ridiculed figures of the twentieth century, the butt of at least one savage skit in the television series *Monty Python and the Flying Circus*. 'Chamberlain', snarled George Costanza in an episode of the acclaimed American sitcom *Seinfeld*, 'You could hold his head in the toilet and he would still give you half of Europe'. The arguments of revisionist historians have clearly made little impression on either the Flying Circus or George. Such perceptions are reinforced everywhere. A curious student seeking a definition of appeasement might turn to Webster's *Ninth New Collegiate Dictionary* where appeasement is seen as an effort 'to buy off [an aggressor] by concessions usually at the sacrifice of principles'.

Appeasement has in fact become one of the great, self-evident 'lessons' of history. This became clear almost immediately after the end of the Second World War. During the early phases of the Cold War people in the West were assured that it was necessary to 'stand up' to the Kremlin. The USSR was portrayed as an expansionist, totalitarian dictatorship that refused to play by the rules of liberal internationalism, just like Hitler's Germany. Failure to 'draw a line in the sand' would have 'dire consequences', while the appearance of weakness would only encourage further attempts at aggression.[1] President Harry Truman argued that the North Korean attack on South Korea in 1950 represented 'the same kind of challenge Hitler flaunted in the face of the rest of the world when he crossed the borders of Austria and Czechoslovakia'. The principle of collective security, to Truman's mind, demanded a firm response:

> It was my belief that if this aggression in Korea went unchallenged, as the aggression in Manchuria in 1931 and in Ethiopia in 1935 had gone unchallenged, the rest of the world was certain to be plunged into another world war.[2]

Such thinking may have been partially responsible for the American intervention in Vietnam in the early 1960s. Dean Rusk, a prominent presidential adviser during the Vietnam era, said, 'once again we hear expressed the views which cost the men of my generation a terrible price in World War II. We are told that Southeast Asia is too far away – but so were Manchuria and Ethiopia'.[3] President Lyndon Johnson justified the war in Vietnam on the grounds that an American withdrawal meant surrender, and surrender would not bring peace: 'We learned from Hitler at Munich that success only feeds the appetite of aggression.'[4] The massive arms build-up of the 1980s – the period of the so-called Second Cold War – were justified on similar grounds. President Carter considered that the Soviet invasion of Afghanistan in December 1979 paralleled Hitler's occupation of the Rhineland in 1936, an idea that he based on a reading of Churchill's *The Gathering Storm*. In Britain, the appeasement analogy was used by the prime minister Anthony Eden to justify the British–French–Israeli attack on Egypt in 1956. Eden compared President Nasser of Egypt, whose nationalization of the Suez canal prompted the crisis, to another Hitler. Many leading British politicians and most British newspapers repeated the analogy or accepted it without question.[5] The appeasement analogy found enthusiastic adherents everywhere. Accepting his Nobel Prize for literature in 1972, the Soviet dissident

Alexander Solzhenitsyn berated the West for laxness in the face of tyranny: 'The spirit of Munich', he said, 'is an illness of the will-power of rich people'.[6] The appeasement analogy also came in handy for politicians who wanted to discredit an opponent. In 1960 Lyndon Johnson, vying with John F. Kennedy for the Democratic Party presidential nomination, recalled that Kennedy's father, as American ambassador to Britain in the late 1930s, had supported appeasement: 'I wasn't any Chamberlain-umbrella policy man. I never thought Hitler was right.'[7]

Most recently, the appeasement analogy resurfaced during the Persian Gulf crisis and the Gulf War of 1990–91. On 13 August 1990 *Time* magazine noted that 'Iraq's land grab drew inevitable comparisons with the 1930's, when Hitler began to gobble up Europe in pieces small enough not to provoke a military response by the other powers of the day'.[8] The reporter Bruce W. Nelan furthered such comparisons by arguing that in the 1930s

> America's resolution came very late – almost too late – in the game. Now the slow reactions that helped produce World War Two [were] weighing anew on decision makers' minds in the wake of Iraq's anschluss with Kuwait.[9]

George Will, conservative columnist for the *Washington Post*, noted that 'Saddam Hussein is not Hitler, but the dynamism of his regime is Hitlerism. That suggests he will not be stopped other than by superior force'.[10] Other commentators compared the Iraqi Republican Guard to the Waffen SS, while 'a British analyst observed that Saddam and his government resembled the Nazis "but without their human warmth"'.[11] The analogy was extended to all aspects of the crisis. Iraq's claim that, historically, Kuwait belonged to Iraq conjured up Nelan's 'anschluss' metaphor. Writing of the conflict a year later, an American author noted that claims to 'what might be called Iraq irredenta' recalled 'pre-1939 German demands that ethnic German areas in countries like Austria and Czecho-slovakia be united with the Reich'.[12] President George Bush, a veteran of the Pacific theatre during World War Two, undoubtedly shared similar views and repeatedly referred to Saddam Hussein as 'Hitler revisited'. Failure to take action, thought Bush, would only encourage further aggression. For once (one of the few occasions during his presidency) Bush knew exactly what to do.

The instinct to use historical analogy is so strong[13] that it is difficult to see how the appeasement analogy might fall into disuse. It apparently has universal applicability. A Canadian newspaper columnist recently wrote that those who expressed reservations about expanding NATO membership on the grounds that it might inflame Russian nationalism were actually advocating a policy of appeasement.[14] On 15 February 1997 Jesse Helms, a US Senator, appeared on the Cable News Network programme *Evans and Novak*, where he accused the Canadian government of following a policy of appeasement towards Cuba. As was noted in the introduction, large portions of modern Western society have no historical grasp of the inter-war period. Of those which do, many may have got it wrong. Or they may have got it right, but for the wrong reasons. The constant use by the media and government officials of the appeasement analogy to justify foreign policy decisions alone shows the necessity for a basic familiarity with the inter-war era.

In retrospect it seems clear that the British were dealt a near-impossible hand from the very beginning of the period under study. One could compile a daunting list of 'structural' problems that Britain faced at the end of the First World War: the apparent withdrawal of the United States from European political affairs, German grievances – real or imagined – arising from Versailles (especially reparations), the contradiction between the promise of 'Wilsonism' and French security needs, additional commitments arising from the expansion of empire, and post-war economic problems. By the late 1920s the load had arguably lightened somewhat, because of Locarno. The incalculable consequences arising from the Great Depression were well beyond the control of any diplomat.

That a policy of appeasement should have been pursued in the 1930s has appeared inevitable and logical to many revisionist historians. To the foregoing list of 'structural' problems one might add the emergence of the triple threat, the perceived lack of reliable allies, Britain's weakened economic and military position, and public anti-war sentiment. In addition, Britain's leaders, particularly Chamberlain, realized that another war would bankrupt the nation and lead to the disintegration of the Empire.[15] It was therefore easier to postpone the day of decision. To pursue a policy that would lead to the loss of empire and the weakening of Britain was inconceivable to most members of Chamberlain's generation and outlook. It might be more interesting to start thinking of Chamberlain not as an appeaser to the very end but rather as the son of Joe Chamberlain, Birmingham imperialist, to the very end. That is certainly how he presented himself to Ivan Maisky, an apostle of a very different social order, at a Soviet embassy reception in February 1939.[16]

In 1938 Chamberlain remarked to Halifax that Britain 'must hope for the best while preparing for the worst'.[17] It is a comment that might well apply to the period as a whole. There was certainly no end of hoping for the best. Readers can judge for themselves whether or not Britain was prepared for the worst by 1939, but, hopefully, not before taking some revisionist arguments into account, if only to balance the scales.

Notes

1   See E. May, *Lessons of the Past: The Use and Misuse of History in American Foreign Policy* (New York, Oxford University Press, 1973), especially chapter two.

2   H. Truman, *Memoirs by Harry S. Truman, Volume Two, Years of Trial and Hope* (New York, Doubleday, 1956), p. 463.

3   R. Jervis, *Perception and Misperception in International Politics* (Princeton, Princeton University Press, 1976), p. 221

4   D. Halberstam, *The Best and the Brightest* (New York, Random House, 1972), p. 729.

5   H. Thomas, *The Suez Affair* (Harmondsworth, Penguin, 1967), *passim*.

6   T. Taylor, *Munich: The Price of Peace* (New York, Vintage, 1980), p. 1004.

7   R. Dallek, *Lone Star Rising: Lyndon Johnson and His Times* (Oxford, Oxford University Press, 1991), p. 573.

8   Lisa Beyer, 'Iraq's power grab', *Time*, 13 August 1990, p. 12.

9   B. W. Nelan, 'Can the US turn off Iraq's oil?', *Time*, 13 August 1990, p. 15.

10 Will is quoted in the 'Notes and comments' section of the *New Yorker*, 20 August 1990, p. 25.

11 N. Friedman, *Desert Victory: The War for Kuwait* (Annapolis, Naval Institute Press, 1992), pp. 20–1.

12 Friedman, *Desert Victory*, p. 371.

13 D. Fischer, *Historians' Fallacies: Toward a Logic of Historical Thought* (New York, Harper and Row, 1970); C. Thorne, *Border Crossings: Studies in International History* (New York, Basil Blackwell, 1988), especially chapter two,

'International relations and the promptings of history'; and Jervis, *Perception and Misperception in International Politics*, especially chapter six, 'How decision makers learn from history'.

14 Marcus Gee, 'How to handle Russia', *The Globe and Mail*, March 26 1997, p. A23.

15 Which is exactly what happened.

16 See above, page 251.

17 D. Dilks, 'Appeasement revisited', *University of Leeds Review*, June 1972, pp. 28–56.

BIBLIOGRAPHICAL GUIDE

The following list is not intended to be a comprehensive survey of works on British foreign policy in the inter-war era. Readers desiring such a survey should consult S. Aster, *British Foreign Policy, 1918-1945: A Guide to Research and Research Materials*, second edition (Wilmington, Scholarly Resources, 1991). The purpose of the following guide is simply to highlight those monographs which newcomers to the field will find most useful and informative.

Readers seeking a general orientation to the period as a whole should consult: M. Kitchen, *Europe Between the Wars* (London, 1988); P. M. H. Bell, *The Origins of the Second World War in Europe* (London, 1986); Akira Iriye, *The Origins of the Second World War in Asia and the Pacific* (London, 1987); and G. Ross, *The Great Powers and the Decline of the European States System, 1914-1945* (London, 1983).

The military dimension is covered by D. C. Watt in *Too Serious a Business: European Armed Forces and the Approach to the Second World War* (London, 1975) and by Williamson Murray in *The Change in the European Balance of Power, 1938-1939: The Path to Ruin* (Princeton, 1984). Anthony Adamthwaite offers a valuable introductory essay and an excellent selection of documents in *The Making of the Second World War* (London, 1977). The same author's *The Lost Peace: International Relations in Europe, 1918-1939* (London, 1980) focuses more on the 1920s. The summative essays in W. Mommsen and L. Kettennacker (eds), *The Fascist Challenge and the Policy of Appeasement* (London, 1983), are helpful, if highly specialized.

Surveys of British foreign policy in the twentieth century include: C. Bartlett, *British Foreign Policy in the Twentieth Century* (London, 1989); D. Dilks (ed.), *Retreat From Power: Studies in Britain's Foreign Policy of the Twentieth Century*, 2 volumes (London, 1981); and D. Reynolds, *Britannia Overruled: British Policy and World Power in the Twentieth Century* (London, 1991).

275

Versailles

A valuable and brief orientation to the controversies surrounding the Treaty of Versailles can be found in Ruth Henig, *Versailles and After, 1919–1933* (New York, 1984). More recent are A. Sharp, *The Versailles Settlement: Peacemaking in 1919* (London, 1991), and E. Goldstein, *Winning the Peace: British Diplomatic Strategy, Peace Planning and the Paris Peace Conference, 1916–1920* (Oxford, 1991). The most comprehensive survey of the British role at the Paris Peace Conference can be found in M. Dockrill and J. Goold, *Peace Without Promise: Britain and the Peace Conferences, 1919–1923* (London, 1981). British attitudes towards the League of Nations are detailed by G. Egerton in *Great Britain and the Creation of the League of Nations: Strategy, Politics and International Organization, 1914–1919* (Chapel Hill, 1978). British thinking on reparations is analysed by Robert Bunselmeyer in *The Cost of War, 1914–1919: British Economic War Aims and the Origins of Reparations* (Hamden, 1975). Britain's role in the post-war Middle East is covered in J. Darwin's *Britain, Egypt and the Middle East: Imperial Policy in the Aftermath of War, 1918–1922* (London, 1981).

The 1920s

The British role in the immediate aftermath of Versailles can be found in Anne Orde, *Great Britain and International Security* (London, 1977) and *British Policy and European Reconstruction after the First World War* (London, 1990). A general overview of the 1920s is provided by Sally Marks in *The Illusion of Peace: International Relations in Europe, 1918–1933* (London, 1976). Relations with the United States are covered by B. McKercher in *The Second Baldwin Government and the United States, 1924–1929, Attitudes and Diplomacy* (Cambridge, 1984). British Foreign Office coverage of the Weimar Republic is analysed by F. Carsten in *Britain and the Weimar Republic* (London, 1984). The Washington conference is studied in E. Goldstein and J. Maurer (eds), *The Washington Conference, 1921–22, Naval Rivalry, East Asian Stability, and the Road to Pearl Harbour* (London, 1995).

Appeasement

The most recent general overview of appeasement as a whole is given by R. A. C. Parker in *Chamberlain and Appeasement* (London, 1993), but Paul Kennedy's *The Realities Behind the Diplomacy: Background Influences on British External Policy, 1865–1980* (London, 1980) is also worth searching out. For a recent collection of essays, see R. Boyce and E. Robertson (eds), *Paths to War: New Essays on the Origins of the Second World War* (New York, 1989).

A view from an American scholar is provided by R. J. Q. Adams in *British Politics and Foreign Policy in the Age of Appeasement, 1935–1939* (Stanford, 1993). C. Barnett's *The Collapse of British Power* (London, 1972) is highly critical. For a controversial work that seeks to draw a connection between domestic and foreign policy see M. Cowling's *The Impact of Hitler: British Politics and British Policy, 1933–1940* (London, 1975).

Some older works on appeasement are also valuable, especially C. Thorne, *The Approach of War* (London, 1967), or W. Rock, *Appeasement on Trial: British Foreign Policy and its Critics, 1938–1939* (Hamden, 1966).

Works that focus on the functioning of the cabinet under Chamberlain include I. Colvin, *The Chamberlain Cabinet* (London, 1971), and C. Hill, *Cabinet Decision on Foreign Policy: the British Experience, October 1938 – June 1941* (Cambridge, 1991).

G. Post applies some insights from social sciences to appeasement studies in *Dilemmas of Appeasement: British Deterrence and Defense, 1934–1937* (Ithaca, 1993). A book that examines the role of the Dominions is R. Ovendale, *'Appeasement' and the English Speaking World: Britain, the United States, the Dominions and the Policy of 'Appeasement', 1937–1939* (Cardiff, 1971).

Conservative anti-appeasers receive attention in N. Thompson's *The Anti-Appeasers: Conservative Opposition to Appeasement in the 1930s* (Oxford, 1971). Information on Labour foreign policy can be found in K. Harris, *Attlee* (London, 1989), and H. Winkler, *Paths Not Taken: British Labour and International Policy in the 1920s* (Chapel Hill, 1994).

Military policy

British military policy in the inter-war era is covered most definitively by Brian Bond in *British Military Policy Between the Two World Wars* (London, 1980) and also by Michael Howard in *The Continental Commitment: The Dilemma of British Defence Policy in the Era of the Two World Wars* (London, 1972). Uri Bialer covers original ground in *The Shadow of the Bomber: The Fear of Air Attack and British Politics, 1932–1939*, while John Ferris throws light on a comparatively neglected period in *Men, Money and Diplomacy: The Evolution of British Strategic Policy, 1919–1926* (London, 1989).

Specific aspects of British military problems are addressed in: L. Pratt, *East of Malta, West of Suez: Britain's Mediterranean Crisis, 1936–1939* (London, 1975); William R. Louis, *British Strategy in the Far East: 1919–1939* (London, 1971); L. Montgomery Hyde, *British Air Policy Between the Wars, 1918–1939* (London, 1976); B. Powers, *Strategy Without Slide-Rule: British Air Strategy, 1914–1939* (London, 1976); and S. Roskill, *Naval Policy Between the Wars* (London, 1975).

Intelligence

The influence of intelligence on policy-making is explored by W. Wark in *The Ultimate Enemy* (Ithaca, 1985). Other relevant works on intelligence include: C. Andrew and D. Dilks (eds), *The Missing Dimension* (London, 1984); C. Andrew and J. Noakes (eds), *Intelligence and International Relations, 1900–1945* (Exeter, 1987); C. Andrew, *Secret Service: The Making of the British Intelligence Community* (London, 1985); and E. May (ed.), *Knowing One's Enemies: Intelligence Assessment Before the Two World Wars* (Princeton, 1984).

Public opinion

The role of public opinion is examined in: P. Kyba, *Covenants Without the Sword: Public Opinion and British Defence Policy,*

1931–1935 (Waterloo, 1983); M. Ceadel, *Pacifism in Britain, 1914–1945: The Defining of a Faith* (London, 1980); F. Gannon, *The British Press and Germany, 1936–1939* (London, 1971); and B. Morris, *The Roots of Appeasement: The British Weekly Press and Nazi Germany During the 1930s* (London, 1991).

Two very critical accounts of government–media relations are R. Cockett's *Twilight of Truth: Chamberlain, Appeasement and the Manipulation of the Press* (London, 1971) and J. Margach's *The Abuse of Power: The War Between Downing Street and the Media from Lloyd George to Callaghan* (London, 1978).

British propaganda efforts in the inter-war period are examined by P. Taylor in *The Projection of Britain Overseas: British Overseas Publicity and Propaganda, 1919–1939* (London, 1981).

The effect of the Spanish Civil War is studied by K. Watkins in *Britain Divided: The Effect of the Spanish Civil War on British Public Opinion* (London, 1963).

Economics

The relationship between economics and foreign policy forms the focus of G. Peden's *British Rearmament and the Treasury, 1932–1939* (Edinburgh, 1979) and R. Shay's *British Rearmament in the Thirties: Politics and Profits* (Princeton, 1977). More generally, see D. Kaiser, *Economic Diplomacy and the Origins of the Second World War: Germany, Britain, France and Eastern Europe* (Princeton, 1981).

Crises of the 1930s

The crises of the 1930s have generated much writing. Ethiopia is examined by F. Hardie in *The Abyssinian Crisis* (London, 1974) and G. Baer in *Test Case: Italy, Ethiopia and the League of Nations* (Stanford, 1977). The Rhineland episode is analysed by J. Emmerson in *The Rhineland Crisis: 7 March 1936* (London, 1977). The standard reference for the Spanish Civil War is H. Thomas, *The Spanish Civil War* (Harmondsworth, 1961), but A. Beevor, *The Spanish Civil War* (London, 1982), is also valuable. J. Edwards looks at

British government policy towards the war in *The British Government and the Spanish Civil War* (London, 1979), while *Britain Divided* by K. Watkins (cited above) covers public opinion.

Two dramatically contrasting views of Munich are offered by T. Taylor in *Munich: The Price of Peace* (New York, 1979) and Roy Douglas in *In the Year of Munich* (London, 1977). A more general background from the British perspective is R. Shepherd's *A Class Divided: Appeasement and the Road to Munich, 1938* (London, 1988).

The Far East

For British Far Eastern policy, see *British Strategy in the Far East* (cited above) by William R. Louis, as well as: C. Thorne, *The Limits of Foreign Policy: The West, the League and the Far Eastern Crisis of 1931–1933* (London, 1972); A. Trotter, *Britain and East Asia: 1933–1937* (London, 1975); B. Lee, *Britain and the Sino-Japanese War, 1937–1939: A Study in the Dilemmas of British Decline* (Stanford, 1973); P. Lowe, *Great Britain and the Origins of the Pacific War: A Study of British Policy in East Asia, 1937–1941* (Oxford, 1977); S. Pelz, *Race to Pearl Harbour: the Failure of the Second London Naval Conference and the Onset of World War Two* (Cambridge, 1974); S. Endicott, *Diplomacy and Enterprise: British China Policy, 1933–1937* (Manchester, 1975); and I. Nish (ed.), *Anglo-Japanese Alienation* (Cambridge 1982).

1939

The events of 1939 are covered in massive detail by D. C. Watt in *How War Came: The Immediate Origins of the Second World War* (New York, 1989), but S. Aster's *1939: The Making of the Second World War* (London, 1973) should not be overlooked. S. Newman in *The British Guarantee to Poland: A Study in the Continuity of British Foreign Policy* (London, 1976) offers a controversial view of the British guarantee of 1939. Also useful are R. Douglas (ed.), *1939: A Retrospect Forty Years After* (London, 1983), and Anita

Bibliographical guide

Prazmowska, *Britain, Poland and the Eastern Front, 1939* (London, 1989). Peter Dennis analyses the British decision to introduce peacetime conscription in 1939 in *Decision by Default: Peacetime Conscription and British Defence, 1919–1939* (Durham, 1972).

Britain and its foreign relations

British relations with specific countries are examined in: N. Rostow, *Anglo-French Relations, 1934–1936* (London, 1984); M. Thomas, *Britain, France and Appeasement: Anglo-French Relations in the Popular Front Era* (Oxford, 1996); G. Gorodetsky, *The Precarious Truce: Anglo-Soviet Relations, 1924–1927* (London, 1977); S. White, *Britain and the Bolshevik Revolution: A Study in the Politics of Diplomacy, 1920–1924* (London, 1979); F. S. Northedge and A. Wells, *Britain and Soviet Communism: The Impact of a Revolution* (London, 1982); C. Keeble, *Britain and the Soviet Union, 1917–1989* (London, 1990); D. Reynolds, *The Creation of the Anglo-American Alliance, 1931–1941: A Study in Competitive Co-operation* (London, 1981); and C. MacDonald, *The United States, Britain and Appeasement* (London, 1981).

Biographies

Biographies of British prime ministers and foreign secretaries include: D. Marquand, *Ramsay MacDonald* (London, 1977); K. Middlemas and J. Barnes, *Baldwin: A Biography* (London, 1969); P. Rowland, *Lloyd George* (London, 1975); D. Gilmour, *Curzon* (London, 1994); G. Bennett, *British Foreign Policy During the Curzon Period, 1919–1924* (London, 1995); D. Dutton, *Austen Chamberlain: Gentleman in Politics* (Bolton, 1985); D. Dutton, *Simon: A Political Biography of Sir John Simon* (London, 1992); J. Cross, *Sir Samuel Hoare: A Political Biography* (London, 1977); D. Carlton, *Anthony Eden* (London, 1981); R. James, *Anthony Eden* (London, 1986); A. Peters, *Anthony Eden at the Foreign Office, 1931–1938* (New York, 1986); and A. Roberts, *The Holy Fox: A Biography of Lord Halifax* (London, 1991).

281

Biographies of senior bureaucrats include N. Rose, *Vansittart: Study of a Diplomat* (London, 1978), and S. Roskill, *Hankey: Man of Secrets*, 3 volumes (London, 1970–1974).

Biographies of Chamberlain include K. Feiling, *The Life of Neville Chamberlain* (London, 1947); H. Montgomery Hyde, *Neville Chamberlain* (London, 1976); L. Fuchser, *Neville Chamberlain and Appeasement: A Study in the Politics of History* (New York, 1982); and D. Dilks, *Neville Chamberlain*, volume one (Cambridge, 1984). J. Charmley tries to portray Chamberlain in a sympathetic light in *Chamberlain and the Lost Peace* (London, 1989).

Memoirs and diaries

The memoir and diary literature is rich and valuable. The most instructive works are listed here: R. Butler, *The Art of the Possible* (London, 1971); D. Dilks (ed.), *The Diaries of Sir Alexander Cadogan* (London, 1971); H. Dalton, *The Fateful Years: Memoirs, 1931–1945* (London, 1957); B. Pimlott (ed.), *The Political Diary of Hugh Dalton* (London, 1986); A. Eden, *Facing the Dictators, 1928–1938* (London, 1962); J. Harvey (ed.), *The Diplomatic Diaries of Oliver Harvey, 1937–1940* (London, 1970); N. Henderson, *Failure of a Mission* (London, 1940); G. Jebb, *The Memoirs of Lord Gladwyn* (London, 1962); I. Kirkpatrick, *The Inner Circle: Memoirs of Ivone Kirkpatrick* (London, 1959); H. Knatchbull-Hugessen, *Diplomat in War and Peace* (London, 1949); V. Lawford, *Bound for Diplomacy* (London, 1963); B. Liddell Hart, *Memoirs* (London, 1958); F. Maclean, *Eastern Approaches* (London, 1949); H. Macmillan, *Memoirs, Volume One, Winds of Change, 1914–1939* (London, 1966); O. O'Malley, *The Phantom Caravan* (London, 1954); F. S. G. Piggott, *Broken Thread* (London, 1950); W. Strang, *Home and Abroad* (London, 1956); F. Roberts, *Dealing with Dictators: The Destruction and Revival of Europe, 1930–1970* (London, 1991); K. Strong, *Intelligence at the Top: Recollections of an Intelligence Officer* (London, 1968); Viscount Templewood (S. Hoare), *Nine Troubled Years* (London, 1954); and R. Vansittart, *The Mist Procession* (London, 1958).

Curiously, memoirs by two foreign secretaries – Lord Halifax, *Fulness of Days* (London, 1957), and Viscount Simon, *Retrospect* (London, 1952) – are too vague to be helpful.

Collections

Students might also find the following collections of essays useful. C. Abramsky and B. Williams (eds), *Essays in Honour of E. H. Carr* (London, 1974); M. Bentley and J. Stevenson (eds), *High and Low Politics in Modern Britain* (Oxford, 1983); G. Craig and F. Gilbert (eds), *The Diplomats* (Princeton, 1953); D. Dilks (ed.), *Retreat from Power: Studies in Britain's Foreign Policy in the Twentieth Century*, volume one (London, 1981); R. Langhorne (ed.), *Diplomacy and Intelligence During the Second World War: Essays in Honour of F. H. Hinsley* (Cambridge, 1985); B. McKercher and D. Moss (eds), *Shadow and Substance in British Foreign Policy, 1895–1939, Memorial Essays Honouring C. J. Lowe* (Edmonton, 1984); G. Peele and C. Cook (eds), *The Politics of Reappraisal, 1918–1939* (London, 1975); A. Preston (ed.), *General Staffs and Diplomacy Before the Second World War* (London, 1978); A. J. P. Taylor (ed.), *Lloyd George: Twelve Essays* (London, 1971).

Finally, two recent collections have appeared: D. Richardson and G. Stone (eds), *Decisions and Diplomacy: Essays in Twentieth Century International History* (London, 1995), and M. Dockrill and B. McKercher (eds), *Diplomacy and World Power: Studies in British Foreign Policy 1890–1950* (Cambridge, 1996).

INDEX

Abyssinia 168, 175
  see also Ethiopia
Admiralty, 5, 57, 63, 100–1, 119,
  170, 172, 184, 186, 199,
  205–6
Albania 10, 112, 242
Alliance, Triple 8–9, 14, 46
Alsace and Lorraine 8, 37–8, 67
Anglo-German Naval Agreement
  (1935) 169–71, 173–5, 183,
  237
Anglo-Soviet negotiations (1939)
  246–64
Anschluss 41, 220–3, 225, 243, 247
Anti-Comintern Pact (1936) 204,
  244
anti-war sentiment in Britain 160–4
appeasement 16, 125, 190, 192,
  chapter nine *passim*, 246,
  269–73
Asquith, Herbert 14–15, 28
Attlee, Clement 178, 200
Australia 44–5, 63, 72, 91, 113,
  230
Austria 41, 61, 110, 112, 116–17,
  168, 171–2, 192, 204, 213,
  216
  Anschluss (1938) 220–3, 228,
  243
Austria-Hungary 8–12, 14–15,
  40–1, 46, 48, 128, 213

Baldwin, Stanley 1, 16–17, 75–6,
  83–5, 89, 102–3, 105, 123,
  157, 166, 173–5
  Ethiopian crisis 163, 183–4
  last months in office 203–5
  perceptions of Hitler 157–8
  rearmament and 178, 193–4
  Spanish Civil War 197, 199

Balfour, Arthur 25, 87
Balfour Declaration (1917) 46
Balfour Note 58
Ball, Joseph 208–9, 220, 241
Baltic states 253–5, 259
Belgium 12–13, 27, 37–8, 42, 59,
  64, 73, 88, 114, 165, 192,
  218, 241–2, 268
Beneš, Eduard 230
Bismarck, Otto von 8–9, 60, 75
Boer War 3–4
Bolsheviks 15, 31–2, 49, 65, 69–70,
  92, 199
  see also Soviet Union
Bonar-Law, Andrew 73, 75
Bonnet, Georges 232, 234
Brazil 94–6
Brest–Litovsk, Treaty of (1918) 15,
  31
Briand, Aristide 66–7, 86, 89, 95,
  100, 102, 115–17
Brüning, Heinrich 117–18, 126
Bulgaria 10, 112, 240

Cadogan, Alexander 22, 137,
  140–1, 147, 218–20, 222,
  230–4, 236, 242, 244, 253–4,
  256
Campbell case (1924) 82–3
Canada 1, 31, 63, 72, 91, 113
Cannes conference (1922) 66
Cato 17, 19, 269
Cecil, Lord (Robert) 36, 51, 75,
  80–1, 85, 96, 101–2, 104,
  127, 175
Chanak crisis (1922) 68–73, 184
Chamberlain, Austen 84–5, 92–3,
  99, 101, 149, 165, 194, 214
  attitude to France, 85
  confronts anti-colonialism, 96–8

Index

CPSIA information can be obtained at www.ICGtesting.com
Printed in the USA
LVOW11s0226100114

368629LV00006B/28/P